A VERY DIFFERENT AGE

AMERICANS OF THE PROGRESSIVE ERA

ALSO BY STEVEN J. DINER

A City and Its Universities: Public Policy in Chicago
Compassion and Responsibility:
Readings in the History of Social Welfare Policy in the U.S.

A VERY DIFFERENT AGE

AMERICANS OF THE PROGRESSIVE ERA

STEVEN J. DINER

HILL AND WANG

A DIVISION OF FARRAR, STRAUS AND GIROUX

NEW YORK

Hill and Wang
A division of Farrar, Straus and Giroux
19 Union Square West, New York 10003

LIBRARY OF CONGRESS CATALOGING-IN-PUBLICATION DATA

Diner, Steven J., 1944–
    A very different age : Americans of the progressive area / Steven
J. Diner. — 1st ed.
        p.   cm.
    Includes bibliographical references and index.
    ISBN 0-8090-2553-1 (alk. paper)
    1. United States—History—1865–1921.   2. Progressivism (United
States politics)   3. United States—Social conditions—1865–1918.
I. Title.
E661.D56   1997
973.8—dc21   97-3801

FOR HASIA, SHIRA, ELI, AND MATAN

ACKNOWLEDGMENTS

When Eric Foner and Arthur Wang invited me to write this book, my first thought (which I did not share with them) was: "Do we really need another book on the Progressive Era?" Each generation may need to write its own history, but several excellent narratives had recently appeared, in addition to an already voluminous literature. As I mulled the matter over, however, it struck me that no one had written a book on how Americans of diverse backgrounds lived in this era, although in the last twenty-five years or so historians had produced a rich literature of specialized studies on which such a history could be based. Five years later, I am grateful to them for stimulating me to write this book. Eric Foner has made invaluable suggestions at every stage of the project. Arthur Wang has been a constant source of encouragement, prodding me graciously, in his inimitable way, to hurry up and finish, and a skillful editor of the penultimate draft. I thank them both. I also thank Lauren Osborne of Hill and Wang, who guided the manuscript through final editing and production with skill and enthusiasm.

I owe a profound debt to colleagues who read the manuscript and made detailed suggestions: Roy Rosenzweig, Lynn Gordon, Jim Gilbert and Stephen Whitfield. Roy Rosenzweig also offered insightful comments on the preliminary outline I wrote at the start of the project. I hope I have made good use of their valuable suggestions. I assigned an early version of this manuscript to my graduate students in a course on the Progressive Era at George Mason University in the summer of 1995. I thank all of them for their candid assessment of the work of the instructor about to give them a final grade. And I especially thank those students who took time to give me their written suggestions: Betsy Burstein, Mary Dellinger, Michael Jackson, Marc Levesque, Una Mahar, and Sue Moutoux.

The office staff of the History Department at George Mason University saved me many hours of work by typing revisions of various drafts. My thanks to Rachel Giesey, Jo Ritter, Erina Moriarty, and especially Betsy Rowe, who somehow managed to free staff members to work on my manuscript and acted as if it was her top priority. Charlene Hurt, Director of Libraries at George Mason University, bent rules to allow me to keep far too many books for far too long a time. William Carpenter checked citations and bibliographic information thoroughly and cheerfully.

I did the bulk of the research and writing during a study leave in the 1994–95 academic year, made possible by the George Mason University Faculty Study Leave program and support from the Krasnow Institute for Advanced Studies at George Mason. I owe special thanks to Mark Friedlander, chair of the Krasnow Institute Board of Directors, for his strong support. The chairs of my department, Marion Deshmukh and Jack Censer, provided secretarial support, funds for photocopying, and warm personal encouragement.

My interest in the social history of the Progressive Era began nearly three decades ago as a graduate student studying with the late Arthur Mann at the University of Chicago. This book owes a great deal to his sharp historical insights, his masterful ability to teach graduate students how to think about history and how to write, and his mentoring.

In everything I do as a scholar, my largest debt is always to Hasia Diner. She alone read multiple drafts of the manuscript from beginning to end, discussed the project with me at every stage, and suffered through too many dinner conversations about the Progressive Era. For her critical insights and suggestions, her ruthless editing, her constant encouragement, and her love I am sincerely grateful.

Contents

We have come upon a very different age from any that preceded us. We have come upon an age when we do not do business in the way in which we used to do business,—when we do not carry on any of the operations of manufacture, sale, transportation, or communication as men used to carry them on. There is a sense in which in our day the individual has been submerged. In most parts of the country men work, not for themselves, not as partners in the old way in which they used to work, but generally as employees,—in a higher or lower grade,—of great corporations. There was a time when corporations played a very minor part in our business affairs, but now they play the chief part, and most men are the servants of the corporations. . . .

Yesterday, and ever since history began, men were related to one another as individuals. . . . To-day, the everyday relationships of men are largely with great impersonal concerns, with organizations, not with other individual men.

Now this is nothing short of a new social age, a new era of human relationships, a new stage-setting for the drama of life.

—WOODROW WILSON, 1912

A VERY DIFFERENT AGE

AMERICANS OF THE PROGRESSIVE ERA

They lived in a world that offered exciting new possibilities even as it destroyed traditional opportunities. They celebrated pioneering achievements and unprecedented abundance, yet they bemoaned the loss of their independence, their self-reliance, even their freedom. Americans of the Progressive Era watched new technologies, exploited by giant corporations, produce ever larger amounts of wealth, create millions of new jobs, offer a stunning array of consumer goods, and open life choices previously unimagined. And they watched the forces of change sweep away familiar modes of economic life, alter the way they lived and worked, rearrange the familiar hierarchies of social status, and redefine their relationship to their government. It looked as if all the rules had changed. Living increasingly in an interdependent society comprised of large institutions, individual Americans made numerous choices and competed with each other as never before to control their own lives. From those choices and contests, from the new institutions, from the losers as well as the winners, from the actions of both the powerful and the powerless, modern America emerged in all its complexity.

An Englishman writing about his visit to America in 1900 proclaimed that "life in the States is one perpetual whirl of telephones, telegrams, phonographs, electric bells, motors, lifts, and automatic instruments."[1] By 1910, Americans could buy electric sewing machines, fans, irons, washing machines, vacuum cleaners, stoves, heaters, phonographs, and a host of other devices. The telegraph transmitted messages almost instantly, and telephone use skyrocketed at the turn of the century, connecting one million homes and offices by 1910. Improved railroads made it possible to travel at speeds of sixty miles an hour; and electric trolleys and elevated railroads allowed people to commute from outlying residences to downtown jobs, shopping, and entertainment. Movie projectors revolutionized mass entertainment after the turn of the century. In 1900, Americans owned perhaps eight thousand automobiles; by 1920, eight million! The gross national product grew to unprecedented heights, from $11 billion in the middle of the 1880s to $84 billion in constant dollars by the end of World War I.

Giant corporations like U.S. Steel or International Harvester, impersonal entities headed by remote managers who seemed invisible, produced most of these new goods and services and held enormous power. Many middle-class Americans who enjoyed the material benefits of industrial capitalism feared that individuals had less and less control over their lives. Self-employed entrepreneurs declined in economic importance, and more and more people worked for corporations. An individual's security depended increasingly on the activities of the corporation and the decisions of a few senior executives. Their own efforts and abilities seemed less important. Nor did corporate capitalism distribute its material benefits equitably. As early as 1890, the richest 1 percent among American families owned 51 percent of the country's real estate and personal property, and the poorest 44 percent only 1.2 percent.

Class conflict erupted in the countryside and in the cities. Workers formed unions and went on strike, employers used violence to defeat them, and workers responded in kind. Farmers faced an unpredictable world market for their produce, with agricultural prices, railroad rates, and the cost of credit determined by powerful but invisible capitalists. They organized Alliances and built the Populist Party in the early 1890s to end the domination of the wealthy over the nation's toilers, but without success. The proportion of farmers who owned their own land declined steadily. Tenants and sharecroppers went from 26 percent of all farmers in 1880 to 37 percent by 1910. Moreover, farmers of all kinds were becoming a minority in an urban nation. In 1890, 35 percent of all Americans lived in cities; by 1920, 51 percent did so.

Immigrants, mostly Catholics and Jews from the unfamiliar countries of Southern and Eastern Europe, poured into America in record numbers to work in its expanding industrial economy. Often living in dense urban neighborhoods where foreign tongues predominated, they created their own churches, synagogues, and communal institutions. A few brought radical political ideas. Not surprisingly, many old-stock Americans feared losing control of their culture to foreigners.

Industrialism and urban culture also threatened the rules governing men and women. Early-nineteenth-century Americans had rigidly limited middle-class male and female spheres, giving men responsibility for public life and confining women to the home and family. Yet as industrialism advanced, the separation weakened. Women assumed new public roles, demanded the right to vote, attended high school and college, and worked in offices alongside men. Young women and men patronized dance halls, amusement parks, and movie houses. Here too, it seemed, the rules had changed.

In the early 1890s, middle-class Americans began looking to government to do something about these wrenching changes in America's economy and culture. They saw corrupt political bosses dominating cities and many state governments, pandering to immigrants and working-class voters with petty patronage while growing rich on bribes from traction companies, railroads, public utilities, and contractors. And they watched as the trusts manipulated members of Congress and used the courts and federal power to suppress dissent from farmers and workers. Government, which according to American ideals should represent the will of the people, appeared a captive of special interests.

Many middle-class Americans concluded, therefore, that they had lost control not only of their society but of their own lives. The idea that control of land, tools, knowledge, and other resources needed to produce wealth defined a man's worth had deep roots in colonial and early-nineteenth-century America. In the new agrarian nation, where land remained plentiful, wage labor had stigmatized a man for his dependence. Women, whose labor legally belonged to their husbands or fathers, had been thought naturally dependent by virtue of their sex. The market revolution after the 1820s began a steady increase in the number of wage laborers, both male and female, forcing a reassessment of the meaning of independence. Defenders of the new market economy insisted that men remained independent so long as they could sell their labor freely. Northerners opposed to slavery in the Southern states decried "the peculiar institution" for robbing African-Americans of this right to profit from their labor. Critics of the market economy, on the other hand, saw industrial employment as "wage slavery," arguing that laborers, completely dependent upon their employers, had lost the control over their lives that had always defined free American men. At the same time, the growing number of single women entering wage labor challenged traditional ideals of female dependency.

After the Civil War, the rapid growth of large corporations and the ensuing struggles between capital and labor exacerbated traditional fears of wage slavery as the decline of small entrepreneurs and independent farmers and craftsmen accelerated. These anxieties culminated in broad-based reform movements, which became known as progressivism, that began to transform local government in the 1890s and state and national government at the turn of the century. Benjamin Parke De Witt, an enthusiastic student of the era's politics, summed it up neatly in his treatise *The Progressive Movement*, published in 1915. "Complex conditions that were bringing wealth to the magnate and the railroad king were bringing difficult social and economic problems to the masses of people. . . . The individual could not hope to compete with the wealthy corporation which employed him," De Witt explained. "Men became economic slaves. . . . Slowly, Americans realized that they were not free."[2]

Many students of America's past have shared De Witt's conviction that progressive reform, a reaction against the excesses of corporate capitalism, dominated America from the 1890s to World War I. Historical narratives of this period focus largely on society's dominant institutions—corporations, government, reform organizations, and political parties—and the people who led them. Numerous accounts explore the efforts and probe the motives of progressive reformers and government officials to rein in big business and mitigate the human consequences of industrialization by expanding the scope and role of government.

Other historians, however, point to corporate capitalism as the dynamic force from which everything else, including politics and reform, followed. Corporate conglomerates, by virtue of their sheer size and complexity, needed to control whatever affected production and profit: the supply of materials, the workforce, the demand for their products, the price they could charge, and the actions of government. The needs of the great corporations dominated politics, economics, and society.

Still others argue that the growth of corporate capitalism constituted only one dimension of the economic and social revolution let loose by industrialization, transforming America's isolated local communities into an interdependent, modern bureaucratic society. America's organizational revolution, these scholars argue, created not only corporate capitalists but also professionals and middle-class reformers who believed that modern scientific knowledge made it possible for government to influence, if not master, social forces. Thus, corporate capitalists who sought control of the market, physicians or scientists who claimed a special role in society by virtue of their expertise, and progressive reformers who sought control of the forces of change all fostered the bureaucratic values of a modern organizational society.

These accounts, centered on corporations, government, and reform movements highlight crucial aspects of a changing America, but they paint an incomplete picture. In the last several decades, social historians have explored the ways in which people behaved during this transformation of American society. A rich literature documents the experiences of workers, immigrants, farmers, African-Americans, women, families, children, and other groups. These specialized social histories deepen our understanding of the period, but they fragment it by presenting groups of Americans largely in isolation from each other and from political and institutional change.

My narrative seeks to combine political, institutional, and social history. It concentrates primarily on the story of people confronted with change, but tells it against the backdrop of politics, corporate capitalism, and the organizational society. Americans in different circumstances acted in distinct ways when faced with the changes wrought by industrialism, corporate capitalism, progressive reform, and a complex society of large-scale organizations. Their varied responses to change constitute the essence of the story I tell.

I have organized my discussion primarily around people with common characteristics: those who earned their living in similar ways, men and women, immigrants, African-Americans, and others of common ancestry. I refer to people of the same sex, ancestry, or occupation as "groups," although significant differences divided people of common ancestry or occupation. Moreover, groups overlapped. A Lawrence, Massachusetts, textile worker might be male, an immigrant, a Catholic, an Italian-American and an industrial operative. All of these groups warrant consideration in a social history, but the categories are not mutually exclusive.

We can readily define groups like men, women, immigrants, or farmers, but I have defined other groups by how people saw themselves and how others saw them. Thus, men and women who worked in offices or department stores took pride in being "white-collar" employees, although they usually earned less money than skilled craftsmen. Physicians, lawyers, social workers, teachers, and librarians all took pride in being "professionals," although their incomes and working conditions varied dramatically. Social history, then, requires that we talk about groups, but we must recognize that group "membership" remained fluid, group boundaries permeable, and differences within a group could be as significant as differences among groups.

The chapters that follow examine how Americans sought to control their lives and their government during the transformation of America. What did different groups need and want from the emerging new society? How did they pursue their goals? To what extent did they succeed or fail? A small number left behind explicit statements of their life goals and experiences in letters, diaries, autobiographies, interviews, and the like, but we also can surmise a great deal about people's goals by looking at how they lived, at the choices they made in their work, family, community, leisure, and politics. Most people pursued three broad goals in life. They sought *economic security*, a reasonable level of material comfort. They sought *personal autonomy*, the ability to make life choices, exercise initiative, build families, and sustain communities, without undue interference from others. And they sought *social status*, respect and recognition from their peers or from society at large.

People faced radically different options. Men had more choices than women, wealthy people more than the poor, whites more than African-Americans or Native Americans, European immigrants more than immigrants from Asia. Different groups, and different individuals within groups, pursued these goals in distinct ways and attached varying importance to each. Poor common laborers or Southern sharecroppers worried more about economic security than social status. Those with somewhat greater economic security, such as skilled craftsmen, bitterly resisted changes in factory organization and technology that encroached not simply on their income but also on their ability to direct their own work at their own pace, their autonomy, and they struggled to hold on to the respect, the social status, traditionally accorded a craftsman. Middle-class women who needed to earn money maintained their social status by taking "respectable" positions as teachers or office clerks.

The goals and needs of one group often impinged on those of another. People competed continually, and sometimes violently, to gain advantage or to maintain the status quo as institutions changed. The most dramatic and sustained conflicts pitted corporate leaders, who demanded control of production, against workers who needed economic security and autonomy in the workplace. Late-nineteenth-century farmers in the Great Plains and the South likewise fought vigorously with railroad managers, bankers, manufacturers, and other corporate capitalists about freight charges, credit, and the price they received for their commodities on the world market.

These and other dramatic instances of organized protest are an important part of the story of institutional and political change, but people also pursued economic security, autonomy, and social status in informal and unorganized ways. Rather than accept oppressive conditions, permanent impoverishment, or declining economic security and social status, for example, industrial workers and farmers commonly moved from place to place. Peasants and artisans in Europe and elsewhere left for America, African-Americans left the rural South for Southern cities and for the North, sharecroppers went from one landlord to another, and children of Midwestern farmers went farther west to buy land. Workers changed jobs constantly, causing continuous turnover on the new assembly lines and in mechanized textile mills. Factory workers, domestic servants, agricultural wage workers, unskilled laborers, and others limited their pace of work, frustrating the foremen and scientific managers who struggled to speed up production. Through these unorganized actions, industrial workers, sharecroppers, domestic servants, and others contested the power of corporate managers, landlords, and mistresses.

Informal competition and overt conflict also occurred outside the workplace. Working-class men in cities, who enjoyed relaxing at a saloon, fought for autonomy in their leisure time against middle-class temperance advocates. Working-class people also resisted efforts by civic leaders to restrain their boisterous use of parks and public spaces. They defied child labor and mandatory schooling laws, enacted through the efforts of reformers, when their economic security depended upon children's earnings.

Changing gender roles sometimes pitted men against women. Male workers in some industries, especially during the labor shortage of World War I, fought to keep women out of their trades because the lower wages employers paid women threatened men's economic security and lowered their sense of social status. Many male physicians and lawyers likewise sought to exclude women practitioners for status reasons.

Competition in the quest for economic security, status, and autonomy occurred within groups as well as between them. Some professional engineers sought autonomy from their corporate employers while others strove for economic security and social status by identifying completely with corporate managers. Foremen in large corporations tried to protect their authority to supervise workers in their shop as they saw fit, their autonomy, from new personnel managers and time and motion engineers. Competing immigrant leaders vied for influence and social status within their communities. African-Americans who organized a mass exodus from the South during World War I challenged the economic security and social status of the ministers, businessmen, and other established leaders of Southern black communities. In these situations, and numerous others, Americans struggled to control their lives as they encountered the inexorable forces of change. In an increasingly interdependent society, the search for economic security, autonomy, and social status often produced competition, if not conflict, with someone else.

On the other hand, coalitions of several groups often united to pursue common goals. In the successful campaigns to unionize the ladies' garment industry, both male and female Jewish and Italian immigrant workers united with Jewish business and professional leaders, female progressive reformers, and affluent clubwomen. Urban political machines, despised by most reformers, united immigrants and native-born workers of many different nationalities, and in some places even worked in coalition with reformers to enact labor and social welfare legislation. The National Association for the Advancement of Colored People linked a group of African-American leaders with some of the leading figures of progressive reform. In these and many other situations, groups came together around particular issues.

Moreover, a common discourse dominated American political debate by the early twentieth century. Struggling to redefine the meaning of American democracy in the age of corporate capitalism, Americans of diverse backgrounds asked how government could protect its citizens against the negative effects of industrialism and economic concentration and how the polity could use government to regain control of the nation's destiny. To be sure, not all Americans participated in this dominant political discourse, and those who did often embraced divergent solutions. But for a decade and a half before the United States entered World War I, many Americans brought their search for economic security, autonomy, and social status into a spirited conversation about the relationship of citizens to their government and how that government should shape the future of an industrial nation.

Of course, people at other times and in many different places also coped with change and struggled to control their lives. I do not want to suggest that only in Progressive Era America did humans struggle for economic security, autonomy, and social status. Still, the quest for control by ordinary Americans provides a particularly useful lens with which to view America between 1890 and the end of World War I, because in these years corporate capitalism and the emergence of a complex society forced millions to adapt to change in order to control their lives while at the same time optimistic reformers proclaimed that government could indeed control the forces of change to make Americans efficient, good, and free.

I refer to this period as the "Progressive Era," even though the term describes at most only the period's reform movements and politics, because historians routinely use this label and readers recognize it more readily than any other. I begin in 1890, when settlement house residents and local citizen groups initiated a variety of reform movements, and end with World War I and its immediate aftermath because the war accelerated change and placed the actions and goals of different groups in bold relief. However, I do not mean to imply that reform dominated all aspects of life in these years or that everything that happened in the period, or for that matter everything done under the banner of reform, constituted positive change. In the years between 1890 and World War I, corporate managers violently suppressed strikes; millions of rural and urban Americans lived in poverty; lynching of African-Americans soared while white Southerners completed the segregation and disenfranchisement of black citizens. These and many other aspects of the period are not "progressive" by any modern definition.

I do not attempt to apply the lessons of the Progressive Era to the present. I must confess, however, that I am struck by many similarities between that period and our own. At the turn of the century, all Americans struggled to control their individual lives and some also tried to control the forces of economic and social change as industrialism and corporate capitalism changed all the rules. At the end of that century, it seems that Americans are again struggling for control amidst new and wrenching transformations brought on by the global information-age economy. Unlike their forebears a hundred years earlier, Americans today look cynically on the possibility of human perfectibility and on the capacity of government to direct social change. Still, because it is reminiscent of our own times in so many other ways, the story of how Americans in the Progressive Era coped with change compels our attention.

ampaigning in rural Kansas in 1890 for candidates backed by the Farmers' Alliance, Mary Lease, an Irish Catholic schoolteacher and lawyer, dissented eloquently from the dominant political ideology of Gilded Age America. "Wall Street owns the country," she declared. "The great common people of the country are slaves, and monopoly is the master."[1]

Farmer activists like Lease, labor leaders, and a good number of writers and intellectuals shared Lease's criticisms of corporate economic and political power. But in 1890 they stood outside the ideological mainstream. The prevailing conservative social Darwinism of the post-Civil War era reinforced a deep-seated American belief in limited government. Social theorists argued that human beings progressed through competition for survival and adaptation comparable to the biological evolution described by Charles Darwin in *On the Origin of Species* (1859). Organized society could not control this inevitable evolutionary process; and government had no significant role in redirecting the concentration of economic power or in mitigating its social effects. In reality, government subsidized railroad construction, maintained high protective tariffs and a tight money supply, used its power to crush strikes, and in other ways supported the nation's most powerful economic interests. But the laissez-faire myth still framed political debate.

The rise of monopolistic corporations accompanied America's rapid industrialization. The American business system at the start of the nineteenth century consisted of numerous small and modest-sized enterprises managed by their owners. In mid-century, businessmen organized the first large-scale corporations to build and operate canals, railroads, the telegraph, and iron and steel factories. By offering shares of stock in the company and distributing profits, dividends, to the share owners, they assembled large amounts of capital, separating company ownership from its management. By the 1870s, the railroad network enabled corporations to ship goods produced in one place to a national and international market, the telegraph and the telephone facilitated the conduct of business across long distances, and industrial technologies made continuous mass production possible. Large economic enterprises grew rapidly.

Nonetheless, producers faced severe competition and declining profits despite the economies of mass production and distribution. To control the supply and marketing of their goods, manufacturers in most industries entered into various kinds of combinations, creating still larger corporate enterprises. In Standard Oil, John D. Rockefeller created perhaps the most controversial combination, or trust, in American history. When Edwin Drake drilled the nation's first oil well in 1859, hundreds of businessmen flocked to the new industry. At first, refining crude oil into kerosene and other products required relatively little capital. The prices and the supply of crude oil shifted dramatically, however, making profits in this volatile market uncertain. Rockefeller entered the industry in 1863, and assembled a group of partners to form Standard Oil in 1867. By 1870, Rockefeller's company owned two large refineries in Cleveland and refined about one-tenth of the nation's crude oil. Using his company's great size as leverage, he forced the railroads to reduce Standard Oil's shipping rates. With lower costs than his competitors, he persuaded several Cleveland producers to sell out.

In 1872, Standard Oil joined with other refiners in forming the National Refiners' Association headed by Rockefeller. Hoping to avoid price fluctuations and uncertain profits, the group allocated production quotas to its members, but nonmember companies undermined the Association's attempts to control overall production, and even its own members commonly exceeded their quotas. So Rockefeller, giving up on voluntary cooperation, began to buy out companies throughout the country by giving their owners stock in Standard Oil and promising them higher profits. By 1880, the Rockefeller conglomerate controlled 90 percent of the country's oil-refining capacity.

In the 1880s, Rockefeller started to integrate this *horizontal* combination of refining firms into a firm that engaged in all aspects of the production and sale of petroleum products. He purchased oil fields, built pipelines for crude and refined petroleum, and developed his own marketing system. This *vertical* combination enabled Standard Oil to control nearly everything affecting production and profit, from the price and supply of crude oil to the distribution and marketing of finished products. Other aggressive entrepreneurs soon emulated Rockefeller's strategy. Gustavus Swift built a vertically integrated corporation in the 1880s that controlled all aspects of meat processing and distribution. Sugar processors formed the American Sugar Refining Company in 1891.

To dissenters like Mary Lease, the concentration of economic power in such large corporations demanded government response. And despite the dominant laissez-faire ideology, Congress responded in limited ways. After several states passed laws regulating railroads within their borders, in 1887 it created the Interstate Commerce Commission with authority to void rates that were not "just and reasonable." In 1890, Congress passed the Sherman Antitrust Act, which banned "unlawful restraints and monopolies." Government officials did little to enforce these vague statutes, however, and neither law had much impact until the next century.

But the federal government did support industrial corporations by maintaining a tight currency and a high tariff on imported goods. These policies hurt farmers, particularly in frontier areas of the Great Plains, where many had purchased land and agricultural machinery on credit. The federal government, which had issued paper money during the Civil War, now required that the national currency be backed fully by precious metals, usually gold. By limiting the supply of money, the government caused the value of the dollar to increase over time. This policy of currency contraction forced farmers to pay back loans with money dearer than that which they had borrowed.

Farmers faced other problems also. Dependent on the railroads to ship their produce to market, they resented paying shipping rates well above those charged to big customers like Rockefeller's Standard Oil. Protective tariffs raised the cost of foreign goods purchased by farmers. Compounding their problems, the price of most agricultural commodities fell steadily throughout the late nineteenth century, as the amount of corn, wheat, or cotton farmers produced increased. Farmers discovered that although they worked harder, cultivated more land, or invested in new technologies, they sold their produce for less money per bushel or per pound.

American farmers organized in various ways, in the decades after the Civil War, against these threats to their economic security and autonomy. The Grange, founded in 1867, created purchasing and marketing cooperatives, and although its charter officially eschewed politics, Grange leaders won elected office in several states. In Iowa, Illinois, Minnesota, and Wisconsin, Grangers worked for state laws regulating railroads and grain elevators. In the South, where landowners and opponents of black suffrage controlled the Grange, many African-Americans and poor whites joined other protest organizations like the Union League, the Cotton Pickers' League, and the Agricultural Wheel. In the 1870s large numbers of farmers also supported the Greenback-Labor Party, which advocated currency reform and inflation.

The Farmers' Alliance, begun in 1877 in Lampasas County, Texas, sent lecturers to rural communities beginning in the mid-1880s. They urged farmers to act collectively against falling farm prices, high interest rates, and farm foreclosures. The movement spread rapidly. By 1889, three Alliances—the Southern (for whites), the Colored (for African-American Southerners), and the Midwestern—claimed more than four million members. Alliance lecturers fanned out into farm communities throughout Texas and then elsewhere in the South and the West, giving farmers a common understanding of their economic problems and the determination to seek political remedies. Alliance lecturers created broad farmer support for public ownership of railroads, currency reform, and especially control of the credit system through federal "subtreasuries." Under this plan, the federal government would create warehouses in every agricultural county in the United States where farmers could deposit their produce and obtain loans, secured by their crops, at minimal interest. By solving farmers' credit problems and undermining commercial banking, Alliance members argued, the subtreasury plan would "emancipate productive labor from the power of money to oppress."[2]

After lobbying unsuccessfully for these reforms, the Alliance backed candidates for office, winning majorities in eight Southern and two Western legislatures. When these legislators failed to deliver on their promises, 1,300 delegates from the Alliances and a number of other groups met in Omaha in 1892 to form the People's Party, commonly known as the Populists. Their platform advocated the subtreasury plan, government ownership of railroads and telegraphs, an end to government grants of land to railroads, a flexible currency based on free coinage of silver to inflate the money supply and thereby lower farmers' debt, a graduated income tax, postal savings banks, direct election of U.S. senators, and the eight-hour day. The Populist candidate for President in 1892, former Union general James B. Weaver of Iowa, carried Kansas, Colorado, Nevada, and Idaho, winning twenty-two electoral votes.

Industrial workers faced a different set of problems. Most worked long hours for low wages. Better-paid skilled craftsmen worried that advances in industrial technology would eliminate skilled jobs and routinize factory labor. Workers organized, but less effectively than farmers. The Noble and Holy Order of the Knights of Labor, begun in 1869, embraced all "toilers" in a single national association, advocating reform of the economic system. The Knights enrolled approximately three-quarters of a million members by the mid-1880s, supporting numerous strikes across the country in a campaign to establish the eight-hour day. Workers also initiated national boycotts of products made by oppressive employers. Still, lacking an effective structure and a sharply defined program, the Knights of Labor collapsed during the depression of the mid-1890s.

The American Federation of Labor (AFL), formed in 1886 by craft unionists and dissenters from within the Knights, limited union efforts largely to skilled craftsmen, rejecting radical challenges to the economic system in favor of concrete collective bargaining over wages, hours, and working conditions. By 1892, forty weak national unions had affiliated with the AFL.

A dramatic strike at the Carnegie Steel Works at Homestead, Pennsylvania, in 1892 dramatized the political weakness of organized labor. Henry Clay Frick, a ruthless opponent of unions, assumed direction of the plant after installation of new open-hearth technology for steel manufacture which reduced the company's dependence on unionized skilled craftsmen. Frick soon announced a cut in wages. When the union refused to accept the reduction, he closed the plant and announced that thereafter it would operate as a nonunion mill. Frick sent two barges filled with armed Pinkerton guards to Homestead, and in a violent battle, strikers defeated the Pinkertons. So Frick asked the governor to break the strike, and three days later, the Pennsylvania National Guard occupied Homestead and protected the steel mills. Frick gradually reopened the works with nonunion labor. The state tried and convicted members of the strike advisory committee on charges of murder, riot, conspiracy, and insurrection.

Workers and farmers from the 1870s onward, then, challenged the dominant political ideology of limited government, protection of property rights, and conservative Darwinism. But a severe economic depression beginning in 1893, the worst the nation had

known, broadened their challenge to the dominant political discourse by demonstrating the depths of human suffering that a
corporate-industrial economy could produce. Just ten days before
the inauguration of Democrat Grover Cleveland as President in
1893, the Pennsylvania and Reading Railroad collapsed into bank-
ruptcy. A few weeks later, the National Cordage Company, commonly referred to as the "the twine trust," went under. By year's
end, 16,000 businesses and 500 banks had failed; 20 percent of
the workforce stood jobless by 1894. The unemployed walked the
streets of the big cities and wandered from town to town in search
of work, quickly exhausting the limited relief funds of private charities and local governments.

The depression caused many comfortable citizens to question the
nation's economic and political system. Local civic leaders in cities
and towns had often undertaken campaigns to replace corrupt politicians with "the best men." But now these civic reformers examined the structure of government and found it wanting. They began
to scrutinize not only corruption among political bosses tied to
working-class constituencies but also public utilities and other corporations that secured lucrative benefits from local governments.
The Milwaukee Municipal League, for example, won broad support
for laws, passed in 1895 and 1897, limiting patronage appointments
by establishing a city civil service system and forbidding political
parties from seeking campaign contributions from local government
employees. Soon thereafter, however, the League moved beyond
these traditional elite concerns, building a broad coalition to end
corporate tax advantages, eliminate tax evasion by wealthy individuals, regulate streetcar companies and public utilities, require utility lobbyists to register with the government, and open party
nominating caucuses to citizen participation. The Civic Federation
of Chicago likewise helped pass the city's first civil service law and
exposed government corruption; but it also organized relief programs during the depression winter of 1893–94.

Meanwhile, middle-class women pressed local and state governments to broaden human welfare services. Since the mid-nineteenth century, they had formed missionary societies, established orphanages and homes for wayward women, and campaigned to improve public sanitation and eliminate prostitution. Economic hard times heightened their concerns about the social consequences of corporate capitalism. During the depression of the 1890s, women's clubs, formed originally to discuss literature and the arts, began a wide range of social service and advocacy projects. The General Federation of Women's Clubs, founded in 1890, campaigned for government food inspection, stricter housing codes, sanitary improvements in public water supplies, laws protecting women in industrial jobs, and services for the poor, the sick, the disabled, and neglected children; they also worked against child labor and prostitution. Mothers Clubs and the National Congress of Mothers, established in 1897 to educate mothers about child rearing, also sought public support for infant health clinics, juvenile courts, probation and detention homes for children awaiting trial, kindergartens, and playgrounds. Middle-class African-American women, although barred because of their race from the General Federation, established their own clubs, forming the National Association of Colored Women's Clubs of America (NACW) in 1896. They educated mothers on child care, campaigned against alcohol consumption, and supported nurseries, kindergartens, and homes for unwed mothers.

In 1889, college-educated women and men began to found social settlements, community centers in the heart of big-city slums, where they lived and learned about their largely immigrant neighbors. The men, mostly Protestant ministers, sought to employ Christian ethics in solving the social problems of their industrializing society. The women, college graduates who by virtue of their sex had limited career options, sought a useful role in society by addressing the problems of poor immigrants in the slums of America's great cities.

Vida Scudder and two friends, all recent Smith College graduates, founded the College Settlement in New York in the fall of 1889. A week later, Jane Addams and Ellen Gates Starr moved into an old mansion on Halsted Street in Chicago, founding what soon became the most influential social settlement of all, Hull House. William Jewett Tucker, a liberal Congregationalist minister teaching at Andover Theological Seminary, founded Andover House in Boston in 1890. Two young nurses, Lillian Wald and Mary Brewster, went looking for an apartment on New York's Lower East Side in 1893 from which they could provide medical care to the poor, staying at the College Settlement before founding the Henry Street Settlement in 1897. Between 1891 and the end of the depression in 1897, the number of settlements in the United States grew from six to seventy-four.

The settlement founders wanted to help their new neighbors in the slums, but they came with no detailed blueprint of what they would do, developing their activities in response to what they found. Jane Addams, the brilliant and eloquent settlement leader, explained in 1892 the "Subjective Necessity for Social Settlements." They constituted, she said, "an experimental effort to aid in the solution of the social and industrial problems which are engendered by the modern condition of life in a great city." Residents must have "scientific patience in the accumulation of facts," arouse public opinion, "furnish data for legislation," and "use their influence to secure it."[3] Most settlements provided classes, clubs, nurseries, recreational programs, summer camps, and other services to their working-class neighbors, but a few became major centers for reform and social research. Leading settlement residents, like the extraordinary group of women gathered around Jane Addams at Hull House, initiated extensive research on their neighborhoods, publicized the plight of the poor, and established organizations which lobbied to expand government's support of economic security and human welfare, pointedly challenging the Gilded Age's Darwinism and commitment to limited government.

The activities of Hull House resident Florence Kelley, daughter of a Republican congressman, in the 1890s illustrate how women helped to undermine the dominant political ideology of the Gilded Age. Kelley, a socialist labor activist divorced from a Russian man she married while studying in Zurich, joined Jane Addams' Halsted Street settlement at the end of 1891. Heading the settlement's new Labor Bureau, which trained immigrant women for work as domestics, she quickly became a leader in the women's campaign to eliminate the manufacture of clothing at home by mothers and their children. Her report for the Illinois Bureau of Labor Statistics on this "sweatshop" system attracted attention. At a legislative hearing, Kelley proposed a law regulating child labor, banning tenement clothing manufacture, and establishing a state factory inspector's office. Jane Addams and Kelley won support for the bill from labor unions, middle-class women's groups, and churches. It passed in 1893, and pro-labor Governor John Peter Altgeld named Kelley Chief Factory Inspector for Illinois, a job she held until Altgeld's defeat in 1897. Kelley became a national figure in women and child labor reform, moving to New York in 1899 to serve as secretary of the newly formed National Consumers' League.

Jane Addams and the Chicago women's reform network also created the nation's first juvenile court almost single-handedly. Nineteenth-century criminal law made few distinctions between adult and juvenile offenders, and judges had limited options in sentencing youngsters who appeared before them. After examining the condition of juvenile offenders in the early 1890s, several charitable and women's groups in Chicago established a school for boys in the Cook County House of Detention. Then they led a four-year effort for legislation creating a separate trial court with a probation program for youthful offenders. When the juvenile court finally opened in 1899, it had no money to hire probation officers. So clubwomen, led by Louise deKoven Bowen, a prominent Chicagoan and volunteer at Hull House, established a committee to provide probation services for the juvenile court. Juvenile courts spread rapidly to other states.

Settlement residents and civic reformers thus helped to change what citizens in many cities expected of government. So did the election in the 1890s of a few mayors committed to improving the lives of working-class people. Among the best-known stood Detroit's Hazen Pingree. One of eight children who grew up on a modest farm in Denmark, Maine, Pingree left home at age fourteen and worked in cotton and shoe manufacturing factories, enlisted in the Union Army during the Civil War, and moved to Detroit in 1865, where he worked in a leather manufacturing plant before starting a shoe factory in partnership with a friend. Successful in business, Pingree won election as mayor in 1889 with backing from the city's conservative Republican business leaders. Once in office, however, he moved steadily from a program of efficiency and administrative reform to a broad social justice agenda, gaining support from working-class people who helped him win reelection three times. He fought to reduce the cost of utilities and public transit to consumers and to force businesses and wealthy individuals to pay greater taxes. He built schools, parks, and free public baths, created work-relief programs for the unemployed, supported laws against child labor, and favored primary elections to select party nominees, a graduated income tax, state regulation of big business, popular election of U.S. senators, and even municipal ownership of street railways and public utilities. Elected governor of Michigan in 1896 and reelected in 1898, he continued his reform initiatives, pushing for legislation to increase taxes on corporations, railroads, and public utilities.

Samuel Jones, who came to America from Wales at the age of three, made a fortune manufacturing oil-drilling machinery. He earned the nickname "Golden Rule" because he gave his workers an eight-hour day and vacations with full pay and refused to employ children. Serving as Toledo's mayor from 1897 to 1903, Jones introduced civil service reform and an eight-hour day for city employees, opened kindergartens and playgrounds, fought against corruption in awarding streetcar franchises, and improved relations between the police and working-class citizens.

The efforts of these mayors, organized citizen groups, and settlement residents to broaden the scope and effectiveness of local and state government made hardly a ripple in Washington in the 1890s. President Grover Cleveland, who feared farmer and labor activism, showed no interest in these reforms. Assuming that the depression stemmed from lack of confidence in the nation's currency, he convinced Congress to eliminate the purchase of silver as backing for paper money. In 1895, Cleveland turned to two of the nation's most powerful bankers, J. P. Morgan and August Belmont, for a $62 million loan to head off a run on the treasury's specie by buying gold. The transaction earned these multimillionaires a tidy profit.

Cleveland reaffirmed his unequivocal commitment to limited government and Darwinian ideas about the causes of social distress when, in the depths of the depression, groups of unemployed workers from all parts of the country organized protest marches to Washington from as far away as Los Angeles, San Francisco, and Montana. The most famous group, headed by eccentric Ohio businessman Jacob S. Coxey, demanded that the federal government issue five hundred million dollars in paper currency to pay unemployed men to build roads. Sympathetic members of Congress introduced Coxey's bill, but the majority would not act on it, so Coxey organized what he called a "petition to Washington with boots on," and Coxey's Army of about a hundred men left his home town of Massillon, Ohio, on Easter Sunday 1894. Picking up marchers along the way, they arrived at the capitol. Police arrested Coxey and two other march leaders for walking on the grass and carrying banners on the capitol grounds, and then indiscriminately clubbed protesters and spectators alike. After the melee, a court fined Coxey and his deputies each five dollars and sentenced them to twenty days in jail.

This show of force paled by comparison with what Cleveland unleashed two months later against the American Railway Union. Workers who manufactured sleeping cars in an industrial community built and operated by George Pullman outside of Chicago

struck after Pullman cut their wages during the depression with no
commensurate cut in the rents he charged them for their houses.
The American Railway Union (ARU) supported the Pullman workers by refusing to work on any trains with Pullman sleeper cars,
thereby shutting down the nation's railroad system. President
Grover Cleveland and his Attorney General, Richard Olney, a former railroad attorney, sent in federal troops to operate the railroads
on the pretext of protecting the U.S. mail, over the objections of
Illinois governor Altgeld and despite the union's announcement that
it would not interfere with mail service. Rioting resulted, taking
thirty-four lives in five days, but the troops broke the strike and the
union. The government brought charges against the ARU's militant
president, socialist Eugene V. Debs, and a judge sentenced him to
jail for six months for interfering with the mail.

Cleveland's hostility to workers and farmers in the midst of the
depression strengthened the Populist Party, which won several congressional seats and state offices in the 1894 elections. Then, in
1896, a young Nebraska editor who had served in Congress, William Jennings Bryan, capitalized on agrarian discontent, the suffering brought on by the depression, and Cleveland's adherence to
tight money and business interests to capture the Democratic Party
nomination for President. Son of an Illinois state senator and judge
who reared him on the values of Jacksonian democracy in a deeply
religious home, Bryan grew up in comfort and went to college. After
an unsuccessful effort to build a legal practice in Jacksonville, Illinois, Bryan moved to Lincoln, Nebraska, where he rose quickly
in politics, winning election to Congress in 1890.

Supporters of a currency based on both gold and silver dominated
the 1896 Democratic Party convention in Chicago. The proposed
party platform, largely written by Governor Altgeld and rife with
anticorporate rhetoric, condemned Cleveland's "trafficking with
banking syndicates" and the "arbitrary interference by Federal authorities in local affairs" during the railroad strike. But the currency
issue overshadowed all others, and the proposed platform advocated

the free coinage of silver. During the platform debate, Bryan, a brilliant orator, turned the currency issue into a metaphor for the burdens of the struggling masses, urging toilers everywhere to reclaim their country from "the idle holders of idle capital." Concluding one of the most effective speeches in American history, Bryan roared, "You shall not press down upon the brow of labor this crown of thorns, you shall not crucify mankind upon a cross of gold." His electrifying speech guaranteed Bryan the nomination, and sounded the theme he would repeat in over six hundred campaign speeches delivered in twenty-one states to an audience of perhaps five million. The Populist Party, divided by Bryan's candidacy, voted to back his bid for President but nominated Tom Watson of Georgia for Vice President. Cleveland gold Democrats broke away and nominated their own candidate.

The Republicans selected Ohio governor and former congressman William McKinley, a strong supporter of high tariffs. Marcus Hanna, a millionaire who made his fortune in coal, iron, oil, and merchandising, fastidiously planned McKinley's nomination and the subsequent election campaign, which contrasted in every way with Bryan's. McKinley campaigned from the front porch of his house, greeting delegations of supporters from many parts of the country brought there by Hanna. The Republican campaign distributed hundreds of thousands of pamphlets, sent reams of copy to newspapers, and distributed campaign posters and buttons everywhere. To fund this elaborate campaign, Hanna raised unprecedented sums, at least $3,500,000, compared with the $300,000 Bryan spent.

Outorganized and outspent, Bryan lost by about 600,000 votes, with McKinley outpolling him 271 to 176 in the electoral college. Bryan lost primarily because free silver had only sectional appeal, offering nothing to the industrial working class in the East and the Midwest, and because many middle-class people who supported the kinds of reforms advocated by the settlement houses and the women's clubs feared tampering with the currency. Still, despite

his defeat and the continuation of limited government in the Mc-
Kinley administration, Bryan's campaign began the process of altering the discourse of politics on the national level. Although
people like Jane Addams, Florence Kelley, Hazen Pingree, and
Samuel Jones had no enthusiasm for Bryan's campaign, he shared
with them the conviction that ordinary Americans had lost control
of their lives and their government in the age of corporate capitalism; and they agreed that an expanded, activist government could
re-empower citizens.

The depression of the mid-1890s also accelerated the process of
corporate consolidation and thus heightened the apparent urgency
of government action to regulate the trusts. Between 1895 and 1904,
157 new holding companies consolidated 1,800 firms; 72 of these
new mega-firms controlled at least 40 percent of the market in their
industries, and 42 firms at least 70 percent. In 1896, fewer than a
dozen U.S. corporations (excluding railroads) had capital assets
worth over $10 million. By 1903, the number jumped to 300 cor-
porations, and 17 had assets of $100 million or more. United States
Steel, capitalized at $1.37 billion on its creation in 1901, became
America's largest corporation.

This startling pace of corporate consolidation, coming on the
heels of Populism and Bryan's campaign, made Americans increasingly receptive to the calls of Mary Lease, Jane Addams, Hazen
Pingree, and many others for a more activist government to protect
citizens from the growing power of economic concentration. After
the turn of the century, debates about how to regulate the trusts,
how to bring about industrial peace, and how to make government
responsive to the electorate would shape American politics.

As this new progressive discourse began to dominate political
discussion, an assassin shot President McKinley. Theodore Roosevelt became President in 1901. He would serve until 1909, gaining a reputation as a "trustbuster" and conservationist, while
muckraking journalists revealed to an eager public one scandal
after another in government and business. Roosevelt's handpicked

successor, William Howard Taft, would govern from 1909 to 1913, unable to contain the growing movement for far-reaching reform within his own Republican Party. The Republican Party would split in 1912, with Roosevelt returning to politics as the candidate of the Progressive Party in a three-way race against Republican Taft and the victor, Democrat Woodrow Wilson. In his first term, Wilson would expand government regulation of business and the economy, enabling him to win reelection in 1916 as a progressive, only to lead the country into the Great European War in 1917. The war, lasting until the end of 1918, would co-opt the progressive discourse and ultimately destroy it.

Yet despite the drama of political events in the early twentieth century, despite the extraordinary ability of settlement house workers, women's clubs, sensationalistic journalists, and flamboyant politicians to engage the public's interest in government and the great debates about corporate capitalism and democracy, politics and reform did not dominate most Americans' lives. The vast majority had to cope first and foremost with the social and economic consequences wrought by industrialism and corporate capitalism. We begin with their stories.

1

OWNERS, MANAGERS, AND CORPORATE CAPITALISM

"We have come upon a very different age from any that preceded us," proclaimed New Jersey governor Woodrow Wilson, Democratic candidate for President of the United States in 1912. Men now work "not for themselves" but "as employees . . . of great corporations."[1] Wilson's words expressed the anxieties of millions of Americans, who watched corporations transform the way they spent their working hours and the way they spent their money. Corporations elevated top managers to positions of unprecedented power and simultaneously destroyed the livelihoods of many small entrepreneurs. We turn first, therefore, to the people who managed American business large and small, those who benefited from the rise of corporate capitalism and those who suffered.

The organizers of the giant trusts, men like John D. Rockefeller, fearful of the exigencies of the traditional competitive market, sought order, predictability, and control of all aspects of production and distribution to ensure steady profits. No one exemplified this quest for total control better than J. P. Morgan, the preeminent business leader of the early twentieth century. A financier, Morgan hated disorder, devoting himself to eliminating price competition in business and bringing about orderly consolidations to maximize profits. In the late 1880s, he began to consolidate and stabilize America's railroads, which had high fixed costs and regularly engaged in price wars. Morgan brought together officers of competing railroad lines to encourage agreements to limit competition. During the depression of the mid-1890s, Morgan consolidated numerous competing railroads into a limited number of large railroad systems in different regions.

Morgan is best known for putting together U.S. Steel, the first billion-dollar corporation in America. The consolidated company manufactured over half the country's basic iron and steel, giving it effective control over prices. Morgan also helped to consolidate the telephone industry and to develop the electrical industry. Because of barons like Morgan and Rockefeller, a small number of corporations in most major industries controlled the majority of their market by the early twentieth century.

Consolidations created a new set of problems for corporate leaders, however. Great size did not automatically make a company efficient or profitable. Giant manufacturers had to develop systems to supply their multifarious manufacturing plants with raw materials, to organize the flow of materials and goods from one stage of production to another, and to coordinate the production output with the transportation system that shipped the goods to distributors. A small manufacturer might know intuitively what it cost to make a product and what profit he made when he sold it, but big corporations needed to assess the costs of every aspect of the operation.

Complex corporations therefore required executives with substantial managerial ability. Professional career managers who did not necessarily own large quantities of company stock became the corporations' administrators and leaders. Although these positions typically went to the sons of businessmen from old-stock families in the Northeast, family background alone became insufficient.

MANAGERS OLD AND NEW

Systematic management, dependent upon bureaucracies rather than on individuals, began to take hold at the end of the nineteenth century. Mechanical engineers initiated the earliest discussions of how to direct large enterprises. Henry Towne, an engineer and lock manufacturer, told fellow engineers in 1886 that the management of industry required men who combined the qualities of a mechanical engineer and those of a businessman. A few heads of corporations experimented with new procedures. Andrew Carnegie required each department at Carnegie Steel to submit detailed figures on the costs of materials and labor. Accountants in his central office processed these figures, and Carnegie reviewed the accountants' cost statements daily and demanded explanations from the head of any department where they increased. One of his managers complained, "The men felt and often remarked that the eyes of the company were always on them through the books."[2]

Many corporate heads clung to familiar modes of operation, however. Often it took a generational change in company leadership to bring systematic management, as at E. I. Du Pont de Nemours & Company, manufacturer of gunpowder. For nearly a half century, Henry Du Pont, the company president, directed the large family business out of a one-room office overlooking the gunpowder mills, writing by hand almost all of the company's correspondence. In addition to running his own company, he bought controlling interests in several other large powder companies and dominated the Gunpowder Trade Association, formed in 1872 to regulate production. Three years after Henry's death in 1899, four of the five Du Pont partners, all elderly or infirm and unwilling to assume the presidency, contemplated selling the company, but Alfred Du Pont, the youngest and least experienced, objected. He convinced his cousins Coleman and Pierre Du Pont to join him in buying the family business. Coleman, who had worked at the company until 1898, left out of frustration with the conservative ways of the elderly partners. At the time of the purchase, Pierre wrote to his brother, "We have not the slightest idea of what we are buying, but we are probably not at a disadvantage as I think the old company had a very slim idea of the property they possess."[3] The new partners integrated the company's diverse holdings, centralized management, developed a specialized research department, and started their own marketing unit.

Foremen and other front-line managers felt the impact of centralized management first. In the late nineteenth century, factory foremen exercised considerable independent authority. They hired, trained, supervised, and fired workers, and usually decided which tools and materials would be used in each job. So long as they got the work done, upper managers left foremen alone.

Foremen cherished the autonomy and social status of a manager. Most began their careers as skilled craftsmen, priding themselves on their superior knowledge of the craft. According to a history of a silversmith firm, foremen "deported themselves with great dignity and customarily reported for work attired in silk hats, cutaway coats, and attendant accessories."[4] Despite their origins as skilled workers, or perhaps because of it, foremen vigorously opposed unions and sometimes treated workers harshly. One analyst observed in 1911 that foremen "spurn the rungs by which they did ascend."[5]

Systematic management undermined the autonomy of foremen and lower-level managers. When Stuyvesant Fish became president of the Illinois Central Railroad in 1896, he complained of "an absence of system in the organization as a whole" and described managers' treatment of employees as "personal and paternal." Fish implemented a code of personnel policies to allow the railroad to function and expand "without the slightest fear of being disturbed by the withdrawal of any man from any position."[6] At Scovill Manufacturing in Connecticut, which made brass products, foremen decided what to pay each of their workers until the company president ordered that timekeepers report to the payroll supervisor the actual hours worked by every employee, including the foremen. Elsewhere, special clerks relieved foremen of responsibility for purchasing materials needed for a job, and engineers began to instruct foremen on the tools to use and the sequence in which tasks should be performed.

Foremen and other front-line managers resisted this attack on their autonomy and status. One manager complained that foremen "resented taking instructions from abrasive, soft-handed college men who had never themselves poured a mold or run a machine."

Superintendents complained vociferously about the number and extent of reports demanded by the central office. Occasionally a foreman might prevail in a conflict with a senior manager. In one instance, an experienced foreman got into an altercation with a supervisor and told him to stay out of his shop for a month. The supervisor complained to a senior manager, who responded, "Well, Mr. Lawrence, the foreman of the plating-room has the reputation of carrying through with his word. If I were you, I think I should keep out of that department for the rest of the month."[7]

Similar tension developed between buyers and managers in big city department stores. These retail corporations, begun in the late nineteenth century, attracted middle-class shoppers by offering package delivery, child care, entertainment, and other services while customers shopped for all kinds of goods under a single roof. Initially, department stores gave considerable autonomy to buyers for each department. They determined what merchandise to sell, managed the department sales staff, wrote advertisements, and arranged floor displays. After the depression of the 1890s, store managers concerned with overall store profits tried to limit the quantity of goods buyers stocked and eliminate harmful competition among departments. To the consternation of buyers, store managers placed goods on sale to meet competition from other stores and readily accepted returned goods. Like factory foremen, buyers resisted these challenges to their autonomy. Store managers, dependent on buyers' relationships with numerous manufacturers of clothing and other goods, sometimes relented. This tug-of-war between buyers and store managers continued for many years.

These conflicts between front-line and senior corporate managers seemed minor when compared with the conflicts between management and labor. Corporations depended upon large numbers of workers. Numerous strikes, frequent worker turnover and absenteeism, and concerted efforts by workers to restrict the pace of production limited managers' control of production. Although most employers responded to workers in the time-honored way—attempting to coerce them to produce more and forcefully breaking strikes—some large corporations also looked for ways to rationalize labor relations without relinquishing control over production. Two general approaches emerged: scientific management and corporate welfare programs.

Frederick W. Taylor, an enormously creative and unyieldingly rigid engineer and industrial manager, devoted much of his career to solving corporate management's labor problem by dramatically increasing the efficiency of workers. This win-win strategy, he argued, made possible both higher wages and larger profits. Taylor was born in Philadelphia in 1856 to wealthy native-born parents. His mother participated in the antislavery and women's rights movements, and his father worked as a lawyer and pursued a gentlemanly interest in literature. As a child, Frederick showed a penchant for orderliness and insisted on elaborate sets of rules when he played games. The young Taylor attended Phillips Exeter Academy to prepare, according to his father's wishes, for Harvard and a career in the law. The son preferred to attend medical school, but in his last year at Exeter he developed headaches and vision problems. Instead of going to Harvard, this eccentric young man became an apprentice pattern maker, despite the fact that the work required him to read complicated mechanical drawings, and his eye problems miraculously cleared up.

His apprenticeship completed, Taylor went to work at Midvale Steel Company, partly owned by a family friend, as a journeyman machinist and took home-study courses in physics and mathematics in his spare time, earning a degree in mechanical engineering from Stevens Institute of Technology. Promoted to chief engineer six years later, he struggled to find more efficient ways for his workers to perform their tasks and attempted, without success, to persuade the workers to increase their productivity by using his new methods.

Taylor left Midvale in 1903 to become a full-time "management consultant." At Bethlehem Steel Company, his most important client, he accumulated extensive information on the speed and effectiveness of tools and machines, and helped develop a steel alloy for use in manufacturing new high-speed machines. He also conducted time and motion studies to determine how quickly workers could do a particular task and when they became fatigued. From this work, Taylor developed a system of "shop management" in which engineers determined the optimum use of each machine and the most efficient pace at which a worker could do a task. He matched each worker to the task that man could do best, and provided substantial wage incentives to get the workers to achieve maximum efficiency.

Taylor's reputation spread among professional engineers, and the American Society of Mechanical Engineers elected him president in 1906. Three years later, officials at federal arsenals engaged Taylor to apply his principles to munitions manufacture. Soon thereafter, liberal lawyer Louis Brandeis, representing clients opposed to a railroad rate increase before the Interstate Commerce Commission, used several of Taylor's disciples as expert witnesses to argue that scientific management could greatly reduce railroad costs, and that the railroads should not charge consumers for their own inefficiency. Brandeis' appeal to scientific management stirred intense national interest. *The American Magazine*, edited by progressive journalist Ray Stannard Baker, serialized Taylor's recently completed manifesto, *The Principles of Scientific Management*.

In *Principles*, Taylor described how he increased daily steel hauling from 12½ to 47 tons per worker at Bethlehem. He watched seventy-five men for three or four days and picked out four "who seemed physically able to handle . . . 47 tons." He and his associates looked up the men's histories and made inquiries about their "character, habits and . . . ambition." They selected a "little Pennsylvania Dutchman who had been observed to trot back home for a mile or so after work in the evening, about as fresh as he was when he came trotting down to work in the morning." Then they called out the man, whose name was Schmidt, and offered to raise his pay from $1.15 to $1.85 a day if he agreed "to do exactly as this man tells you to-morrow, from morning till night," with "no back talk."

Schmidt started to work, and all day long, and at regular intervals, was told by the man who stood over him with a watch, "Now pick up a pig and walk. Now sit down and rest. Now walk—now rest," etc. He worked when he was told to work, and rested when he was told to rest, and at half past five in the afternoon had his 47½ tons loaded on the car. And he practically never failed to work at this pace and do the task that was set him during the three years that the writer was at Bethlehem.

"One man after another was picked out and trained to handle pig iron at 47½ tons per day," Taylor boasted, until all of the pig iron was handled at this rate, and the men were receiving 60 percent more wages.

Taylor made sweeping claims for his system, describing it as a "science" resting "upon clearly defined laws, rules and principles." Scientific management will "double the productivity of the average man engaged in industrial work," provide cheaper and better goods to consumers, increase both profits and wages, and thereby "eliminate the wage question as a source of dispute."[8] In short, Taylor proposed to increase dramatically the autonomy of management engineers and simultaneously reduce that of both workers and traditional corporate managers, promising in exchange greater economic security for workers and greater profits for owners.

Taylor's system never worked nearly as well as he claimed. Unions resisted it, often through strikes, and individual workers sabotaged Taylor's time and motion studies. After civilian government workers struck against the introduction of Taylorism at the arsenal in Watertown, Massachusetts, in 1911, Congress held hearings on the Taylor system, and investigators concluded that scientific management did not enhance the welfare of workers. In 1916, Assistant Secretary of the Navy Franklin D. Roosevelt banned the Taylor system in government arsenals and navy yards.

Workers understood that Taylorite engineers sought to take away from them all matters of judgment about their jobs: what tools to use, in what order tasks should be performed, how many pounds they should lift at one time, how fast they should work, when they should rest—in short, every aspect of control over work. "In the past, the man has been first," Taylor declared, but "in the future the system must be first."[9] Although workers surely wanted higher wages, few would willingly sell their autonomy for Taylor's wage incentives. Moreover, workers recognized better than Taylor that corporate managers, faced with pressures to control costs, would not maintain high wages once they had established higher standards of worker productivity. In the end, workers rejected scientific management because it threatened both their autonomy and their economic security.

Many managers resisted Taylorism as much as or more than their workers. Taylor's system limited their autonomy too, circumscribing their responsibilities and assigning key decisions to planning departments. Systematic management had already restricted the autonomy of foremen over materials, costs, and methods of production. Taylor proposed to go further, eliminating traditional foremen altogether in favor of a "functional foremanship." A "gang boss" would have responsibility for the movement of materials, a "speed boss" would oversee the organization of production, an "inspector" would ensure a quality product, a "repair boss" would maintain machinery, and a "disciplinarian" would hire and fire workers.

Foremen and superintendents fought the Taylorites wherever they appeared. When developing his methods at Midvale Steel, Taylor designed a bulletin board on which he posted tags giving work assignments to different machines in the shop. He had to cover it with thick glass, however, to keep the foremen from tearing off the hated tags. As a consultant to Simonds Roller Bearing Machine Company of Fitchburg, Massachusetts, in 1897, he set up a planning office. All of the foremen quit in protest. When machinists at the Watertown Arsenal walked out in opposition to Taylor's reorganization, several of the foremen supported the strikers. At Bethlehem Steel, managers successfully opposed Taylor's elaborate cost accounting system. Although some fifty companies employed elements of Taylorism, in the years before World War I only two companies embraced it completely. By threatening the autonomy and economic security of workers and managers alike, scientific management failed to fulfill corporate managers' quest for control of production costs.

Welfare capitalism offered an alternative, equally unrealistic, way to make labor reliable, efficient, and pliant. Its advocates proposed a wide variety of employee benefits to secure worker loyalty and prevent unionization and walkouts, including subsidized housing, free health care, libraries, social clubs, company cafeterias, and recreational activities. Some employers even offered company stock. Others allowed workers to elect representatives to advise management about worker concerns and set up procedures to hear employee grievances.

At least forty companies initiated substantial welfare programs before World War I. Some also established personnel departments to deal with all aspects of employee recruitment, training, and supervision, incorporating welfare work within them. The National Civic Federation, formed by corporate leaders in 1900 to find ways to mediate labor-management conflict and to discourage worker radicalism, established a Committee on Welfare Work in 1904 to promote these activities.

Although some executives claimed altruistic motives, most sought to stabilize their labor force and to increase productivity. George Perkins of International Harvester candidly asserted that his company undertook welfare programs "in a purely business spirit." Another businessman proclaimed crudely, "When I keep a horse and I find him a clean stable and good food I am not doing anything philanthropic for my horse." Elbert H. Gary of U.S. Steel got to the heart of the matter when he explained in 1914 that "we must make it certain that the men in our employ are treated as well, if not a little better than, those who are working for people who deal and contract with unions."[10]

Foremen and front-line managers, their autonomy and status al-

ready challenged by centralized administration and scientific management, now had to contend also with welfare and personnel
directors. One personnel manager, after studying the way foremen
hired and fired workers in several factories, declared that "in no
other phase of management is there so much unintelligence, reck-
lessness of cost, and lack of imagination." Some personnel administrators viewed foremen as mere workers. Officials of Henry Ford's
"sociological department" at his Dearborn auto factory visited the
homes of Ford workers beginning in 1915 and ensured that they
had orderly and wholesome habits. Ford's "sociologists" initially
visited foremen as well as workers, but the foremen refused to submit to inspections and senior managers backed down. "We were
trying to teach other fellows how to live," one foreman explained,
"and they wanted to investigate us at the same time."[11]

Historians, in describing how corporate capitalism transformed
work in America, have understandably focused on industrial workers and their struggle with capital. But corporate capitalism also
transformed, albeit less dramatically, the work lives of its managers.
Personnel directors, management engineers, and the senior executives who centralized control of corporate conglomerates secured
a leading place in the new economic order. Foremen and other front-
line supervisors, although much better off than the workers they
often drove ruthlessly, still lost status and autonomy. Like the workers they supervised, they found ways to resist.

SMALL BUSINESSMEN

The spread of giant corporations also challenged the economic security of self-employed entrepreneurs. Small companies managed
by their owners could hardly compete with large manufacturers of
steel, petroleum products, or processed foods. Still, the vast expansion of the national industrial economy created opportunities in the
interstices of the giant industries. The number of manufacturing
firms actually increased 37 percent in the 1890s and by smaller

percentages in succeeding decades, even as a limited number of corporations came to dominate most major industries.

Small metal fabricators and machinery makers in New England, for example, succeeded by making specialized products in quantities too limited for large enterprises. A company begun in 1901 made steel core plugs used in tar paper, floor coverings, and newsprint manufacture. Another, founded in 1917, manufactured miner's cap lamps; still another, founded in 1908, produced equipment for distilling water. Small manufacturing firms, headed by men who had been skilled industrial craftsmen or proprietors of other small businesses, often excelled at providing deliveries on short notice and offering personal service. A former office worker told an interviewer that he started a metal business because he "had ambition." Another explained, "I had a family, and I needed more money." A toolmaker started his own business because he resented the fact he received only 30 cents of the $1.50 his employer charged for the product he made.[12]

Similarly, small textile manufacturers in Philadelphia survived by producing limited quantities of specialty fabrics which required highly skilled labor, leaving the continuous production of basic cloth to large, automated mills in New England and the South. These family businesses produced wool and worsted fabrics, carpets, upholstery, knit goods, and lace curtains, for example, and they shifted quickly from one product to another as the market changed. A textile industry publication reported in 1907 that "a Philadelphian has a set purpose to have a business of his own, no matter how small, and young men are starting in business today with two or three looms, making worsteds or rugs." The proprietor "is the designer, operator and owner for a time" and as his business increases he becomes a "selling agent and manager" too. Proprietors worked "in overalls, running or directing operations of looms or spindles."[13]

Some small manufacturers, then, maintained family businesses or succeeded in new enterprises by manufacturing goods too specialized for large companies. But for all those who survived and thrived as small entrepreneurs in the corporate-dominated economy, many more lost autonomy and their economic security.

Corporate consolidation and integration hit independent distributors who sold manufactured goods to shopkeepers particularly hard. Many corporations developed their own sales and distribution networks staffed by their own employees, freeing themselves from dependence on self-employed distributors. At the same time, new retail corporations—department stores, mail-order companies, and chain stores—purchased goods in huge quantities from manufacturers and sold them directly to consumers, hurting both small wholesale and retail merchants.

Manufacturers of consumer and agricultural machinery, such as Singer Sewing Machine, Remington Typewriter, and McCormick Harvesting, established distribution networks by the 1880s. Only people who could explain to prospective buyers how the machines worked and provide instruction, service, repair, and technical assistance to customers could sell their products. In the 1890s, food processing and distribution corporations established networks of offices that shipped fruit from plantations in the Caribbean or meat from regional slaughterhouses to stores across the country. Chicago's William Wrigley manufactured and packaged chewing gum and sold it directly to shopkeepers. Asa Candler produced Coca-Cola syrup in Atlanta, employing a worldwide sales force to sell it to druggists and other retailers. National Biscuit Company, formed out of a horizontal combination of three regional companies, shifted from making bulk crackers for store cracker barrels to the manufacture of attractively packaged Uneeda Biscuits. It centralized manufacturing in large New York and Chicago plants, used extensive advertising to increase consumer demand, and built an international sales network that brought the crackers into the stores. Although shopkeepers made only a small profit on this product, consumer demand proved so great that merchants had little choice but to stock Uneeda Biscuits.

Before companies developed their own distribution networks and built demand through mass advertising, one manufacturer explained, they "stood on the merchant's doorstep begging him to buy his product." But an advertising trade journal gloated early in the new century, "The manufacturer selling an advertised trademarked article is absolutely independent. The only class to whom he is responsible is the consumer."[14] Companies like National Biscuit and Wrigley thereby reduced the autonomy of shopkeepers throughout the nation.

They also eliminated many independent entrepreneurs who had worked as wholesale distributors for corporate manufacturers. Elliot S. Rice, a casualty of the management reorganization and integration at Du Pont, began his business career as a wholesale grocer in Erie, Pennsylvania, before the old Du Pont management persuaded him to move to Chicago to serve as a general agent for the company in the Midwest. Technically self-employed, Rice received a salary from Du Pont along with a commission on sales. After Du Pont's new management established a sales department in Wilmington, Rice complained to Coleman Du Pont that a company official had bypassed him in hiring a freight manager for Chicago. "I cannot believe that the foregoing was ever authorized by you," he wrote. Du Pont's reply stunned him. "I beg to advise you that your office in Chicago will be entrusted with just so much of our business as we think you can handle, always reserving the right to ourselves to decide the question."[15] Not long thereafter, an auditor in the corporate office asked Rice to justify certain expenditures, and Rice refused until Coleman Du Pont intervened personally. Other demands for information followed. When the vice president for sales concluded that Rice was inefficient and overpaid, Rice resigned.

The rise of mass retail corporations posed the biggest threat to the autonomy of wholesalers and distributors. In the middle of the nineteenth century, specialty stores in cities sold specific types of

goods, like gloves, umbrellas, or women's hats; small-town general
stores sold many different kinds of items. In succeeding decades,
big city department stores began offering a wide variety of goods
under a single roof. Meanwhile, mail-order houses, offering many
of the goods sold in department stores as well as appliances, hard-
ware, and furniture, began to distribute catalogues and take orders
from people across rural America. Montgomery Ward and Sears,
Roebuck began in the 1870s, but the mail-order business really
took off in the mid-1890s when Sears greatly expanded its offerings
and cut costs, manufacturing many goods itself and buying large
quantities directly from the producers. Sears's profits soared from
$68,000 in 1895 to $2,868,000 in 1905. By 1906, Sears owned
sixteen manufacturing plants and filled 100,000 orders daily. Chain
stores, selling inexpensive consumer goods in small retail outlets
across the country, grew rapidly after 1900. The most successful
chain stores included the Great Atlantic and Pacific Tea Company
(A&P) with nearly five hundred general grocery stores by 1912, and
Frank W. Woolworth's five-and-ten-cent stores.

Small retailers fought back. In several states, they pressed state
legislatures for laws restricting department stores, failing everywhere but Missouri. There, the state Supreme Court overturned
their legislative victory. When chain stores began to grow some
years later, urban merchants again failed to secure restrictive laws.
Rural merchants had a different target—the United States Post Office. Until the first years of the twentieth century, farmers had to
pick up letters at tiny post offices located in general stores and
packages at railroad stations. With rural free delivery, the Post
Office closed many of these substations, depriving proprietors of
their modest income as postal agents and also reducing the need
for farmers to come to their stores. Moreover, rural people could
now order through the mail, picked up daily at their homes, the
vast array of goods offered by catalogue companies. Then, to make
matters worse, postal officials extended rural home delivery to packages. Small-town merchants and private delivery companies vigorously opposed this, but Congress bowed to the desires of rural

consumers, establishing rural parcel delivery in 1912. In its first year, orders to Sears increased fivefold.

The shopkeepers responded with spirited campaigns to convince people to buy local, even labeling catalogue buyers "traitors" to their community. One flyer read: "What's the use of sending money east when we can buy just as cheap at the Popular Store?" Some merchants collected Sears and Ward catalogues and ceremoniously burned them in the town square. Others appealed to neighborly loyalty. "When you want to raise money for some needy person in town do you write to the 'Fair' store in Chicago or do you go to your home merchant?" the editor of a rural Iowa newspaper asked rhetorically in 1904. "When your loved one was buried, was it Marshall Field and Co. who dropped a tear of sympathy and uttered the cheering words, or was it your home merchant?" This same newspaper sharpened its admonition the following year. "People who continually buy goods away from home," it declared, "are helping to kill the town in which they live by destroying its businesses and lowering the price of its real estate and driving out its population."[16]

Mail-order companies, chain stores, and the new sales departments in manufacturing corporations also hurt traveling salesmen and small distributors, who vented their anger at hearings before the U.S. Industrial Commission in 1899. Hoping to spark federal action against the "retail trusts," people like P. E. Dowe, representing an organization of traveling salesmen, asserted that no longer could his members attain their own business "as an equitable return for years of hard work under trying conditions." Instead they must give up their independence and work for huge corporations. "Trusts have come . . . as a curse for this generation and a barrier to individual enterprise," he lamented.[17] His plea, mingling with those of the small city merchants and rural general store proprietors, evoked broad sympathy but no government action. Some tradesmen retained autonomy and economic security by distributing goods not sold by corporate retailers. Many others lost out, becoming, for better or for worse, employees in an economy dominated by corporate capitalism.

CORPORATE CAPITALISM AND GOVERNMENT
REGULATION

When shopkeepers and small distributors railed against the trusts and demanded government action to protect traditional entrepreneurship, they echoed a familiar theme of the Progressive Era. Organized farmers demanded regulation of railroad rates and grain elevators and called on government to give farmers control over the marketing of their crops. Middle-class reformers, troubled by industrial violence, child labor, and horrific work conditions, demanded government regulation of factory and mine safety, child and female labor, working conditions and hours.

The national government did not regulate economic life substantially in the late nineteenth century, although it vigorously promoted corporate interests by subsidizing railroad construction, maintaining a tight currency, and keeping tariffs on imported goods high to protect domestic producers. By the end of the century, however, many Americans looked to the national government to mitigate the negative effects of industrial capitalism. With so much economic power concentrated in the hands of giant corporations, many argued, the federal government must now regulate the market and supervise corporations in the public interest. The "trust question" and "the industrial question" became central issues of national politics in the early twentieth century.

However, the debates on these issues did not neatly pit businessmen against consumers, farmers, workers, and social reformers. They also pitted smaller businessmen against larger ones, and businessmen in one industry against those in another. While politicians, reformers, and journalists demanded government control of the trusts, most businessmen did not rigidly oppose regulation, but tried to control it for their own purposes.

Many states established public utilities commissions to protect consumer interests by regulating local gas, electric, and steam companies. Utilities executives generally supported state regulation as an alternative to regulation by several different city commissions, discovering quickly that they could influence the public utilities commissions to restrict competition, rationalize service, and secure profits. Public outrage at several prominent mine disasters caused coal industry executives to join with others in an effort to bring about uniform state safety legislation for mines. This approach won the support of the coal mine operators represented by the American Mining Congress, who thought uniform safety standards would equalize the costs of safety across the industry. The movement for uniform laws failed, however, because mine operators in different states could not resolve their differences in this highly competitive industry.

Businessmen in many industries and in many different states supported workmen's compensation laws in the second decade of the century. For many years, common-law doctrine held that workers injured as a result of their own negligence, the negligence of another worker, or at jobs that inherently involved high risk could not sue their employers for damages. As accidents increased in the late nineteenth and the early twentieth century, both court rulings and changes in state legislation altered these common-law principles, making the outcome of injury suits against employers unpredictable. Workers wanted a system that provided immediate compensation to injured laborers and reformers wanted incentives to improve industrial safety. Businessmen joined labor unions and reformers in supporting state workmen's compensation to eliminate uncertainty about employer liability and to simplify compensation.

On the federal level, the trust question preoccupied the administrations of Theodore Roosevelt, William Howard Taft, and Woodrow Wilson. Leaders of the large corporations, facing uncertain and inconsistent enforcement of the Sherman Antitrust Act, sought a clearer federal policy that would not force the breakup of large corporations or intrude too heavily upon management's prerogatives. In 1903, Congress established, at President Roosevelt's request, a cabinet-level Department of Commerce and Labor with a Bureau of Corporations within it. The bureau could investigate corporations and publish its findings, but had no direct regulatory authority. George W. Perkins, a senior officer of J. P. Morgan & Company and a friend and political ally of Roosevelt, mobilized business support for the new department and the bureau. Smaller manufacturing firms, owned and operated by individual entrepreneurs, feared the power of both large corporations and labor unions. Through the National Association of Manufacturers (NAM), they lobbied for vigorous enforcement of antitrust laws and opposed any concessions to organized labor. A textile manufacturer in the NAM told a congressional committee in 1904 that "the so-called organized labor and the organized capital in the shape of trusts are not antagonistic to each other" and he expressed alarm "as to what will become of the commercial and manufacturing conditions in the United States if one class of labor gets control of all labor, and one class of capital gets control of all trade."[18]

The National Civic Federation, which represented the large corporations, played a significant role in discussions of federal antitrust policy that culminated in the passage of the Federal Trade Commission Act and the Clayton Antitrust Act in 1914, two major achievements of President Wilson's administration. The former declared illegal "unfair methods of competition" and empowered the commission to issue cease and desist orders, to require annual and special reports from corporations, and to investigate antitrust violations. The Clayton Act outlawed certain kinds of corporate consolidations, including interlocking directorates in firms capitalized at over a million dollars, and price discrimination. Similarly, both powerful Eastern bankers, like Morgan, and Western and small rural bankers played a role in reforming the nation's monetary system through the Federal Reserve Act of 1913. Although progressive politicians and journalists portrayed these laws as the product of a public uprising against the trusts, corporate leaders played a major role in shaping them.

.   .   .

The leaders of the major corporations that dominated industrial America above all sought control of production and the market for their products. To restrict competition, they formed voluntary trade associations and created massive horizontal combinations. To control the supply and price of goods and raw materials and the distribution of their products, they purchased mines, plantations, and transportation facilities, creating great vertical combinations. To regulate costs and the flow of materials through the production process, they developed systematic central management. To control labor, they provided welfare benefits to their workers and developed personnel departments. To protect themselves against the uncertainties and inconsistencies of America's courts and legislative bodies and from the growing demand for solutions to the "trust question," they played a major role in developing government regulatory policy in the Progressive Era.

Corporate leaders' quest for control threatened many people. Foremen and middle managers lost autonomy and social status to central office executives. Small manufacturers adapted or went out of business. Independent distributors and merchants reluctantly relinquished their economic security and autonomy. Corporations also changed the nature of work in America, creating new kinds of jobs in offices, department stores, and company bureaucracies, transforming the way farmers produced and marketed their crops, and fundamentally altering the work lives of industrial laborers and craftsmen. In each of these instances, people both resisted change and adapted to it creatively, challenging corporate control however they could.

2

INDUSTRIAL WORKERS' STRUGGLE
FOR CONTROL

A tug-of-war between workers and corporate capitalists shaped America's twentieth-century industrial system. Corporate leaders sought to lower labor costs but also wanted reliable and pliant employees. Workers needed economic security for their families, but they also demanded autonomy in performing their jobs. Industrialists experimented with Taylorite methods, installed mass production machinery, broke down complex industrial jobs into shorter and simpler tasks, kept wages as low as possible, and insisted on strict factory discipline. Workers formed unions and went on strike over wages and hours, work rules and control of the shop floor. They changed jobs readily, took days off at will, and slowed the pace of production. In this uneven contest in which industrialists held most of the power, workers still fought for economic security, challenged managers' control over the workplace, and protected the autonomy of their families.

Many factories, mills, and mines from the mid-nineteenth century on required workers with considerable skill to perform complex tasks. Skilled craftsmen themselves determined the manner and pace of their jobs. Labor leader John Brophy, a turn-of-the-century coal miner, recalled "the skill with which you undercut the vein, the judgment in drilling the coal after it had been undercut and placing the exact amount of explosive so that it would do an effective job of breaking the coal" with little or no supervision. A miner, Brophy continued, "was his own boss within his workplace."[1]

Many skilled laborers in 1890 shared Brophy's experience, and some still proudly performed their jobs without much direction in 1920. But most of American industry moved in the opposite direction, reducing the skill and therefore the autonomy of workers. A superintendent at the Swift meatpacking plant in Chicago explained how the assembly line gave him control of production: "If you need to turn out a little more you speed up the conveyor a little and the men speed up the pace."[2]

Wages increased faster than prices in the late nineteenth and the early twentieth century, but not enough to ensure that a laborer with limited skill could support a family, even if work remained steady. In many factories, however, busy periods alternated with slack times, and most workers continually feared unemployment. They also dreaded the poverty that befell a family of a worker injured or killed in an industrial accident, a fate frighteningly common in this period.

Workers did not accept their lot passively. They tried to achieve economic security for their families and to control conditions and rules in the workplace. On the job, they organized unions but also established informal codes of behavior to maintain control over the nature and pace of work. As citizens and voters, they sought help from the government. As members of families, they subordinated individual preferences to collective needs. And as members of culturally distinct ethnic and working-class communities, they created and defended their own institutions and systems of mutual support.

SKILLED CRAFT WORKERS

Mid-nineteenth-century industry depended heavily on skilled craftsmen, who labored independently and commanded substantial wages. Iron craftsmen, for example, worked largely as internal contractors. Collectively they negotiated with management a price per ton of iron, hiring and paying unskilled laborers to assist with heavy work. They controlled the pace of work and the rules of the mill.

Skilled craftsmen trained their assistants, and could pass their craft positions on to their sons or other relatives. Organized into fraternal unions, these craftsmen maintained monopolies on the skills needed to produce iron, and vigorously guarded their control of the workplace. They developed a code of ethical behavior and penalized violators. The workers themselves defined the "stint," a reasonable day's work, and ensured that no craftsmen exceeded it. They expected craftsmen to treat each other with respect, support fellow workers' grievances, and act in a proud and manly manner toward management. Skilled cigar makers, for example, refused to display any deference to factory owners or foremen. They would not run errands for their bosses or perform any task other than rolling cigars. Their union rules also forbade them from renting houses from their employers. They wore attractive clothing, symbolically asserting their social equality with their employers.

Managers, dependent upon skilled craftsmen, could not significantly increase production or lower unit costs except by introducing new technologies which did not require skilled labor. Open-hearth machinery for steel production, for example, installed by many companies in the late 1880s, reduced the need for powerful craftsmen, dramatically cutting labor costs. This technology enabled Henry Clay Frick, no longer dependent on skilled craftsmen, to break the Amalgamated Iron and Steel Workers Union in the Homestead strike of 1893. When Pennsylvania judge Edward Paxson sentenced the strike leaders, he explained that the real issue in the strike was control of the mills, chiding the convicted unionists for "the assertion of imaginary rights, . . . a deliberate attempt by men without authority to control others in the enjoyment of their rights."

The defeat of the union and of craft control enabled Carnegie Steel to realize spectacular increases in productivity as it cut wages and increased profits. In the next eight years, production tripled and profits soared from $4 million in 1892 to $40 million in 1900. A few skilled workers became low-level managers, but the craftsmen's day had passed. As one of Andrew Carnegie's associates put it, no longer was "the method of apportioning the work, of regulating the turns, of altering the machinery, in short, every detail of working the great plant . . . subject to the interference of the Amalgamated Association."[3] In 1901, after J. P. Morgan bought out Carnegie and created U.S. Steel, the new corporation forced a final confrontation with the remaining unionized plants and completely routed the Amalgamated.

Machinists faced a similar challenge to their control of production, but they resisted more successfully. Like ironworkers, the men who built machines and machine parts took pride in their work, their mutual responsibility, and their manliness. The young Frederick Taylor, working as a gang boss at the Midvale Steel lathes, complained that the machinists "carefully planned just how fast each job should be done." When he tried to increase production they brought "such pressure to bear (both inside and outside the works) upon all those who started to increase their output that they were finally compelled to do about as the rest did, or quit."[4]

The number of machinists grew rapidly after 1880 as expanding factories needed more and more machinery and parts. Some firms made standardized machine components, but production machines still had to be customized to specification, and no great technological breakthrough, like the open-hearth steel process, lessened management's dependence on skilled workers. As competition among machine manufacturers grew, however, they sought to cut costs and increase worker productivity through scientific management. Taylor stated proudly that, in his system, management engineers gathered the knowledge of production which craftsmen had kept to themselves so that it could be used to maximize efficiency. Machinists understood how managerial innovations like piecework, undergirded by time and motion studies, endangered their autonomy and status as well as their income. As they saw it, Taylor sought to accomplish by management what Frick had done with guns and political power.

Machinists, who rarely went on strike before the depression of the 1890s, lost some ground during those years but bounded back by the end of the decade, using the strike weapon with some success. The International Association of Machinists (IAM) grew, its new members pledging never to work two machines at once or accept pay below the union's established minimum. Machinists passed around copies of Taylor's *Principles of Scientific Management*; just the appearance of engineers with stopwatches on the shop floor commonly caused a job action. As one machinist from Davenport, Iowa, explained: "Now we object to being reduced to a scientific formula, and we do not want to have the world run on that kind of a basis at all."[5] When the union's national leaders attempted to negotiate reduced hours and minimum pay by accepting management authority over shop rules, machinists at the local level refused to cede control.

In other industries, craft workers similarly struggled to maintain high pay and control of shop rules. Where new technology undermined their position, as in the textile industry, they quickly lost their autonomy and their pay declined. In crafts not substantially affected by technological or managerial change, like the building trades, skilled workmen held on to the craftsmen's traditional status and rewards. But the great expansion of America's industrial economy during the Progressive Era relied primarily on semiskilled operatives in dozens of new industries.

INDUSTRIAL OPERATIVES

Unlike craftsmen, who exercised judgment and independence, operatives performed a single, easily learned task repetitively. Employers typically paid operatives piece rates. Foremen supervised them strictly, imposing penalties for lateness or defective work. Whereas skilled craftsmen came from the ranks of native-born or immigrant males from Western Europe, huge numbers of new immigrants, men and women, from Eastern and Southern Europe worked as operatives alongside a smaller number of native-born workers. Managers frequently assigned certain tasks exclusively to women, whom they paid less than men. Children also worked as operatives. Only rarely did factory managers employ African-Americans, however; racism relegated black workers mostly to jobs as unskilled laborers or domestic servants.

Managers used new technologies and new ways of organizing factory labor to reduce the skill needed by industrial workers. Jobs for industrial operatives grew rapidly. The manufacture of light-bulbs, for example, involved thirty-five processes. Young women constituted 94 percent of the workers who manufactured or assembled bulb components, according to a 1907 federal government study. The women who worked with filaments did the equivalent of threading a fine needle two to three thousand times a day. Foremen established piece rates for each process by determining the daily output of a fast worker. They set the rates so that these "fast" women earned no more than what managers thought normal for young female factory workers. "We keep rates so low that they have to keep right at it to make a living," bragged one supervisor.[6] Managers fined operatives for poor-quality work and infractions of shop discipline, and sometimes paid a small bonus to workers who produced well above average.

In the textile industry, power looms had replaced hand weavers even before the Civil War, but in the late nineteenth century, manufacturers introduced improved spinning and weaving machines and thereby reduced the skill needed for most tasks. They also increased output by requiring workers to tend more machines. "Year by year they've been adding new machinery and making one man gradually increase his work until he was doing that of two," a textile worker explained to a Georgia reporter in 1898.[7]

Textile managers also assigned different tasks to men and women. The relatively well-paid male operators of mule spinning machines, developed in the 1850s, needed considerable strength and modest skill. By the 1890s, textile manufacturers had begun to replace the mules with new, easily operated ring spinning machines, which could be handled by lower-paid workers. One mill superintendent boasted that when the mule spinners in his mill demanded an increase in pay, "one Saturday afternoon, after they had gone home, we . . . smashed up a room full of mules with sledge hammers. When the men came back on Monday morning, they were astonished to find that there was no work for them. That room is now full of ring frames run by girls."[8]

In other industries, changes in work organization rather than in technology swelled the ranks of specialized operatives at the expense of skilled workers. The meatpacking industry pioneered in assembly-line production precisely because the killing and processing of animals of different size and quality did not readily lend itself to mechanization. Until the 1880s, in many slaughterhouses, a single skilled butcher killed the animal and cut it up, controlling the pace and manner of his work. Two decades later, a "killing gang" of 157 men, each performing a single operation, did the same work, but still manually. A few highly skilled jobs remained, but most workers exercised little control over the pace and manner of work. A trade journal explained that with the installation of the Armour Company conveyor system, the men "must keep steadily and accurately at work, for it keeps coming, and each man must complete his task in an appropriate time or confess himself incompetent for the job."[9]

Henry Ford, on the other hand, developed a fully mechanized assembly line between 1910 and 1914 to produce identical Model T cars. Before he created the assembly line, teams of skilled craftsmen made each car. Now these skilled laborers worked as toolmakers, draftsmen, pattern makers, troubleshooters, and supervisors, with the actual production work performed by operatives. By the early 1920s, operatives made up nearly two-thirds of the employees in the auto industry, and craftsmen only 9 percent. One Ford engineer explained that in hiring operatives the company had "no use for experience." Ford "desires and prefers machine-tool operators who have nothing to unlearn, who have no theories of correct surface speeds for metal finishing, and will simply do what they are told to do, over and over again, from bell-time to bell-time."[10]

Without the craftsmen's monopoly of skill, operatives could not demand the craftsmen's autonomy. But assembly-line workers did not acquiesce in poor pay, unsteady work, or the discipline of the assembly line. In informal ways and through unions, these workers contested their employers' claim to hegemonic control of the factory and its labor force.

First, they protested with their feet. Workers resisted management control by leaving their jobs whenever they could. A 1919 study found that fully one-third of all men hired by factories stayed in their jobs for less than a year. Despite high pay, Ford workers facing the monotony of assembly-line work quit readily. To maintain a workforce of 13,000 for a twelve-month period in 1912 and 1913, Ford employed 54,000 different individuals, an annual turnover rate of 416 percent. Magnus Alexander, personnel director for General Electric, found that twelve metalworking firms employed 42,571 workers to fill 6,700 new jobs during 1913. Operatives on repetitive jobs quit most often, and it took several months for a new worker to achieve maximum proficiency.

Boredom and physical strain did not cause all the turnover, however. In the Amoskeag textile mills in Manchester, New Hampshire, studied by historian Tamara Hareven, workers tried to reconcile "job security and continuity of employment" with "some freedom and control over their own schedules . . ."

> Men wanted to go hunting and fishing in season. Some wanted to return to Canada to tend a farm or to assist relatives; others wished to alternate factory work with farm work in New Hampshire or with lumbering in Maine or Canada. Women also wanted to be able to withdraw temporarily after childbearing or to alternate housekeeping with factory work as family needs dictated.[11]

Sometimes relatives replaced each other at the same job; other times workers just quit.

Rural white workers in Southern mills routinely failed to show up for work. "Most men had the Monday drunks, I reckon," recalled a mill worker about her experience in the 1910s. Employers rarely fired absent workers, she explained, because the entire family would pick up and move, creating an immediate labor shortage. And, if they did fire them, "they'd hire them back the next day when they sober up." Officials of one Southern mill complained to investigators in 1907 and 1908 that there was "a considerable falling off in the number [of workers] who report for work directly after pay days, and on one particular Monday following pay day . . . 150 looms were idle at one of the mills." Workers also moved from mill to mill. "I never did have to take anything," a mill worker told an Atlanta reporter in 1899. "If they don't treat me right, I just walked out. I could always walk into another door."[12] In 1904, Eagle and Phoenix Mills in Georgia and Alabama employed 4,986 workers to fill fewer than 1,800 jobs.

Managers in other industries and in other parts of the country told similar stories. H. A. Worman, an executive of International Harvester, headquartered in Chicago, complained in 1908 that "two or three Monday-idle machines in any group make serious inroads on the department's earnings." A management engineer who visited the Ford assembly line in 1914 attributed high turnover among operatives in part to "the desire to do something different, after drilling the same-sized hole, in the same place, in the same piece, day after day, for several months."[13]

Like skilled craftsmen, industrial operatives enforced production quotas, albeit informally. A gang leader in a U.S. Steel mill in Fort Wayne complained that "as soon as the night boss turns his back . . . [immigrant workers] just drop down and sleep." One Ford worker reported an "unwritten law" restricting the pace of work. The "hungry bastards" who violated it "were ostracized, and no one would talk to them. Every time one of them went for a drink of water or to the washroom, the belts on his machine were cut, the grinding wheel was smashed, his personal tools were damaged, the word

'RAT' was chalked on his machine in block letters."[14] Henry Ford won acclaim for offering workers high wages, fringe benefits, and profit sharing, but like other corporate heads who embraced welfare capitalism, Ford did so to retain and motivate assembly-line workers.

Nor did piece-rate pay readily overcome worker resistance to production speedups. Workers knew that if they increased their productivity, employers would cut rates. A young woman bookbinder told an investigator in 1911 that "I worked very hard, but I tried to keep a schedule because if one girl turns out too much in a day, they're apt to cut the rates."[15]

In short, industrial operatives, unable for the most part to prevent changes in technology and work organization from diminishing their autonomy in the workplace and threatening their economic security, still kept managers from gaining unquestioned control over labor force efficiency and productivity. Progressive economist John R. Commons saw clearly that workers "are conducting a continuous, unorganized strike."[16]

UNSKILLED LABORERS

Commons' observation applied equally to unskilled laborers, often called "common laborers" or "day laborers." The transformation of industrial production had little impact on them because they worked with their hands and bodies and did not operate machines. These men—and most were young, single males—built and repaired train tracks, loaded freight in railroad yards and on docks, hauled building materials, dug ditches, paved streets and roads, shoveled coal into industrial furnaces, and moved goods inside factories. Far from the cutting edge of industrial development, their numbers remained considerable.

Laborers' work varied from day to day. Researchers for the U.S. Immigration Commission reported that a gang of workers on New York City's new aqueduct "may work in the stone quarry one day, on concrete work the next, or in moving the track for the dirt trains the following day."[17] Common laborers found work more easily in warm weather than in the winter, when rural construction work generally ceased. Even more than operatives, laborers moved constantly from job to job, looking for better pay or fleeing oppressive gang bosses.

Immigrants from Eastern and Southern Europe, most often single or with wives and families still in Europe, made up the largest group of laborers. They came to earn money and often had no intention of staying in America. Many, particularly Italians, worked for a *padrone* or labor recruiter of the same nationality who provided transportation and negotiated their employment. In Southern African-American farm families, men did common labor at slack times while women and children tended the crops. Single, native-born white men from rural areas, commonly called "hoboes," also moved in search of manual work.

With the exception of longshoremen, common laborers migrated too often to join a union. Like operatives, they went from job to job, and refused to show up for work when it became too exhausting. Social worker Grace Abbott reported in 1914 that American-born white railroad construction laborers rarely stayed at a job more than ten to fifteen days. In the winter, most returned to Chicago to shovel snow, cut ice, and do odd jobs, and the rest went to lumber camps.

Like operatives and craftsmen, laborers regulated their pace of work. A middle-class writer who took a job as a laborer in a steel mill described his first day:

When I started in I figured I'd keep going as long as I could and loaf after I was played out. I couldn't get on with the programme. First the little Italian boy tapped me on the shoulder and advised, "Lotsa time! Take easy!" I slowed down a notch or two. A little later the Russian, wiping off the sweat as he sat for a moment on a pile of bricks, cautioned, "You keel yourself. Twelve hours long time." Finally, after every one had remonstrated, I got down to a proper gait—so you'd have to sight by a post to see if I was moving.[18]

Pittsburgh laborers told a researcher that they took off to celebrate "Saint Monday" as they pleased. Those whose work required only muscle and stamina, consigned to strenuous and dirty jobs for low pay, still decided for themselves when, how, and how hard they would work.

Workers' Collective Action

Some workers, however, joined together to protect or improve their economic condition and work situation. They formed unions, went on strike, and voted for prolabor and socialist candidates. The Knights of Labor collapsed in the depression of the 1890s. The AFL survived, but just barely. By the end of the 1890s depression, its membership numbered only 447,000, not even 5 percent of American wage workers. But with the return of prosperity after 1897, AFL president Samuel Gompers pursued conservative policies with some success.

The AFL sought to negotiate industry-wide contracts and eliminate spontaneous grass-roots strikes. From 1897 to 1904, union membership rose to 2,073,000. Coal miners, typographers, machinists, railroad employees, and building trade workers, among others, won eight- or nine-hour days and other improvements. Concentrated in the crafts, the AFL made little effort to penetrate the growing ranks of mechanized factory operatives and unskilled laborers. Some politicians, including President Roosevelt and later President Wilson, grudgingly accepted the legitimacy of unions, while businessmen in the National Civic Federation sought an accommodation with organized labor.

Formidable obstacles kept the unions from growing very much more until World War I. The National Association of Manufacturers, bent on their destruction, launched an "open shop" campaign. Employers' associations provided strikebreakers, maintained industrial spies, and blacklisted union activists. Unions lost members during the depression of 1908 and 1909. But organized labor limited its own growth by ignoring factory operatives, the fastest-growing segment of industrial labor. A few AFL leaders recognized the need for industrial unions encompassing all workers, irrespective of skill. James O'Connell, president of the machinists' union, stated that "every day our trade is becoming more and more specialized, and if we hope to protect our craft it is necessary that our qualifications for membership be radically changed," but most AFL leaders did not agree.[19]

The experience of the meatpackers' union between 1901 and 1904 illustrates the obstacles to labor-management cooperation. The heads of the two largest packing companies, Louis Swift and J. Ogden Armour, active members of the National Civic Federation, sought an agreement with the butchers' union which would eliminate work stoppages and produce a steady and reliable workforce. Amalgamated Butchers and Meatcutters Union (ABM) president Michael Donnelly and treasurer Homer Call eagerly sought a national union contract for all meatpacking workers, not just the dwindling number of skilled butchers. "Today, it is impossible to draw the line where the skilled man leaves off and the unskilled man begins," declared the ABM journal, "and makes it necessary to organize all working in the large plants under one head."[20] The union rapidly signed up new members and negotiated contracts with Swift, Armour, and other large companies.

These industry-wide contracts on wages and hours did not readily address the problems of the ordinary packinghouse workers, however, who wanted work organized to guarantee steady employment. Cattle butchers won a ten-hour day in 1902; the company could not keep workers longer unless the foreman guaranteed full work for the next day. The union also secured promotions based on seniority and a last-hired-first-fired rule in the cattle-killing department, significantly eroding the discretion of foremen, who had traditionally extracted payments from workers in exchange for promotion or rehiring after layoffs. But workers also wanted to eliminate seasonal unemployment by getting the companies to employ everyone part-time, if necessary, during slack periods; the companies refused.

The contract in the Chicago stockyards established elected

"house committees" in each department of the plant to settle management and worker grievances. These committees began to reduce the pace of work. John R. Commons concluded in 1904 that they had cut production between 16 and 25 percent. One worker in the Beef Luggers local explained, "We used to load 60 to 70 cars of beef with 5 or 6 men," "and now we load 60 cars a day with 8 men, thereby putting more carriers to work; and where we had only 37 carriers before we organized, we now have 53, and they do no more loading than the 37 used to do." The packinghouse workers accomplished this by short and often spontaneous strikes, without union endorsement, around specific issues during busy periods. Donnelly spent a good deal of his time trying to control these workers and settle local strikes.

The actions of workers on the local level soured the packers on their experiment in collective bargaining. The union had not stabilized labor relations as promised, but it substantially limited management control over production. When the union, responding to grass-roots concerns, demanded a minimum pay scale for all workers including the common laborers hired daily at the gate, the employers refused, precipitating a long strike. The packers used strikebreakers, including African-Americans from the South, and routed the union. A spokesman for the packers explained that "the dominating of the packing plants by the union gradually had become unbearable. The proprietor of an establishment had forty stewards to deal with and nothing that failed to suit them could be done."[21]

Grass-roots workers displayed similar militance in clothing manufacturing, but with happier results. Jewish and Italian immigrant women predominated, but immigrant men held the better-paying skilled jobs. The manufacture of ready-made clothing required only modest capital, producing a large number of employers and making industry-wide organizing difficult. The owners lacked organization, however, and did not command the political power and resources that enabled large industrialists to defeat strikes.

Male garment workers had attempted unionization sporadically since the 1880s. Tailors who sewed men's clothing formed the United Garment Workers in 1891, and men who made women's clothing founded the International Ladies' Garment Workers' Union (ILGWU) in 1900, although neither made much headway. By 1906, only 2,500 of 40,000 cloak makers in New York City had joined the ILGWU. Beset by conflicts between skilled cutters and less skilled workers, and between ideological socialists and pragmatic unionists, the ILGWU nearly fell apart by 1908.

Owners imposed rigid discipline on female garment workers. Some charged the women for needles and supplies, for their clothes lockers, and for the chairs on which they sat. They fined them for being even a few minutes late. Employers usually paid workers by the garment, keeping piece rates low. Rebecca August, who led a protest of buttonhole makers in Chicago in 1907, recalled, "They paid 3½ cents for a button hole. I was very fast because there was an urge behind it. The more money I made, the sooner we could send for my mother and the six children." When her foreman realized she was making $25 a week, he cut the piece rates, saying "it was an *outrage* for a *girl* to make $25 a week."[22] August organized an unsuccessful protest, for which her boss fired her.

In 1909, young women workers in New York's shirtwaist industry struck spontaneously in three separate factories. The employers of Rosen Brothers, the first to go out, won a union agreement after five weeks. But the owners of the Triangle Shirtwaist Company and Leiserson's refused to settle, hiring thugs and prostitutes to harass the picketers. (The tragic death of 146 young workers in a fire two years later at the Triangle Shirtwaist Factory would bring public outrage against the conditions under which these women worked.) The strikers pressed the ILGWU to call a general strike in the shirtwaist industry, but the union hesitated. To placate them, union leaders called a mass meeting attended by Samuel Gompers and prominent socialist leaders. After a series of speeches, Clara Lemlich, a young immigrant strike leader, passionately addressed the audience in Yiddish. "I am a working girl, one of those striking against intolerable conditions. I am tired of listening to speakers who talk in generalities," she declared. "What we are here for is to decide whether or not to strike. I offer a resolution that a general strike be declared—now."[23] Pandemonium erupted and the assembled garment workers overwhelmingly approved the strike.

The "uprising," by 20,000 mostly female workers lasted nearly three months, shutting down most shirtwaist factories. Prominent women reformers, including settlement house leaders Lillian Wald and Mary Simkovitch, used their political connections to protect strikers and to press manufacturers to settle. Strikers demanded union recognition, a fifty-two-hour week with overtime pay and the elimination of fines. Despite having to bargain with 450 different factory owners, strikers got 300 shops to accept at least some of their demands, although many bosses refused to recognize the union. Workers at the remaining factories won nothing, but union membership skyrocketed, and the uprising set off a wave of strikes in garment factories elsewhere.

Five months after the shirtwaist strike, the predominantly male Cloak Operators Union in New York undertook a carefully planned walkout. A fund-raising committee, headed by a radical Yiddish poet, raised $250,000. As the strike dragged on, Jewish leaders asked Louis Brandeis to mediate. The "Protocol of Peace" which he negotiated gave preference to union members in cloak shops without requiring all workers to join the union, raised wages, established a fifty-hour week, and abolished inside contracting.

Workers in the men's clothing industry made less progress because the ineffective United Garment Workers organized only skilled craftsmen. Despite an unsuccessful strike in 1910, Sidney Hillman, a young Jewish immigrant with ties to Jane Addams, negotiated a contract with substantial improvements for the workers at Hart, Schaffner and Marx after settlement house leaders and rabbis convinced Joseph Schaffner to cooperate with the union. Four years later, Hillman formed the Amalgamated Clothing Workers Union to organize all men's garment workers.

By 1920, the Amalgamated enrolled 170,000 members, but the AFL still recognized the rival United Garment Workers. The ILGWU had grown to 102,000 members, making it the sixth-largest AFL union. Women constituted two-thirds of the ILGWU membership and one-third in the Amalgamated; women garment workers made up 42 percent of all unionized women in the United States. Neither union had women in its leadership, however.

Why did unionization between 1909 and World War I progress only in the garment industry? First, striking female garment workers benefited from the support of influential women reformers. Second, the small manufacturers who dominated women's clothing manufacturing lacked the power of industrialists to demand the government's help in breaking the strike. Most owners were Jews, many of them immigrants operating small shops. Since both employers and employees were Jews, prominent Jews could mediate their labor conflicts. More fundamentally, Jews in New York, Chicago, and Philadelphia lived in ethnic communities in which class consciousness and socialist ideology flourished, as it did in the cities of Russia and Poland from which many of them had come. More Jews read the socialist *Forward* than any other Yiddish daily, and leftist fraternal and political societies played a major role in immigrant Jewish life. Significant numbers of garment workers fused their identities as Jews and as workers. They built good relations with the smaller number of Italian immigrant women who also worked in the trade, so industrialists could not divide them by nationality as they did in other industries. In short, a combination of strong class culture based on ethnicity, relatively weak and divided employers, and support from powerful women reformers enabled garment workers to gain a modicum of control over their work lives through collective action.

If women garment workers challenged the AFL's conservatism from the grass roots, a small number of radical unions, under the banner of the Industrial Workers of the World (IWW) challenged it through revolutionary politics and militant industrial unionism.

Founded in 1905, the IWW, popularly known as the Wobblies, sought to "confederate the workers of this country into a working class movement that shall have for its purpose the emancipation of the working class . . . having in view no compromise and no surrender."[24] A broad range of radical unionists and political leaders joined the nascent organization; but many left during the next three years, frustrated with the IWW's bitter internecine struggles. Nonetheless, the Wobblies assisted spontaneous strikes at the Pressed Steel Car Company at McKees Rocks, Pennsylvania, in 1909, the Lawrence, Massachusetts, textile mills in 1912, and the Paterson, New Jersey, textile mills and the rubber works of Akron, Ohio, in 1913. The IWW succeeded in organizing significant numbers of itinerant farmworkers, miners, lumberjacks, and others in the Western states. Unlike the AFL, which denied membership to black workers and favored immigration restriction, from the start the IWW organized African-Americans, new immigrants, and women. Although at its peak in 1916 the IWW boasted only about 100,000 members, it aroused fear among employers and middle-class Americans with its sharp class rhetoric and ability to organize unskilled workers in militant, and occasionally violent, collective action.

In addition to forming unions and protesting labor conditions, workers who could vote attempted to use the political system to advantage. Politicians representing working-class constituents generally supported factory laws, workmen's compensation, regulation of female and child labor, a progressive tax system, the direct election of senators, initiative, referendum, and other devices to enhance voter power and improve economic security. Gompers had long eschewed political action by unions, arguing that workers should gain benefits through collective bargaining and not through government largesse. Faced, however, with the hostility of government and especially the courts, the AFL adopted a legislative agenda which it entitled "Labor's Bill of Grievances" in 1906. The Federation first sought support from President Theodore Roosevelt, who on occasion worked with unions to avert labor unrest. When

Woodrow Wilson actively courted labor support during his successful 1912 campaign and thereafter, the AFL entered into an alliance with the Democratic Party.

Many workers rejected both major parties in favor of socialist politics. The Socialist Party of America, founded in 1901, grew steadily until World War I, drawing support from working-class voters. Strong socialist movements developed in Milwaukee, New York City, Bridgeport, Butte, and the shoe towns of Massachusetts. Workers sent socialists Victor Berger from Milwaukee and Meyer London from New York's Lower East Side to Congress, and numerous socialists served in state legislatures and city councils. Although the political system responded slowly and grudgingly to the demands of workers, workers did not passively accept employers' monopoly of government power. Their political efforts, and their various forms of collective action, kept "the labor question" as a central issue in the policy debates of the Progressive Era and a continuing problem to corporate managers.

WORKERS' LIVES AND WORKING-CLASS CULTURE

Despite efforts to improve their economic security through unionization and political action, few industrial workers could support families on their own incomes alone. And although they resisted, individually and collectively, bosses' attempts to control factory rules and the pace of production, workers achieved at best a modicum of workplace autonomy. But workers' lives did not begin and end in factories, mines, or railroad freight yards. In their families and communities, workers devised ways to enhance their economic security. At home, and in their leisure hours, they asserted their autonomy much more effectively than they could at work.

Working-class people depended upon their families for economic security, subordinating individual desires to the needs of the family. According to one study in 1912, barely half of all industrial families in the United States lived solely on the husband's earnings. In the

Chicago stockyards district, according to a University of Chicago study in 1911, the earnings of family heads comprised only 54.4 percent of family income. In rural communities, here or abroad, from which large numbers had only recently arrived, families had labored together in farming and domestic industry. Industrial families continued to expect all members to contribute to the family economy.

Children began work in childhood. "It stands to reason that the father expected, when there was nine or ten children, that they're all gonna start working and pitch in," recalled a worker in the Amoskeag mills. "When we worked, we gave our pay at home." Parents in poor families commonly took their children out of school to work full-time. "We older ones couldn't be educated because there was no money coming in," a Polish coal miner explained years later.[25]

Married women in industrial families only occasionally worked outside the home. The U.S. Immigration Commission concluded in 1911 that the wages of married women provided on average about 5 percent of the income of working-class families in most cities and 10 percent in New York City. These figures greatly understate married women's contributions to working-class family incomes, however. Married women earned money in ways consistent with their values and other responsibilities. Although southern Italians frowned upon married women working outside of their home, in Buffalo southern Italian women and children traveled together to work at nearby canneries in the summer. They considered such work respectable because the women remained under the scrutiny of members of their communities.

To earn extra income, some immigrant women and children made clothing, artificial flowers, and other goods in their homes. In New York City, at least 250,000 married women and other family members did such "homework" in 1911. Reformers despised home manufacturing, arguing that it exploited children, created an unhealthy home environment, and spread disease. Labor leaders argued that

homework lowered wages and undermined unionization. But homework allowed married women to supervise their young children and
socialize with other women while earning needed income. One study
of the period found that homeworkers provided about 20 percent of
their families' income.

More commonly, married women in working-class families
earned extra money by taking in boarders, usually single immigrant
men of their own nationality. A study of Lawrence, Massachusetts,
in 1912 found that 90 percent of immigrant families in which the
husband was the sole wage earner took in boarders, and 50 percent
of families with more than one wage earner also did so. Nationwide,
according to the U.S. Commissioner of Labor in 1901, 24 percent
of working-class families took in boarders. In the Chicago stockyards district, a remarkably large number of immigrants managed
to buy their houses so that they could rely upon lodger income when
their children grew up or in hard times. Rose Popovich, daughter
of a Croatian immigrant steelworker and his wife, remembered that
they had "a room just for boarders" in their house in Pennsylvania.
"They would pay ten dollars just to have their clothes washed and
for their rooms."[26] Misunderstanding the role of these nonfamily
members in the household economy, reformers often complained
that lodgers weakened families and provided negative influences
on children. In fact, boarding generally strengthened families by
improving their economic security and enabling mothers to supervise their children at home.

Workers relied upon their extended families too. They found jobs
for newly arrived relatives and gave them temporary lodging. John
Parraccini came to America in 1911 from Umbria in Italy and
worked initially in Scranton, Pennsylvania, with his brother-in-law.
His cousin offered to get him a job in the mines, but "then a friend
of my family found out that I was here, and he said, 'Come to work
with me.' He said, 'If your father know that you come to the same
town that I am, and not take you to work with me, your father would
be mad at me.' "[27]

Working families formed tight enclaves, usually held together by strong ethnic ties and a host of community institutions, and occasionally by a working-class consciousness transcending ethnic differences. In the shoe manufacturing town of Lynn, Massachusetts, workers of English, Irish, Italian, Greek, Scandinavian, and Jewish origin lived in the same neighborhoods, participated in a variety of worker-controlled institutions, ate together in central city lunchrooms near Lynn's numerous small shoe factories, and spent their leisure time in union halls where they played cards, pool, and billiards and sang union songs. The union sponsored mutual benefit associations; a socialist club and a labor church thrived here; and in 1890 workers in Lynn elected a prounion mayor. Long a stronghold of militant unionism, the town supported shoe workers during bitter strikes in 1890 and 1903. Local merchants often refused to sell goods to imported strikebreakers.

Italian, Spanish, Cuban, and Afro-Cuban cigar workers in the Ybor City area of Tampa likewise developed strong unions, class-oriented mutual aid societies, and a tradition of worker militance transcending ethnic and racial differences. All four groups had come to Tampa from places with histories of worker protest and built a class-conscious island surrounded by Southern nativism and racism. "When in 1902 I landed in Tampa," explained an immigrant from Sicily, "I found myself in a world of radicals for which I was prepared, and when I listened to speeches against the Catholic Church and the priesthood, I was not at all surprised." In the cigar factories, a "lector" read aloud radical tracts and analyses of class struggle.[28]

In Butte, Montana, on the other hand, Irish workers arriving after 1870 created a conservative class culture. Marcus Daly, head of Anaconda Copper, himself an Irish immigrant, made a fortune in mining and encouraged Irish people to come to Butte. Daly gave generously to Irish communal institutions and maintained good relations with the miners. Mining towns had traditionally attracted transient common laborers, but the Irish of Butte built a family-based community with strong local institutions. Irishmen owned most of Butte's businesses and held almost all elected offices.

The Irish miners, determined to maintain their stable, family-oriented community at all costs, allowed only reliable workers who wished to settle permanently in Butte into the dangerous underground copper mines. After its inception in a strike in 1878, the Butte miners' union became the most accommodating in the West. For thirty-six years, the miners engaged in no strikes or job actions. "The key to this working class conservatism," explains historian David Emmons, "was the control the Irish exercised over the work force. By cooperating with the more powerful, Irish workers became active partners in a collaborative effort to maintain the community."[29] Not until the 1910s, when increasing numbers of non-Irish transients sought work in the mines and a corporate merger placed the Butte mines under non-Irish and militant antiunion management, did the stable Irish workers of Butte lose control of their unique worker enclave.

Places like Butte, Lynn, and Ybor City proved to be exceptions, however. Ethnicity divided most working-class enclaves. And in company towns like Pullman, Illinois, U.S. Steel's Gary, Indiana, and a variety of Southern mill towns, employers controlled workers' housing, the local government, churches, schools, and sometimes local stores. In Fall River, Massachusetts, dispersed mills fostered separate ethnic enclaves in different parts of town. No common working-class area brought all the textile workers together, as in Lynn. Skilled English and Irish weavers opposed the employment of unskilled French Canadian, Polish, and Portuguese workers. They rejected industrial unionism, and during a strike in 1904 maintained separate relief funds for union and nonunion members.

Ethnicity also divided workers in large cities. Few immigrant groups occupied entire neighborhoods to the exclusion of all others, but neighborhood churches, fraternal associations, businesses, and ethnic or religious schools normally served members of a single group, reinforcing the primacy of nationality over class. Members of ethnic groups occupying the same neighborhood often clashed.

Even when segmented by nationality or race, in enclaves workers enjoyed autonomy in their daily lives. Here they built institutions, raised children, went to church, and socialized with neighbors without the constraints of the workplace. Many men gathered in saloons, for example, where they ate, drank, sang songs, told jokes, listened to music, and socialized loudly. They could read newspapers for free, cash checks, and learn about work opportunities. "The saloon," argues historian Roy Rosenzweig, "clashed with the values of industrial America not just in its communality and mutuality but also in the unwillingness of some patrons to endorse fully the work ethic of that society." Industrialists and reformers, convinced that drinking undermined family welfare and industrial discipline, got city governments to regulate the saloons and impose licensing fees. Temperance reformers appealed to men to abstain from liquor on moral and religious grounds, establishing coffeehouses and other substitutes for the saloon, but with little success. One observer aptly noted, "The tired, over-worked laborer enters [the saloon] unobtrusively. No one meets him at the door with a clammy handshake and stereotyped inquiry into the health of his wife and family. No one bustles about to see that he is amused. No one makes any strained attempt at intimacy."[30]

Workers also used public park space in boisterous and rowdy recreation that offended middle-class sensibilities. They celebrated the Fourth of July loudly with bonfires, alcohol, and ethnic festivals. A newspaper in Lawrence complained that "bands of foreigners and trouble makers," who had no idea of how to celebrate the holiday properly, marched to the center of town "filled with the spirit of the day and armed with trumpets, cowbells, augmented by their own shrill voices," where they lit huge fires and "pandemonium reigned."[31]

Leading citizens organized the Safe and Sane Fourth of July Movement to ensure order on the nation's birthday and to encourage "American" rather than "foreign" modes of holiday observance. Lawrence banned the traditional worker parade and bonfire after the 1912 textile strike. Playground reformers sought to supervise

working-class children in public recreational spaces. The leader of
the playground movement in Pittsburgh explained in a speech in
1896 that immigrant and working-class children did not know how
to play.

Workers resisted these attempts to control their leisure hours.
They used parks regularly for ethnic group outings and refused to
attend the classes, concerts, and athletic facilities reformers created
for them. In 1912, the *Worcester Telegram* quoted children's complaints about organized playground activities. "I can't go to the
playgrounds now," said an eleven-year-old from a working-class
neighborhood. "They get on me nerves with so many men and
women around telling you what to do."[32]

By the early twentieth century, however, new commercial amuse-
ments began to alter the nature of working-class recreation. Many
young working men and women spent a portion of their earnings at
amusement parks, dance halls, and the nickelodeon, challenging
both their parents' standards of sexual propriety and the norms of
middle-class society. Workers of all ages crowded into the cheap
storefront movie houses of the early-twentieth-century cities.
"Those who cannot afford $5 for grand opera must take their plea-
sure at . . . the humble five-cent picture show," asserted the *Milwaukee Sentinel* in 1907.[33]

Industrial workers lived difficult lives in the Progressive Era. Most
earned less than they needed to live, and faced the constant fear of
unemployment and the dangers of death or dismemberment. Unions
protected only a minority of workers, and in a political and legal
system hostile to collective bargaining their status remained tenu-
ous. As managers reorganized production and adopted new technologies, jobs required less skill and workers lost autonomy in the
workplace.

Workers coped with these difficult conditions creatively and at
times resisted aggressively. They enhanced their economic security
by tapping the earnings of all family members able to work. Many

formed unions, went on strike, and engaged in political activity. They regulated the pace of work despite the efforts of scientific managers and personnel directors to increase production, and they coped with the monotony of assembly-line work by erratic attendance and by changing jobs frequently. Their continuing strikes and informal protests made "the labor question" a central issue of public policy and a continuing problem for management. Unable to achieve autonomy in the workplace, they protected it vigorously in their neighborhoods and in their leisure-time activities. These were small victories, however. In their continuing contest with corporate capitalists, the capitalists held most of the power, and workers won few clear victories.

3

IMMIGRANTS IN
INDUSTRIAL AMERICA

In 1883, Emma Lazarus, a thirty-four-year-old Jewish poet and writer whose family had lived in America for several generations, wrote "The New Colossus," a sonnet inspired by her volunteer work with immigrant refugees at Ward's Island in New York. Years later, schoolchildren learning about their nation's historic mission as a refuge for the oppressed would recite her words, posthumously mounted on the pedestal of the Statue of Liberty in 1903. "With silent lips," Miss Liberty cries:

> *"Give me your tired, your poor,*
> *Your huddled masses yearning to breathe free,*
> *The wretched refuse of your teeming shore.*
> *Send these, the homeless, tempest-tost to me. . . ."*

Progressive Era crusaders on behalf of immigrants routinely echoed Lazarus' message, if not her poetry. Kate Holladay Claghorn, a professor at the New York School of Social Work, wrote of the immigrant's "sheer helplessness." Reform journalist Robert Hunter detailed the suffering of newcomers "drawn from the miserable of every nation."[1]

A powerful metaphor indeed, but not accurate. Most of the immigrants who came to America between 1890 and World War I sought economic opportunity more than personal liberty; many intended to return home once they earned some money. Most immigrants, although poor, did not come from the poorest of the poor, and few lacked homes. Emigration cost money, a carefully calculated investment enabling the sojourners to earn in America the funds needed to increase their modest landholdings and possessions back home. They could hardly be described as tired. Young, ambitious, and accustomed to hard work, immigrants acted boldly and deliberately to gain control over their lives. These artisans and farmers, refusing to accept passively the negative effects of industrial capitalism in their homelands, came to America to find economic security for their families.

More immigrants arrived during the Progressive Era than before or after, fifteen million in the twenty-four years between 1890 and 1914, although the foreign-born *proportion* of the U.S. population remained nearly the same in 1910 (14.5 percent) as in 1860 (13.2 percent). The sources of immigration changed substantially, however. Before 1890, most immigrants had come from Great Britain, Ireland, Canada, Germany, Scandinavia, Switzerland, and Holland. Immigrants after 1890 came disproportionately from the Austro-Hungarian Empire, Italy, Russia, Greece, Romania, and Turkey. Eighty-seven percent in 1882 arrived from the countries of Northwestern Europe, but by 1907, 81 percent hailed from the South and the East. A majority of the "new" immigrants were not Protestants, and they spoke languages, such as Polish, Yiddish, Lithuanian, Czech, and Greek, that were completely unfamiliar to Americans.

To be sure, immigrants continued to come to America from Northwestern Europe. Between 1890 and 1920, 874,000 people entered from Ireland, 991,000 from Germany, 571,000 from Sweden, 352,000 from Norway, but they drew little attention when compared with the 3,807,000 from Italy, for example. Substantial numbers also came from outside Europe, particularly from French and English Canada, Japan (until excluded by diplomatic agreement in 1906), Mexico, and Syria.

These fifteen million souls left amidst diverse economic and so-

cial circumstances, moved all over the country, and held thousands
of different kinds of jobs. Yet they shared certain goals. Like all
workers, they struggled for the economic security of their families,
whether back home or in America. They also demanded autonomy
over their family lives, their communities, and their culture, selectively taking elements from the Old World and the New. Finally,
many newcomers to America sought to enhance their social status.
If, as outsiders and poor laborers, they could not hope to acquire
prestige within the larger American society, they could still compete
for respect and social position within the ethnic communities and
institutions they built in America.

WHOEVER HAD A GOAL

The sources of immigration changed with the spread of industrial
capitalism. Although the exact causes of migration varied from
place to place, in general the expansion of railroads and other transportation networks brought cheaper manufactured products into
once-isolated rural areas. This undercut artisans and peasants who
had produced goods at home for local sale. Simultaneously, industrial capitalism increased the demand for food for the growing number of industrial workers in cities, encouraging the consolidation of
land in the hands of a few large owners and a decline in subsistence
agriculture. The move to surplus farming created economic hardships for peasants, small landowners, and agricultural laborers.

In response to these developments, young men began to travel
from their homes in search of wage work to augment agricultural
income, or in the case of artisans in search of remote customers for
the products they made at home. Temporary emigration to America
seemed a natural extension of that practice, a way to earn some
money to buy land and improve life. Areas completely removed from
the transportation networks emanating from industrial cities, or areas unsuited to large-scale agriculture, like the mountainous sec-
tions of the Balkans, rarely sent emigrants, even though their
residents were as poor as or poorer than others in the same countries

who had emigrated. In other words, emigration appealed to energetic individuals who had the means to pursue this solution to economic challenges, and not to those desperate or demoralized. In Italy, for example, areas where too many small landowners competed with each other for scarce land registered the heaviest migration. These small farmers journeyed to America to earn money to buy land back home. In areas in which large landowners held most of the land, few people left, and militant farmer-laborers organized unions to demand improved pay and conditions. In Mexico, President Porfirio Díaz abolished communal lands in the central states and built railroads from the agricultural areas to the U.S. border, enabling large haciendas to grow export crops. Ironically, the same railroads enabled displaced Mexican peasants to reach higher-paying jobs in the United States. In Russia, Jews fled to America when the czarist government, seeking scapegoats to deflect growing peasant discontent, encouraged violent attacks on Jews; but Jewish shoemakers, tailors, carpenters, printers, and blacksmiths also faced increased competition from cheap manufactured goods and Jewish peddlers in rural areas had to travel to ever more remote areas to find customers.

Hope, not desperation, drove most emigrants. "Whoever had in mind a goal that couldn't be fulfilled by lifelong work at home began deliberating at night about going overseas," explained an observer in Central Europe. One peasant wrote in his diary, "I lived with this single thought: to earn money and to return home and to buy a farm even better than my father's."[2] Not all went to America. Many European immigrants headed for Canada, Australia, New Zealand, Argentina, Brazil, and elsewhere in Latin America. But no country rivaled America's rapidly expanding economy and demand for labor.

Immigrants commonly returned home, some for good; but others came back to the United States. A government study concluded that 9,949,740 immigrants entered America between 1908 and 1923 and 3,498,185 left. Among Italians, perhaps 50 percent of those who came to America went back, among Jews a mere 4 percent, with most groups falling between these extremes. At the age of twenty, a Hungarian named Lajos, born in 1883 to a farming family, left for America, where his sister already lived. He worked in the mines of West Virginia, had a child with a woman named Lea from his home village, and abandoned them to return home after five years. In Hungary he married a woman named Hermina; they lived on his parents' farm. In 1913, Lajos and Hermina returned to America, leaving their two children with grandparents. Living first in West Virginia, they moved from job to job and Hermina gave birth to three more children. After World War I, the family returned to their native village in Hungary, reunited with their older children, built a house, and purchased about an acre and a half of land with money saved in America. In the early 1920s, Lea returned to the same village with her daughter; she subsequently married a local man and bore four more children.

VOTING WITH THEIR FEET

The emigrants organized and financed the migration themselves; steamship companies and American labor contractors played little role in convincing people to move, although critics of immigration claimed they did. Most immigrants participated in a chain migration, in which one or more family members came to America and sent back information and transportation money, enabling relatives and close friends to follow. Researchers for the U.S. Immigration Commission concluded in 1909 that letters "from persons who have emigrated to friends at home have been the immediate cause of by far the greater part of the remarkable movement from Southern and Eastern Europe in the last twenty-five years."[3]

Immigrants commonly lived with relatives upon initial arrival. An Italian woman who moved to Providence in 1890 later recalled that, before they left, Italians would "make the arrangement to stay in the house of some relatives" and then "when they stay here for a little bit they used to send for the wife and family." Antonia Bergeron, an immigrant to Manchester, New Hampshire, from Quebec, remembered how she started a family migration. "When my neighbors went to the U.S., I decided to go with them." Upon arrival in Manchester, she "met a woman who had taught me school in Canada when I was small" who "found me a job in the mills. . . . My mother came up later with my little brother and my little sister. . . . As time went on, we'd have another person come up, and another, and finally the whole family was here."[4]

Relatives in America demonstrated the advantages of emigration by sending substantial sums back home. American researchers who went to Europe to study immigration in 1907 discovered that "men in Italy and in various Slavic communities" who had lived in America refused to accept low wages, making "a vivid impression" with the money they displayed. "They are dispensers of information and inspiration, and are often willing to follow up the inspiration by loans to prospective emigrants." In Ireland, people eagerly awaited the "America cheque" before Christmas.[5] One scholar estimates that between 1890 and 1940 Croats sent back home about $180 million, Serbs $40 million, and Slovenes $80 million.

Local elites and home governments often discouraged emigration. To counteract the exodus to New England, Catholic church leaders in Quebec implored rural Quebec residents to stay, offering financial inducements to landless citizens if they agreed to settle in frontier colonies in the province. They got few takers. The Magyar rulers of Hungary distributed publications denigrating life in America. A Ruthenian paper published in the United States with Hungarian government money declared on its front page in 1911:

> Dear Countrymen! Do not forsake your homeland for always. When fate forces you to emigrate, at least don't sell your lands, so that you will leave something to come back to. Go for the sake of making money. Be thrifty and don't lose your savings on drinking. Return with the money earned and use it to improve your farms/households.[6]

Italy simplified the process by which returnees could renounce American and regain Italian citizenship. The government of Greece offered financial incentives for poor overseas nationals to return home. Antiemigrationists in Sweden tried to lure their American countrymen back with offers of jobs. The Turkish government placed military officers at the ports to prevent migration of Syrians to America.

When hacienda owners in central Mexico complained that emigration northward created labor shortages, the Díaz government sent reports of unemployment and discrimination against Mexicans in the United States to Mexican newspapers. The revolutionary government ordered state governors to stop emigration by any means necessary and placed specific restrictions in the 1917 constitution on the temporary departure of laborers. These policies did not slow emigration. Eastern European rabbis also sought to stem the flood of immigrants to America. "Whoever wishes to live properly before God must not settle in that country," declared Rabbi Israel Meir Ha-Kohen Kagan in 1894 from Warsaw. "America is a *treif* [not kosher] land where even the stones are impure," wrote Rabbi Jacob David Willowski a decade later.[7] Yet neither clerics nor coercive governments could stop determined people from leaving. Seeking economic security, immigrants to America voted with their feet.

IMMIGRANT ENTERPRISE

With family economic security foremost, immigrants adapted their traditional values to the necessities of their new country, making pragmatic choices at every stage. The vast majority of immigrants worked for wages, pooling the wages of men, women, and children and the money earned from home manufacturing, laundering, and boarders. During the Progressive Era, only a few recent immigrants could write and speak English well enough to qualify for white-collar office or department store jobs, and a modest number became independent farmers. Some chose another alternative and became peddlers or shopkeepers. Although department stores, chain stores, and catalogue companies offered a wide array of goods to more and more Americans, opportunities remained for petty merchants, which some immigrants seized. Peddling required little or no capital. A distributor, usually a fellow countryman, supplied a newcomer with goods which the peddler paid for after he had sold them. In cities with large immigrant populations, peddling did not even require a working knowledge of English, since one could sell to fellow immigrants from a pushcart or by going from apartment to apartment. Eastern European Jews, Italians, Greeks, Irishmen, and Armenians dominated big-city peddling.

The *New York Tribune* reported in 1898 that "recently landed immigrants are advised by their friends to take a pushcart until they can establish themselves in some business." A Jewish immigrant in New York went "to the factory where the tinware was made" and a man "gave me a basket filled with a variety of tinware. . . . I felt happy that I had become a businessman. I went back to my lodging feeling that I might become a big businessman—perhaps even a tinware manufacturer."[8] Immigrant women and children also sometimes tended pushcarts.

Other immigrants peddled in small towns and rural areas across America, carrying goods purchased from a countryman on their backs or in horse-drawn wagons. In the mid-nineteenth century, Central European Jews dominated the trade. By the turn of the century, most peddlers were Syrian immigrants, even though as late as 1908 people reported encountering Irish and Swedish peddlers in the Prairie States. The daughter of Francis Abraham Modi recalled that her father's two-hundred-pound pack consisted of "dry goods, mostly cut yardage, and clothing, shirts, work clothing, socks, pants and underwear." He also carried "a hand grip, which held combs, thread, needles . . . shaving soap, straight razors, and just about all the non-toiletries the farm folks would need."

Experienced peddlers taught novices the trade, and shopkeepers provided the recent arrivals with goods on credit. An early Syrian immigrant, Salem Bashara, supplied new immigrant peddlers from his store in Fort Wayne, Indiana. One newcomer, upon arrival in New York, showed Salem's name and address to an interpreter "who put us on the train. Salem met us." A relative remembered that "those who had been here a month or two would teach them a few words . . . to knock on a door and say, 'Buy sumthin', Maam,' or how to say they were hungry and needed a place to sleep."[9] While distributors imported some of the goods from the old country, Syrian women in America sewed or embroidered many of the items sold.

Why did so many immigrants take up either city or long-distance peddling? Peddlers faced hard work and long hours. Established shopkeepers, who disliked the competition, condemned them; reformers complained that pushcart operators cluttered busy city streets. Police officers who enforced antipeddling ordinances shook them down, and thieves stole from them. Nonetheless, peddling offered economic opportunities for those who could sell. Many peddlers dreamed of opening a store, and some succeeded. Moreover, peddling offered greater autonomy than wage labor. Unlike factory workers, Jewish peddlers could observe the Sabbath and religious holidays without penalty.

Small businesses offered immigrants these same advantages on a greater scale. Numerous immigrant enterprises, including kosher butcher shops and bakeries, Irish and German saloons, and ethnic groceries, provided goods or services unavailable elsewhere. Immigrants often preferred to buy American products from countrymen. An early-twentieth-century study of immigrant adaptation noted:

> The Jewish woman in New York buys a steamship ticket for her sister in Russia from a ticket peddler who collects fifty cents a week; the Polish laborer deposits his money with the saloon keeper; and this peddler or saloon keeper will eventually become a joint steamship agent, banker, employment agent, real-estate agent, etc.[10]

These ethnic businesses, protected from mainstream competition, made immigrant neighborhoods distinctive places where newcomers felt comfortable, enhancing the economic security and personal autonomy of the proprietor.

Sometimes, immigrant entrepreneurs, building on relationships with their countrymen, carved out a special niche in the American economy. Settled Norwegian immigrants, for example, owned and worked in Brooklyn businesses catering to Norwegian merchant ships. Greek immigrants opened confectionery shops and restaurants. A number of Eastern European Jews who worked in the garment industry became small clothing manufacturers.

Immigrants from Asia relied especially on small enterprise because white employers refused to hire them for all but the most menial jobs. Congress excluded almost all new Chinese immigrants in 1882, and hostility to Chinese laborers, who had initially worked in railroad construction, mining, and other activities in rural areas of the West, forced them to cluster in urban Chinatowns. About 40 percent of the San Francisco Chinese in these years worked as merchants and shopkeepers, serving both Chinese residents and outsiders who went to Chinatown for exotic foods and imported goods. Even in the smaller inland towns, Chinese shopkeepers ran restaurants, groceries, and laundries. Chinese laborers found work largely in these Chinese-owned service enterprises. By 1920, 58 percent worked in service occupations, compared with only 10 percent of white immigrants. A Chinese laundry worker explained that the work was "very hard" but "there is nothing else to do. . . . This is the kind of life we have to take in America."[11]

Japanese immigrants worked initially as laborers when they began arriving on the mainland in the 1880s, but many quickly established small businesses. By 1909, between 3,000 and 3,500 Japanese immigrants in the West operated hotels and boardinghouses, restaurants, barbershops, poolrooms, tailor shops, supply stores, shoemaker shops, and laundries. Some also fished for abalone, a delicacy in Japan, drying and canning it for sale back home. Most Japanese immigrants became self-employed farmers, however. In the 1890s, some began cultivating sugar beets, beans, potatoes, hops, and other fruits and vegetables, initially for a fixed wage and then for a fixed share of the crop. Having earned a little money, they leased land and eventually bought it outright. In 1909, Japanese-run farms produced 18 percent of the value of Los Angeles County farm products on just 1.5 percent of the farmland, typically selling their produce to Japanese dealers. Nativists fearful of Japanese progress in agriculture and business won passage of the California Alien Land Act of 1913, prohibiting foreigners from owning land in the state. Since Congress had banned the naturalization of Asian immigrants, the authors of the new law expected it to keep Japanese immigrants from owning land. But Japanese parents circumvented the law by placing title to the land in the names of their children born on American soil, who became citizens at birth. In the seven years following the passage of the Alien Land Law, Japanese-owned land tripled.

For European immigrants, self-employment offered an alternative to wage labor in factories and mines. For Chinese and Japanese immigrants, largely excluded from those occupations, entrepreneurship remained the only significant avenue to economic security and autonomy.

RELIGIOUS INSTITUTIONS

Ethnic businesses constituted one strand in a web of institutions through which immigrants established cultural autonomy within their American communities. Of the many others, religious institutions loomed largest. Prayer and religious ritual provided meaning to people continually struggling for the necessities of life. Religious institutions played central roles in immigrants' social lives, both at home and in the New World, providing for the observance of births, weddings, funerals, and other life-cycle events. Because the American government did not sponsor or finance religion, however, immigrants had to create and manage their own houses of worship. As a result, they exerted far greater control of religious life than had been possible back home.

Roman Catholics, who made up a majority of immigrants to America in the Progressive Era, found the Catholic Church here well established. Every city in which substantial numbers of immigrants settled had a Catholic diocese headed by a bishop and numerous Catholic churches. But newcomers wanted priests who spoke their language and churches that honored national or local patron saints and practiced distinctive rituals. Newly arriving Irish, German, Polish, Italian, French Canadian, Slav, Magyar, Slovak, Croatian, and Mexican adherents to the Church of Rome therefore organized their own national parishes and built formidable church buildings. The first Poles in Chicago, for example, built St. Stanislaw Kostka parish and secured a Polish-speaking priest in 1869, with the approval of the local bishop, eventually establishing sixty-one parishes in and around Chicago. By 1916, German immigrants worshipped at 1,890 German Catholic parishes across the United States.

Other immigrants also readily founded national churches and a plethora of denominational organizations. Separate Lutheran synods represented Germans, Swedes, Norwegians, Slovaks, and others. Greek immigrants, who followed the Eastern Orthodox rite, established churches in more than a half dozen cities without much help from the Orthodox hierarchy in America or from church officials in Greece. The mostly Christian Syrian immigrants established Melkite, Maronite, and Orthodox churches in New York in the early 1890s, and about seventy others across the country in the next three decades. By 1916, Armenians maintained ten parishes in Worcester alone. Jewish immigrants from Eastern Europe found well-established synagogues here, but they wanted to pray in congregations that used the familiar rituals of their Old World localities, and they disliked the liberal innovations developed by American Reform Judaism. So they formed their own synagogues, 326 on the Lower East Side of New York alone by 1907.

Immigrants demanded a degree of autonomy within their churches and synagogues unthinkable back home, where religious institutions enjoyed state sanction. Clergymen from abroad who ministered to these congregations, and officials of American church hierarchies, struggled with their congregants to protect clerical authority. Not surprisingly, the most intense battles occurred within the hierarchical Catholic Church. Poles, Slovaks, Lithuanians, French Canadians, and other Catholic immigrants demanded that lay boards of trustees oversee church finances and property, but the mostly Irish church hierarchy insisted that the diocesan bishop maintain control.

Polish nationalists, who viewed American Polish churches as outposts in the struggle to reestablish a Polish nation, bitterly fought the hierarchy. To the nationalists' dismay, the Resurrectionist order, which sent priests from Poland to staff the Polish parishes in America, accepted the authority of American diocesan bishops. In Chicago, Polish nationalists formed a new parish and sought to find a priest to their liking. They struggled for twenty years with the Resurrectionists and the bishop, who closed the church for long periods and excommunicated several of its lay leaders. In 1894, factional disputes disrupted the celebration of mass at one Polish church, and the following year a group of parishioners stormed the church rectory; the police had to disperse the protesters. In frustration, some nationalist Poles established parishes independent of the Roman Catholic Church, uniting in 1911 to found the Polish National Church, encompassing about 5 percent of America's Polish Catholics. The Vatican, fearing further defections, appointed a Polish-American bishop in 1908.

Other groups had similar conflicts with the hierarchy. In 1911, Slovak Catholics at Pittsburgh's St. Matthew's parish sued the diocese over a financial dispute in an unsuccessful effort to force the removal of the parish priest. In 1915, 150 parishioners at St. Elizabeth's asked the bishop to replace a priest who had insulted church members and ignored lay leaders. Slovak organizations also regularly ignored the diocese's prohibition against alcohol at church functions. In New England, where French Canadian Catholics and the Irish hierarchy fought bitterly over the appointment of French-speaking priests, Québecois ritual, and lay control of church property, parishioners at a Fall River church withdrew en masse in 1884 when a bishop appointed an Irish priest to an overwhelmingly

French Canadian parish. In Portland, Maine, the bishop placed Québecois parishioners under an interdict in 1906 after they challenged his control of parish property.

Catholic immigrants from areas like southern Italy and Mexico, where many peasants viewed the church as an agent of wealthy landowners, did not at first attend church regularly in America any more than they had at home; but they continued to practice a folk Catholicism centered on home and local community rituals. Italians placed great importance on the celebration of their town's patron saint's feast day, typically organized by a local lay committee. In 1906, members of an immigrant mutual aid society in Providence complained to the bishop that the pastor of Holy Ghost parish reneged on a promise to reserve seats for society members on their patron saint's day and cursed the saint's name when they brought her image into the church. The bishop took no action against the priest, and heightened the conflict when he prohibited mutual aid societies from christening new Italian and American flags in church. (The societies simply moved their flag christening to an Italian fraternal hall.) When the priest at another Providence parish prohibited fund raising for a feast day celebration, several thousand Italians gathered in a park across from the church on a Sunday morning, threatening to close it and drive away the offending cleric.

Jacob Riis, a prominent progressive reformer and journalist, observed an Italian patron saint *festa* on New York's Elizabeth Street in 1899. He reported, "Between birthdays . . . the saint was left in the loft of the saloon, lest the priest got hold of him and got a corner on him. . . . He was their home patron, and they were not going to give him up."[12] In placing patron saints at the heart of their Catholicism and employing mutual aid societies to organize saint's day celebrations, Italian Catholics sought to establish religious autonomy in America, just as Polish, Slovak, and French Canadian Catholics did by challenging the hegemony of bishops and priests.

No central body controlled synagogues in America; and no entity held the authority of the state-sanctioned kehillah, the organized Jewish community of Eastern Europe. Jewish immigrants welcomed

their newfound religious autonomy, readily forming new congregations in America, often in tenements and storefronts. Rabbis could
not enforce the traditional rules of religious behavior. Many Jews
now worked on the Sabbath, no longer attended daily minyanim
(prayer services), and became more lax in their adherence to kashrut, the dietary laws. And anyone could advertise meat as "kosher."
Synagogues became voluntary associations in which a board of trustees employed and paid the rabbi.

Disturbed by the weakening of rabbinic authority in America, a
group of congregations in the 1880s appointed Rabbi Jacob Joseph,
a distinguished scholar from Vilna, as "chief rabbi" of New York to
rule on religious matters and oversee the inspection of kosher meat.
He soon clashed with butchers, ritual slaughterers, and even other
Orthodox rabbis who refused to accept his authority. Hungarian and
Galician Jews appointed their own "chief rabbi" in 1892. The next
year, a rabbi from Moscow claimed the title "chief rabbi of America." The effort to establish a central rabbinate soon collapsed.

Eastern European Jews also resisted the attempts of Americanized Reform rabbis to impose an unfamiliar liberalized Judaism on
them. The Reform movement, which took hold among the Central
European Jews who had emigrated before 1880, held services primarily in English, eliminated most Jewish laws governing daily life,
including kashrut, and imposed middle-class Protestant decorum
on the traditionally disorderly Jewish prayer service. Jewish immigrants from Eastern Europe rejected these alien practices. In
America, Jews would not allow rabbis to circumscribe their new
religious autonomy either with Old World restrictions or with liberal
reforms.

COMMUNAL INSTITUTIONS

Immigrants of every nationality formed mutual aid societies, collected modest dues from their members, and paid death benefits;
some societies also gave money to members when illness kept them
from working. Such associations did not spring up entirely new in

America. As capitalism had disrupted life in Europe, skilled workers, artisans, and intellectuals formed mutual benefit organizations. By 1893, southern Italians, for example, had established more than 6,000 such associations. Immigrants brought this experience to America, and mutual aid groups proliferated.

In America, these organizations provided not only a modicum of economic security, as they had in the old country, but an opportunity for cultural autonomy and a means by which leaders could achieve social status within their immigrant communities. By 1910, two-thirds of Poles in America belonged to at least one of approximately 7,000 Polish associations. The National Slovak Society boasted almost 37,000 members by 1910. Eastern European Jews created at least 3,000 societies, known in Yiddish as *landsmanshaften*. As late as 1930, the Croat Fraternal Union enrolled 92,458 members.

Typically, men from the same town, region, or province in the old country formed a mutual aid association, although members of a common occupation also organized lodges; a few, like the Arbeter Ring (Workmen's Circle) united Jewish workers irrespective of occupation or geography. As the societies proliferated, they united into federations to enhance their financial stability, and fraternal insurance became a sizable business.

Although founded to provide modest insurance, the mutual benefit societies also served as social clubs, advancing nationalist, socialist, or other political causes. Most lodges limited membership to men and provided life and burial insurance to wives and children, although some accepted women as full members and women also founded a few societies of their own. Mutual aid lodges typically required that all members attend funerals. They also sponsored parties, outings, and social events for members and their families. Historian Irving Howe described the elaborate rules that governed *landsmanshaften*:

The Kolomeir constitution refuses admission to saloonkeepers. The Narevker declares that if a member marries, a committee of seven will be chosen to grace the wedding. . . . The Pukhoveritser is strict as to decorum, insisting that "at the funeral of a member or his wife every member has the duty to dress neatly and arrive on time. . . . Every member must line up and is not allowed to smoke during the funeral, and when someone disobeys he will be fined fifty cents." With the Narevker Untershtitsung Fareyn, a member who marries is to receive a five-dollar gift, but only if he has belonged a full year; and the present must be given personally by the vice-president at the wedding. Virtually all the constitutions declare that if a member marries a gentile, he will be stricken from the rolls.

A member of a Chinese tong (communal society) explained in the early twentieth century: "We are strangers in a strange country. We must have an organization (tong) to control our country fellows and develop our friendship."[13]

The societies thus enabled immigrants to maintain ties to their culture of origin while providing modest insurance against economic disaster. But they also gave some immigrants an opportunity to become leaders and enhance their social status. Rose Cohen recalled in her autobiography the importance of such activity to her immigrant father. "The men often came to our house to talk things over with him and he felt important." She remembered that "before they opened the meeting they always assured mother that they would not keep us up any later than ten o'clock. But when the time came they were so deep in discussion that they never even heard the clock strike the hour." Discussion typically centered on "a piece of burial ground" or "whether as a society they should or should not employ a doctor and pay him out of the society fund." A witness at hearings of the U.S. Industrial Commission in 1901 explained that the officers of tong federations in San Francisco "are called together" with other prominent men in Chinatown "to deliberate and advise on occasions of important events" and often acted as arbitrators "to prevent their people, if possible, from going to the law."[14]

Other immigrant associations also combined economic and social functions. Loan societies helped would-be entrepreneurs and those in financial distress. Jews created more than a thousand free-loan societies by 1917. Poles established building and loan societies to help immigrants buy houses. Many Chinese immigrants financed small businesses through the *woi*, a family or clan loan fund in which each member paid a sum to create initial capital; the *woi* then loaned the funds to members on a rotating basis. Koreans, Japanese, and West Indian immigrants established similar institutions.

Mutual aid and other immigrant associations also participated in nationalist struggles back home. The Polish National Alliance, the largest federation of Polish fraternal associations, from its inception in 1880 pledged to reestablish a sovereign Polish nation-state. The earliest Korean mutual assistance associations in San Francisco, Chicago, New York, and Seattle advocated the liberation of their homeland from Japanese control, and in 1909 the tiny Korean community created the Tae-Hanin Kungmin-hoe (Korean National Association of North America) for the purpose of "regaining the independence of the fatherland." Nationalist organizations sprang up even among nationalities which did not face independence struggles. The Sons of Italy sought to foster "the patriotic spirit and love of fatherland, by the observance of such holidays as Columbus Day and by "providing means for the diffusion of the Italian language."[15]

Immigrant intellectuals launched numerous periodicals to deliver news of the homeland and of America in the familiar tongue. By 1917 immigrants supported 1,323 foreign-language newspapers in the United States, including 522 in German, 103 in Italian, 132 in the Scandinavian languages, 84 in Spanish, 77 in Polish, 63 in Bohemian, 45 in French, 44 in Yiddish or Hebrew, 17 in Japanese, and 6 in Chinese. The Yiddish-language *Jewish Daily Forward*, edited by socialist Abraham Cahan, sold 175,000 copies daily, making it the highest-circulating immigrant newspaper in America, although it competed with four other New York Yiddish dailies.

Some groups also maintained foreign-language theaters. Chicago's Swedish-language theater, for example, performed comedies, farces, and vaudeville presenting a romanticized image of pre-industrial Sweden for a broad immigrant audience. After 1910, films made in Sweden played regularly in Swedish-American urban communities. The vibrant Yiddish theaters on the Lower East Side of New York staged everything from Shakespeare to slapstick comedy. A Chinese theater opened in San Francisco in 1879. Spanish-language musical variety shows put on by touring Mexican performers after 1910 attracted large numbers of immigrants in El Paso.

Most immigrants had not read a newspaper or gone to the theater before coming to America. Here, these and other communal institutions enabled them simultaneously to adjust to life in America and to assert cultural autonomy. Free to choose, they adapted to the culture of their new home neither by strictly re-creating Old World forms nor by simply imitating American practices.

IMMIGRANTS AND SCHOOLS

In the immigrants' dual quest for economic security and cultural autonomy, public schools posed a profound challenge. By the 1890s, most cities and states where immigrants settled mandated compulsory schooling. Schools could foster mobility in the next generation, but threatened immediate economic security by depriving a family of a schoolchild's earnings. Schools also challenged cultural autonomy. Teachers and school administrators rather than parents controlled what children studied; and most public schools set out to Americanize immigrant youngsters. Immigrant groups responded in different ways to these challenges.

Most immigrant families relied on the earnings of working children past the elementary grades. In New York, in the early part of the century, 60 percent of native-born white children began high school, but fewer than 33 percent of German children and only 25 percent of Italians did so. In Chicago and Cleveland, fewer than one in ten Italian, Polish, and Slovak children advanced beyond grade six in 1910. Immigrants commonly violated the compulsory school law. New York City's attendance bureau found the highest rates of truancy in Little Italy and Italian East Harlem, and the schools hired Italian-speaking attendance officers and enlisted the Italian press to publish the names of parents convicted of violating the truancy law. Neither action had much impact. One Italian immigrant conceded after the fact that she kept her daughter home from school occasionally "to work on pieces of embroidery. . . . I was lucky the school inspector [truant officer] was a nice man," she explained.[16]

Immigrants took children out of school from economic necessity rather than hostility to education as such. In a crude cost-benefit analysis, most determined that children needed to read and write, but further study did not compensate for the lost income. Immigrant parents who evaded compulsory schooling felt that they, rather than the state, should decide.

Many immigrant parents, particularly Catholics and Lutherans, also thought the public schools threatened their religious values, and sent their children to alternative parochial schools. Nearly every Catholic parish ran a school. A Polish immigrant child from Johnstown remembered that "our parents, ardent Catholics, were mostly concerned that their children grew up in the same way, so they built magnificent churches and rectories for their priests and erected parochial schools. It was deeply believed," he continued, "that in [public] schools the youth lose their religion and their faith weakens." A Slovak priest in Scranton denounced public schools as antireligious and said they "made loafers of all girls who attended them."[17]

Not all Catholic groups patronized parochial schools with equal enthusiasm, however. Irish children attended at much higher rates than Italians, for example, even though Italian priests endorsed parochial education and built some parish schools. Mexican immigrants, who shared Italians' anticlericalism, also sent their chil-

dren mostly to public schools. A 1912 survey located only six
Spanish-language Catholic schools in the whole country.

Many other immigrants supported parochial schools for linguistic
as well as religious reasons. German, Swedish, and Norwegian Lutheran schools and some Catholic schools taught largely or exclusively in the native tongue. French Canadians, having struggled in
Canada for a century to maintain their use of French in preference
to English, established a network of French-language parish schools
in America which enrolled 63,000 students in 1912. Early Japanese
immigrants opened thirty-one schools in California alone by 1914
to teach the Japanese language and Japan's national curriculum so
that the children could return home. A Jewish religious school,
Machzikei Talmud Torah, established in New York in the 1880s,
offered only one hour a day of English instruction, from five to six
in the evening.

Private foreign-language schools caused the English-speaking
majority to fear that these immigrant children would never assimilate. Several states required that English be taught in all schools.
In 1890, a newly elected governor of Wisconsin discovered that
129 Lutheran and a number of Catholic parochial schools in the
state taught no English at all. He initiated legislation requiring that
all schools teach reading, writing, arithmetic, and American history
in English. Immigrant voters, angered by this intrusion on their
cultural autonomy, defeated the governor at the next election, and
Wisconsin's legislature promptly repealed the law.

German-speaking immigrants in some places went further, demanding that the public schools teach German. In the early twentieth century, largely as a result of German-American influence,
perhaps a quarter of all U.S. high school students studied German
as a foreign language. In 1913, Germans persuaded Nebraska's
legislature to mandate that every public high school and urban elementary school provide instruction in any European language requested by half the parents of that schools' pupils. St. Louis and
Buffalo offered bilingual instruction in German and English.
Smaller immigrant groups had less political success in promoting

instruction in their native language. In the 1890s, a Polish immigrant member of the Wisconsin legislature could not get Milwaukee's high schools to offer Polish along with German as a foreign language.

Immigrant parents who did not send their children to ethnic parochial schools supported supplemental schools which taught language, religion, and group culture to public school pupils. Catholic parish schools offered religious instruction. Norwegian Lutheran summer schools taught language and religion. Rabbis and Jewish educators started numerous religious and language schools in immigrant neighborhoods; others created secular Zionist, Yiddishist, and socialist alternatives. Children of Chinese immigrants attended Chinese-language classes for several hours each evening.

Public school educators generally feared these efforts to foster group autonomy; in their zeal to Americanize youngsters, they often showed disrespect for immigrant cultures. In 1891, a committee of the National Education Association complained that "foreign influence has begun a system of colonization with a purpose of preserving foreign languages and traditions and proportionately of destroying distinctive Americanism." New York School Superintendent William Maxwell explained that a school should be "a melting pot which converts the children of the immigrants of all races and languages into sturdy, independent American citizens." Victor Wong remembered that "in English school they didn't believe in Chinese customs" and that they tried to "dissuade us from speaking Cantonese . . . [and] from everything Chinese. Their view of the Chinese ways was that they were evil, heathen, non-Christian."

Yet some children of immigrants enjoyed public schools, and leaders in some groups warmly embraced public education. Alice Yu recalled her Chinese parents telling her, "Think of all the marvelous things you can learn here. You can get one of the best educations here. This is a wonderful country." Jews built very few parochial schools, although they established other institutions with a vengeance. In 1914, nearly all of the elementary-age Jewish children in New York attended public schools, but less than a quarter received any formal Jewish education. Sam Friedman recalled that preparing to enter school for the first time in 1902 "was a period of great excitement . . . the whole home . . . atmosphere was that of wanting to go to school, how wonderful school is, how much you learn. . . . We went to school full of anticipation."

Still, Jews and other immigrant parents who viewed public schools positively often had to struggle to get what they wanted from them. When the New York City schools sought to track students into vocational curricula on the basis of standardized educational tests, Jewish immigrants rebelled. The plan threatened "parental aspirations" and engendered "deep-seated resentment," concluded a research team.[18] Their outcry eventually caused school officials to drop the plan. Whether immigrants sent their children to public or parochial schools, whether or not they withdrew their children from school so they could work full-time, individual immigrant families made their own decisions as they pursued their dual quest for economic security and cultural autonomy.

RECONCILING IDENTITIES

Once immigrants ceased being sojourners and began raising families in their new home, they sought to become Americans, but on their own terms. Loyalty to their adopted country, they believed, did not require that they abandon ancestral identities. Seeing this strong commitment to cultural autonomy, nativists and many well-meaning leaders in the Americanization movement concluded incorrectly that immigrants did not want to become Americans. In fact, although few knew the term, most immigrants advocated cultural pluralism; they wished to maintain twin loyalties as Americans and as members of ancestral groups.

Throughout their communities, immigrants fused their dual loyalties. Parochial schools taught the English language and American history and government. Foreign-language newspapers reported general American news and discussed the problems of daily life in

America. Many newcomers voted in American elections, and immigrants who won public office became powerful figures and important symbols in their communities.

Immigrant leaders articulated this pluralist vision of Americanization. Abraham Cahan, a native of Russian Poland who edited the Yiddish-language *Forward*, wrote a history of the United States in Yiddish, and his paper regularly published Yiddish translations of the Declaration of Independence and the Constitution. His editorials criticized America's failure to live up to the country's ideals of liberty and democracy in its treatment of workers and black Americans. The Yiddish lexicographer Alexander Harkavy, who grew up in Vilna and came to America at the age of nineteen, wrote numerous books and articles to teach English to Yiddish speakers, or to instruct them on the Constitution, George Washington, Christopher Columbus, and the procedures for applying for American citizenship. About 250,000 students used his *English Teacher*, published in 1891. "The Russian Jew is expected to adapt himself to American conditions of freedom and democracy," he explained in a 1907 article, "but America does not demand of him that he forget the ties that bind him to his mother country, no matter how cruel she may have been, or that he forget his race, no matter how prosperous or how wretched that race may have become."

Polish nationalist organizations, dedicated to the struggle for an independent Poland, celebrated the careers of Casimir Pulaski, a Polish soldier who died in the American Revolution, and Thaddeus Kosciuszko, a Pole who fought on two continents, in the American Revolution and in Poland for independence. Peter Kiolbassa, the founder of Chicago's first Polish Catholic parish, an officer of the Polish Roman Catholic Union, and the most prominent Polish-American leader until his death in 1905, served in the Illinois legislature and as treasurer of Chicago. He insisted that Catholic parishes in Chicago accept the authority of Chicago's Irish bishop, rejecting the nationalist suggestion that they come under the Bishop of Poland. Addressing a rally of 2,000 immigrants protesting Russian persecution of Poles, he linked American political values with the Polish national cause, exclaiming, "We as free-born citizens have a right to ask for assistance and moral support of *other* free citizens of this country." At the outbreak of the Spanish-American War, Francis Fronczak, a member of the New York State legislature and Buffalo's Public Health Commissioner, linked the struggles for Cuban and Polish independence. "Poles loyal to Poland must be loyal to America," he proclaimed. Michael Kruszka, the Milwaukee politician who tried to get the public schools to teach Polish, once explained: "I am an enthusiastic Pole and at the same time a [loyal] American. I do not see where the one contradicts the other."[19] In a similar vein, Italian leaders organized elaborate pageants to celebrate Columbus' discovery of America.

Many Japanese leaders likewise advocated Americanization without abandoning loyalty to the homeland, despite growing white hostility and second-class legal status in the United States. In 1911, the Japanese Association of America began a "campaign of education" to encourage Japanese immigrants to think of themselves as permanent residents and to educate Americans about Japan and Japanese immigrants. A conference of Japanese-American educators soon concluded that their schools should prepare children to live as Americans. "Recognizing the necessity of an American education, Japanese schools will provide supplementary instruction in Japanese and education about Japan" while enrolling children in the public schools, they resolved. The next year, the Japanese Teachers Association deemed textbooks compiled by the Japanese Education Ministry inappropriate for Japanese-American students. Japanese leaders also successfully petitioned the Japanese government in 1915 to allow their American-born children to renounce their Japanese citizenship.

When the United States banned the naturalization of Japanese immigrants in 1906, Japanese leaders in America pressed the government of Japan to seek American naturalization rights for Japanese immigrants already here, but the Japanese government refused. In 1914, a Japanese immigrant, Ozawa Takao, who graduated from Berkeley High School and attended the University of California, challenged the naturalization ban in the courts. In his legal brief, Ozawa stated: "In name, General Benedict Arnold was an American, but at heart he was a traitor. In name, I am not an American, but at heart I am a true American." The Japanese government, not wanting the naturalization issue to interfere with more pressing diplomatic priorities, instructed its consul in San Francisco "to take steps to prevent the Japanese within your jurisdiction from undertaking a test case campaign." In defiance of the Japanese government, several West Coast Japanese newspapers supported Ozawa's appeal to the U.S. Supreme Court, and in 1917, the Pacific Coast Japanese Association Deliberative Council unanimously backed Ozawa and set up a committee to assist his ultimately unsuccessful appeal.[20]

Intellectuals, newspaper editors, politicians, and communal leaders in every group vigorously debated Americanization and group identity, articulating many variations on a single theme: loyalty to ancestral groups did not preclude loyalty to America. Some progressive intellectuals defended immigrants' demand for cultural autonomy, suggesting that cultural pluralism grew naturally from America's democratic values. For ordinary immigrants, such abstractions hardly mattered. Struggling for their daily bread, they had ignored elite admonitions at home against emigration, establishing themselves, their relatives, and their townspeople in a grassroots quest for economic security. They adapted pragmatically and selectively to life in the United States, vigorously asserting their right to cultural autonomy. Their grandchildren might agonize over the meaning of dual identity, but immigrants themselves did not worry about what it meant. They just did it, taking their future and that of their children into their own hands.

4

Rural Americans
and Industrial Capitalism

Farmers experienced the rise of corporate capitalism in America with one foot in the world of Jeffersonian yeomanry and the other in the complex economy of J. P. Morgan. Although farming remained a traditional way of life and family farmers on their own land epitomized American individualism, farms also operated as businesses producing cash crops. Entrepreneurs in fact, if not in self-image, farmers found their autonomy and economic security challenged by remote institutions: the railroads on which they shipped their products to market, the currency and credit system, the corporations which manufactured and sold agricultural machinery, and, most important, the invisible hand that determined the price of farm commodities. But industrialization offered new opportunities as well, including expanding markets for new products, labor-saving technologies, and a wide array of consumer goods.

The number of Americans earning a living from the soil continued to increase until after World War I, but at a slower rate than it had in the mid-nineteenth century. Although fewer people each year farmed in the older agricultural areas of New York, New England, Ohio, Illinois, Indiana, Michigan, and Iowa, farm families in the 1890s began tilling new land in the Great Plains and elsewhere equal to the combined territory of France and Germany; they added an additional 120,000,000 acres between 1900 and 1920 in the Western prairies, the semiarid areas of the Southwest, the Oregon desert, the depleted forests in the Great Lakes area, and elsewhere.

The influx of farmers to these new areas more than offset a shrinking farm population in older regions. The percentage of Americans who worked in agriculture, however, declined steadily from almost 40 percent in 1890 to just over 30 percent in 1920, as the growth in urban and industrial occupations greatly outstripped the growth in farming.

An increase in farm prices after 1897 ushered in two decades of prosperity for most farmers outside the South, putting a damper on the fires of agrarian protest and Populism that had dominated rural America for the preceding two decades; but it did not extinguish them. The economic and cultural effects of corporate capitalism continued to challenge traditional rural life, both North and South. Farmers neither fully embraced nor completely resisted these changes. They approached new conditions and new technologies pragmatically, selecting whatever enabled them to enhance their autonomy and economic well-being, and at the same time vigorously resisting the efforts of outsiders to reshape rural life to accommodate corporate needs and values. Rural America remained contested terrain throughout the Progressive Era.

Northern Farm Families

Small farmers who raised cash crops had always remained as autonomous as possible by employing the labor of all family members, by working very long hours, and by producing on the farm much of what they consumed. When the prices for the products of most Northern farms rose after 1897, these farmers did not abandon their time-honored efforts to minimize their dependence on the market. On average, Northern farm families worked eleven hours a day, according to a 1920 survey, far exceeding the workday of low-income families in cities. Much of this labor produced goods consumed by the family itself and even farmers with substantial land and equipment saw less cash than many urban workers. Most commercial farmers produced and processed fruits and vegetables, poultry, dairy products, firewood, and smoked meats for their own use, selling whatever they did not consume. Women, in addition to caring for children and maintaining the home, took primary responsibility for these enterprises. As late as 1920, 60 percent of farm families churned their own milk and 49 percent baked their own bread.

Children from an early age contributed to the farm economy. Mari Sandoz, a writer born on a Nebraska homestead in 1896, wrote that "all of us knew children who put in twelve-, fourteen-hour days from March to November. We knew seven-, eight-year-old boys who drove four-horse teams to the harrow, who shocked grain behind the binder all day in heat and dust and rattlesnakes, who cultivated, hoed and weeded corn, and finally husked it out before they could go to school in November."[1] In poor or large families, older children sometimes worked for wages for nearby farm or town families, giving most of their earnings to their parents; boys did field labor or unskilled work in town, girls worked as domestics.

Farmers also helped each other fill silos, cut wood, butcher animals, husk corn, or raise barns. When farmers took ill, neighbors helped out. Women's clubs organized cooperative labor for big projects like quilting and sewing bedding, and some collectively marketed women's produce, eggs, and dairy products. Nor did labor-saving technology immediately eliminate the need for mutual assistance. Farmers had long performed threshing, the separation of seeds from straw, chaff, and other debris, cooperatively. Between 1875 and 1895, steam-powered threshers replaced threshing machines powered by horses in much of the Midwest. Few farmers could afford their own threshing machine, so they rented the equipment. The steam-powered technology, although very fast, required a large number of workers for a short but intense period and farmers organized threshing rings of eight to twenty families, with rules governing the obligations of each family.

Farmers also established purchasing and marketing cooperatives. In 1900, farmer groups owned 2,000 enterprises, mostly creameries or cheese factories in the dairy regions. Wisconsin's Pigeon Creamery Association, organized in 1892, denied membership to anyone not engaged in agriculture. Dairy farmers also organized effectively to increase the price of milk. They held milk off the Boston market for six weeks in 1900 to raise prices, and groups serving New York, Philadelphia, Chicago, and other cities subsequently forced price increases in the same way. They also vigorously resisted efforts of city health officials to require tuberculin tests on cows supplying milk to urban consumers. Dairy farmers selling in Milwaukee, for example, withheld their milk before World War I to challenge city government testing of cows. Maintaining unfettered control over the sale of their milk overrode any concern for the health of urban residents.

Other farmers followed the example of dairy producers. The Society of Equity, begun in 1902, organized cooperative grain elevators and other farmer-owned marketing entities. Farm women in Wisconsin started a cooperative laundry. Yet farmers in many places remained frustrated by their inability to control prices. When a federal commission in 1908 asked farmers whether they were "satisfactorily organized to promote their mutual buying and selling interests," 80 percent answered "no." Two out of three farmers did not belong to any organization.[2]

Farmers outside the South also faced the challenge of keeping their grown children on the land. As new farmland became scarce and expensive, and the economic and social attractions of city life beckoned, the potential departure of young people threatened the continuity of farm communities. Farmers responded in different ways.

In old agricultural communities like Chelsea, Vermont, whose population had been declining since the mid-nineteenth century, farmers passed their land on to younger sons with the requirement that they support their parents in old age and provide dowries for their unmarried sisters. Although older sons normally did not inherit the family land because their parents were still farming it when the sons reached adulthood, their parents usually gave them money for a down payment on another farm. They gave older daughters a dowry which might be used to acquire land after marriage. Those young adults in Chelsea who continued to farm stayed in the immediate area and did not seek out new farmland in the West. Only those who chose nonagricultural occupations left Chelsea in significant numbers.

Some northern New England farmers attempted to maintain farm communities in more innovative ways. New Hampshire and Vermont communities initiated "Old Home Week," encouraging children and grandchildren of local residents who had moved to urban areas to return for nostalgic celebrations. Some farmers also began to offer farm vacations, providing meals and lodging to middle-class urbanites whom they encouraged to return to their New England "roots" and enjoy the farm's healthful natural environment. A staff member of the Vermont Board of Agriculture explained that "there is no crop more profitable than this crop from the city."[3] If harvesting tourists in this way significantly altered the nature of farm labor and family life, for many it seemed a worthwhile compromise to maintain farm life in a marginal agricultural area.

Midwestern farmers had a better chance of establishing their children on the land and thereby preserving their rural communities. German farmers in St. Martin, Minnesota, usually rented a portion of their land for a year or two to sons in their twenties, before selling it to them at a modest price; at the same time, they purchased new plots to be leased and sold later to younger male offspring. They also provided a dowry for daughters upon marriage. In one extraordinary case, a German farmer began cultivating 160 acres in 1869, and had ten children, including five sons. When his eldest son turned twenty, he purchased on credit another 160 acres, and four years later took out a mortgage for still more land. He sold a portion of his land to his two oldest sons when they reached their mid-twenties. He sold his original farm to his third son when the young man turned twenty-five, but in succeeding years the father acquired an additional 138 acres, which he sold to his fourth son. When Dad retired at seventy-two, only his youngest son's future remained unsettled. Yankee farmers in the Midwest, unlike Germans or Norwegians, typically held on to their land until their death, so few of their children stayed in the community. Still, in most families at least some grown children had to move farther west in order to farm.

Some Midwestern farmers went south to the western prairie areas of Louisiana, Texas, and later Arkansas to cultivate rice. After the railroads reached this area in 1881, Midwesterners in search of cheap farmland adapted wheat technology and irrigation to rice cultivation. By 1900, 7,000 Northern farmers from Iowa, Illinois, and Nebraska had settled in the area.

Although many farm children moved to less settled agricultural areas or to towns and cities when they reached adulthood, enough stayed to keep Northern farm communities stable. Families in these farm communities achieved economic security and maintained their way of life after the return of agricultural prosperity in 1897. By producing on the farm most of what they consumed, by working long hours and employing the labor of all family members, by cooperating with their neighbors in large tasks, and sometimes by organizing purchasing and selling cooperatives, farmers participated in the capitalist market for agricultural produce without becoming completely dependent on cash for the necessities of daily life. In this way, they enhanced their economic security and maintained greater economic autonomy than the majority of Americans who depended almost entirely on the wage economy for survival.

SOUTHERN FARM FAMILIES

The lot of Southern and Northern farmers differed sharply. The nation's poorest region attracted few immigrant farmers, lacked adequate schools, and lagged behind the rest of the nation in its commerce, industry, and transportation. Race divided farmers, and white fear of African-Americans blinded them to their common plight. In the South, poor farmers raised staple crops on small plots, owned or rented, but with diminishing returns. In 1900, almost two-thirds of Southern farmers tilled plots of twenty to fifty acres. Tenancy rose dramatically during the hard times of the late nineteenth century, from 36 percent of all Southern farms in 1880 to 47 percent in 1900 and 49 percent in 1910. In Deep South states like Mississippi and Alabama, tenancy rates exceeded 60 percent. Among African-Americans, more than three-quarters worked land owned by others in the first two decades of the century.

A small number of Southerners owned substantial acreage, working the land with agricultural wage laborers or more often contracting with tenants and sharecroppers. A substantial number of better-off farmers (about 750,000 in 1900) owned or leased plots of one to two hundred acres. Below them stood small landowners or tenants, who attempted to eke out a living on tiny plots. At the bottom stood sharecroppers, the largest and most exploited group of Southern farmers.

The differences in tenancy arrangements between North and South revealed the relative disadvantages of Southerners. In the North, new farmers commonly rented land for a few years before purchasing. They owned their own work animals and agricultural machinery. Southern renters or tenants paid cash or a portion of their crop for the use of the land, normally owned their own mules and implements and most of their seed and fertilizer, but could not routinely purchase the land they worked as Northerners did. Sharecroppers, on the other hand, owned almost nothing. A landowner supplied a "cropper" with mules, tools, seed, fertilizer, and a house, and determined what crop the tenant would grow. In exchange, the owner took perhaps half of the cash value of the harvest. The landowner also typically provided croppers with food and other essential goods at inflated rates of credit, deducting the amount due from the cropper's share after sale. Sharecroppers, who rarely saw cash under this crop lien system, found themselves trapped in a cycle of poverty and dependence from which few could break loose.

All cotton and tobacco growers, the vast majority of Southern farmers, suffered from falling prices not only in the late nineteenth century but also in the early twentieth century, when Northern farmers prospered. The price of a pound of cotton, which sold for as much as 43 cents right after the Civil War, averaged 5 cents in the 1890s. In 1903, 1905, and 1907, when the price finally rose to 10 cents, Southern farmers grew larger crops, and the price dropped again. Yet few Southern farmers considered raising other crops. The South had poor transportation, and staples like cotton and tobacco did not spoil quickly once harvested. Moreover, in the credit-poor South, even farmers who wanted to invest in new crops had trouble finding someone with money to lend.

Sharecroppers suffered the most from these circumstances. Their hard family labor brought only continuing poverty and little prospect of eventual ownership, denying them both economic security and autonomy. Ned Cobb, an African-American farmer, started picking cotton as a child. When he began sharecropping, he never saw any cash after he settled his debts. "If you don't make enough to have some left you aint done nothin, except givin the other fellow your labor," he later complained. Landowners expected deference from their tenants, and acted at best paternalistically toward them. One white tenant farmer remembered "the worst man I ever worked for was Lem Harris. . . . You can't suit him. Sunday night just 'fore bed-time he drives round to tell you how and what to do first thing Monday mornin'. You start at it; he's there cussin' at you 'fore breakfast Monday mornin' for not doing it another way."[4]

Cotton and tobacco, whether cultivated by tenants or small owners, engaged the whole family, just like corn, wheat, or dairy farming in the North. Typically, men plowed and women and children hoed and picked. Rosa Kanipe, a white woman born in western North Carolina in 1887, remembered that she had to cook dinner at home

as soon as she was old enough, because "the rest of the family was
in the field by six o'clock in the mornin'."

> I stayed at the house and took care of the little ones not big enough to
> work. I had to cook enough for dinner and supper. After dinner was
> over, I hitched a horse to the wagon, piled the younguns in, and drove
> to the fields. . . . I always hoed till seven, then I'd hitch up the horse,
> put the small children back in the wagon and start for home. The rest
> worked long as they could see. Supper would be ready to eat when
> they come in, and the milking done.[5]

Southerners also produced much of what they consumed on the
farm. One small landowning family harvested peanuts, potatoes,
corn, peas, and sugarcane, tended a variety of animals, and canned
peaches and pears in addition to growing cotton. Many sharecroppers maintained vegetable gardens and raised animals, and some
sold firewood, fruits, vegetables, eggs, molasses, pork, or other farm
products, with the sufferance of the landowner. Mary Wigley,
daughter of a white sharecropper, recalled that a new landlord insisted that her father convert their large vegetable garden to cotton
cultivation. "This was a blow to freedom and pride, also to our way
of subsistence farming," she explained. "It drove home the fact that
we were not on our own. We were mere tenants. It made us want
all the more a home of our own."[6] Like the more prosperous
Northern farmers, Southerners also shared large tasks like cotton
picking, fodder pulling, log rolling, hog killing, and quilting, often
turning tedious tasks like shucking corn into festive competitive
events.

Southern farmers, facing a losing battle for economic security
and autonomy, looked occasionally for collective solutions to their
problems after the failure of the Alliance and Populist movements
of the 1880s and 1890s. In 1902, a former Alliance organizer and
rural newspaper editor founded the first branch of the Farmers'
Educational and Cooperative Union of America, popularly known

as the Farmers' Union, in southern Texas. Branches spread quickly in seven Southern states. A secret society dedicated to fighting the "credit and mortgage system," the Union tried to control the marketing of cotton by creating cooperative warehouses where farmers could store their crops until prices rose. In 1905, the Union urged cotton farmers to withhold their crop from market until it brought at least 10 cents a pound, but only a few farmers participated. By 1908, 111,000 families had joined the Union in the South, but membership declined to 44,280 by 1916, and many of its cooperatives failed. Despite its avowed goal of coordinated farmer action to raise cotton prices, the Union refused to admit black families, who in 1908 formed their own Negro Farmers' Union.

Some farmers also tried to restrict the amount of cotton raised or marketed. Organizers proposed to destroy two million bales of cotton, and in 1904, farmers in Gaines, Georgia, dramatically set 3,000 bales on fire in front of the courthouse as they sang hymns. Farmers in a few other places joined in public burnings, but no massive destruction followed. In 1908, night riders in Georgia, Mississippi, Texas, and Arkansas threatened violence against farmers who did not hold back their cotton for a minimum of 10 cents a pound; but to no avail.

In tobacco regions of Tennessee and Kentucky, growers organized purchasing cooperatives for fertilizer and tools in the first years of the new century, and attempted to get farmers to process and market their crops through a pool which would bargain with the tobacco trust. When night riders burned tobacco warehouses and beat farmers who refused to join, law enforcement officers intervened and the effort collapsed. Overall, collective action by Southern farmers in the early twentieth century proved no more successful than it had in the 1880s and 1890s.

Therefore, Southern farmers employed the one form of autonomy still available to them—they moved in search of greater economic security. Like industrial operatives and unskilled day laborers who quit jobs and took new ones regularly, tenant farmers moved frequently from one landlord to another after the annual crop harvest and sale, or from farm work to wage jobs. Between 1880 and 1930, three to four of every ten sharecroppers changed plantations each year. Only 26 percent of white tenants in Cobb County, Georgia, in 1880 still lived there by 1900. M. D. Rice remembered that as a child in Georgia "we never found 'ary place we wanted. Seems like come next year we'd find the right place to suit us, but we never did." When Rice married, he continued this nomadic existence. Interviewed in 1938, he remembered twenty-three moves in forty-two years. Most tenants traveled relatively short distances, but in the early twentieth century significant numbers of black sharecroppers moved away from older cotton-growing regions infested by the boll weevil to new farms in Arkansas, Mississippi, Texas, Louisiana, and Oklahoma.

The South's nascent industrial economy offered some alternatives to farming. Industrial jobs in the South grew rapidly. Southern textile mills employed 10,000 hands in 1870 but more than 97,000 by 1900. Frank and Sally Martin sharecropped until 1914, when, Frank recalled, they "made fourteen bales of cotton, thirty-one barrels of corn and three hundred bushels of potatoes besides a sight of peas. It was one of the best crops I ever knowed . . . and we came out about the poorest we ever done." So they decided to look for "public work," and the family moved to a mill town.[7] Textile mills rarely hired black workers, but some African-Americans worked in Southern steel mills, coal mines, and sawmills. Many rural folk moved back and forth between industrial wage labor and farming, taking jobs in slack season, or trying mill work for a few years and then returning to cropping. In 1908, the Tennessee Coal and Iron plant in Alabama had an annual turnover rate of 400 percent.

Still, a significant number of poor Southern farmers, both black and white, gave up rural life altogether and moved to Southern cities or to the booming urban centers of the North. In the 1890s, the number of Southern-born blacks living in the North grew by 105,000, and black migration accelerated in the early years of the twentieth century. We know less about the much larger migration of white Southern farmers to the North. Historian Jack Kirby puts the number between 1900 and 1920 at 2.3 million. In short, many Southern farmers, unable to gain security despite the hard labor of all family members, moved to different farms, to Southern cities, mills, and mines, or to the North, seeking escape from their region's pervasive rural poverty.

Subsistence Farmers

Although most farmers produced substantial cash crops, some sold little or none of what they produced. In the coastal South Carolina low country, for example, former rice plantation slaves and their children acquired small plots and resisted sharecropping by growing their own food instead of traditional rice and long-staple cotton. They lived simply and frugally, minimized their dependence on the cash market, and avoided buying on credit at local stores. Staying out of debt kept them from losing their land.

Most subsistence farmers experienced much less success in maintaining their autonomy. Appalachia's poor soil did not lend itself to cotton or tobacco cultivation, and inadequate transportation in the mountainous region made it difficult to sell any agricultural produce in the national market. For many years, people there mostly grew corn, the staple of their diet, which they used also to feed farm animals. They ground corn locally, spun their own wool, and wove cloth at home. Some also maintained apple orchards, and each fall they went down to nearby towns to sell the apples, the sole source of cash for the year. Some farmers converted corn into moonshine whiskey, more easily transported down steep mountain paths than corn, and it sold for six times the price. Still others gathered medicinal herbs and roots like ginseng, exchanging these for store goods with local merchants, who sold them to distributors in large cities. In 1890 a merchant in Logan County, West Virginia, announced that "a pound of seng will get you a good pair of boots or a fine suit of clothes."[8]

At the turn of the century, however, industrialists seeking lumber and coal offered to buy land outright or to lease the mineral rights for what seemed like substantial sums. Companies built mining and lumbering towns, and many Appalachians began to work for wages. By World War I, the companies had cut down the forests and worked out the mines. No longer autonomous marginal farmers, Appalachians now depended heavily on declining wage employment for economic survival. Many left their homes for jobs in Northern cities.

Cajuns in the southwestern Louisiana prairie also practiced subsistence agriculture for several generations. Descendants of French settlers of what is now Nova Scotia, Cajuns had come to Louisiana when the British expelled them in the eighteenth century, maintaining their culture and a distinct dialect. In the eastern part of Louisiana's prairie, farmers typically devoted about 40 percent of their modest landholdings to cotton which they sold for cash, 40 percent to corn which they consumed, and the remainder to animal pasture or vegetables. In the thinly populated western prairie, Cajun farmers maintained substantial autonomy by raising cattle on open land and maintaining small gardens in scattered locations; occasionally they also planted "providence rice," rice which would grow only in those years when providence provided sufficient rainfall. Midwestern wheat farmers who moved to the region in the 1880s and 1890s to cultivate rice with modern machinery and irrigation offered Cajun farmers seemingly high prices for their land; sometimes the newcomers traded cotton-and-corn land farther east for Cajun prairie land. As a result, many western Cajun farmers moved to the eastern prairie, where Cajuns continued to farm in the traditional way. The western Louisiana Cajun community largely disappeared.

In New Mexico, Hispanic farmers had long combined subsistence agriculture on small irrigated plots with the grazing of livestock on communal ranges. The Spanish and Mexican governments had granted communal land rights to settlers who built villages; residents owned a house and a small amount of land adjacent to it; and the village community collectively controlled pastureland. When English-speaking settlers began moving to the area in the 1880s, Congress recognized the Spanish-speaking settlers' individual titles, but placed much of the communal land in the public domain for homesteading or national forests. When Anglo cattle ranchers and landowners fenced in these common rangelands, a group of Mexican farmers, calling themselves the White Caps, or Las Gorras Blancas, burned or cut fences and harassed the cattlemen. "Our purpose is to protect the rights and interest of the people in general and especially those of the helpless classes," they explained in their platform, written in 1889.[9] Often jailed by law enforcement officials, the White Caps still managed to slow down the privatization of common lands and temporarily reduced new Anglo settlement in their areas.

Still, they could not stop the process, and by 1900 the government had taken six million acres in New Mexico for national forests and another million for homesteading. Deprived of cash from open-range sheep farming, and confined to insufficient plots, some attempted herding sheep as sharecroppers. More often, however, they entered the wage economy, with men working seasonally in mines or on railroads, while women and younger children tended village plots. After 1900, many sold these parcels and migrated to Colorado to work on sugar beets during the growing season and in cities the rest of the time. Tapping the labor of all family members and providing mutual support within their communities, Hispanic landowners nonetheless lost the autonomy they had enjoyed as subsistence farmers in communal villages.

NATIVE AMERICANS

Government policy and the continued westward movement of settlers eager to bring more land into cultivation also challenged the traditional subsistence economy and the cultural autonomy of Indian peoples, particularly on the Great Plains. Defeated by the army, and undermined economically by the destruction of the buffalo herds, by 1880 most Plains Indians lived communally on reservations in which tribes rather than individuals owned the land and used it for the collective needs of tribal members. Throughout the Progressive Era, U.S. officials attempted to assimilate the Indians by turning them into small farmers with private holdings, by establishing schools to educate young Indians as Americans, by making Native Americans eligible for U.S. citizenship, and by forcibly suppressing Indian culture.

Some advocates of Indian assimilation believed that Indians would benefit from adopting mainstream American ways. Others, unconcerned with the Indians' welfare, eagerly sought to bring reservation land within the capitalist market and open it for settlement. The Dawes Act, passed by Congress in 1887, attempted to break up reservations and give each Indian family an individually owned farm; it also provided for the sale of reservation lands not needed for "allotments" to settlers, the proceeds to be placed in a fund for Indian "education and civilization." Once they received title to their land, they could become U.S. citizens. Advocates of the Dawes Act's allotment policy, the linchpin of a national effort to assimilate the Indians, argued that property ownership would civilize the Indians and make them like whites. Many whites undoubtedly welcomed the opening of "surplus" reservation land for sale and settlement. When the Dawes Act passed in 1887, Indians controlled 138 million acres of land. By 1900, they held only 78 million acres.

Some Indians did well under the allotment system, embracing private property and individualist values. Edward Goodbird, a Hidatsa, moved with his parents from Like-a-Fishhook Village to an allotment in nearby North Dakota. He recalled later that in the old village "four or five families lived in one large earth lodge, but now we built each family a cabin for themselves." As an adolescent, he sought a vision from God, a Hidatsa custom, by subjecting himself to physical pain, but the vision did not come to him. Shortly thereafter, the government outlawed Indian self-torture. This greatly angered his father and many other Hidatsa, but Goodbird quietly approved. "I was glad of it," he explained, "for I could not help thinking that in the matter of torture, the Indian way was a pretty hard way for a young fellow to travel."[10] Goodbird prospered as a farmer and cattle rancher, and worked for the Bureau of Indian Affairs. Later he became a Congregational minister.

Goodbird's experience proved unusual. Most Hidatsa did not flourish under the strict rules enforced by government agents. Goodbird reported that "older Indians, who came from Like-a-Fishhook Village, find life on allotments rather lonesome." When Goodbird went to work for the government, the local agent instructed him, "If an Indian is lazy and will not attend to his plowing, report him to me and I will send a policeman." When the government issued cows to each Indian family, "the agent ordered me to see that every family built a barn." They "were not allowed to kill . . . cattle without a permit from the agent," Goodbird explained. The agents tried to wipe out Indian rituals and traditional dances. "It only creates in them a desire to become worthless with their heathen notions. . . . They can have some other enjoyment, which does not fill their mind with too many Indian notions," wrote one agent in 1909.[11] Hidatsa even needed permission from an agent to leave the reservation.

The federal government mandated schooling for Indian children and the Bureau of Indian Affairs established boarding schools where they hoped to rid young people, removed from parental influence, of Indian ways. The schools prohibited Indian dress, songs, dances, rituals, and the use of Indian languages. Teachers cut boys' hair and gave all children English names. Some Indian parents welcomed this educational opportunity, while others saw it as a threat to traditional culture and kept their children away. John Rogers (named Way Quah by his mother) and his siblings, born on an Anishinaabe reservation in Minnesota, attended boarding school for six years. On return, only his oldest sister still spoke the Anishinaabe language, but their mother insisted that they use their Anishinaabe names and learn tribal traditions.

Despite government assimilation policy, many Indians continued traditional practices, often in private. Goodbird's mother, Buffalo Bird Woman, who never abandoned her ancestral religion, spoke for many when she told an anthropologist in 1908, "I [do not] like white men's laws. I do not understand them nor know how to make them rule my life."[12] John Rogers' father, Pindegaygishig, whom John did not meet until his teens, owned a lumber business employing hundreds of men and lived well. But at night he frequently brought out a traditional drum and taught his family to communicate with the Great Spirit. John recalled that after six years of boarding school, "it was hard to understand . . . about the 'Great Spirit.' " But when he became seriously ill, he prayed in the traditional Anishinaabe way. "Thus it was that I remembered the teachings of my Indian people," he explained years later.[13]

Many Native Americans who accepted Dawes Act allotments found ways to combine traditional economic practices with the opportunities offered by the market, even if such activities met with the disapproval of the government agents. On the White Earth Anishinaabe reservation, Indians on allotment farms gathered wild rice, hunted game, fished, picked wild blueberries, gathered ginseng and snakeroot, and collected maple syrup not only for their own consumption but for sale to white merchants. An Episcopal minister noted in the early twentieth century that the Indians "got hold of a great deal more money in the course of a year than the average white farmer."[14] Like farmers in other parts of the country, men commonly supplemented farm income with seasonal wage labor. After about 1910, Indian income from these sources diminished as the government sold off much of the reservation land. Farmers enclosed large areas and posted "No Trespassing" signs, and logging companies greatly damaged the area's wild rice and other profitable vegetation. By 1915, many White Earth Anishinaabe had left the reservation.

Elsewhere, on much less fertile allotments, even fewer Indians succeeded in becoming independent farmers. By 1895, almost all the Omaha and Winnebago of Nebraska had leased their allotments. In 1906–7 the combined income of the Cheyennes and Arapahos from the sale of farm produce was only $5,312; tribe members' total income of $217,312 came almost entirely from the sale and leasing of individual allotments. Creek Indians formed a society of "Snakes" which rejected the allotment policy and, until suppressed by the army, attacked other Creeks who accepted assigned government farms. For many years thereafter, some Choctaws, Cherokees, and Creeks refused to live on their allotments.

A minority of Native Americans achieved substantial economic security by accepting the concept of private property, Christianity, and the majority culture. Most however, although largely dependent on the government economically, resisted forced assimilation.

SCIENTIFIC AGRICULTURE AND
THE COUNTRY LIFE MOVEMENT

In 1908, President Roosevelt, the only American President born in New York City, appointed agricultural educators, editors, rural organizers, and public officials to a Country Life Commission headed by Liberty Hyde Bailey, dean of the New York College of Agriculture at Cornell University. Charged with studying the condition of rural America, it concluded that farmers had failed to adjust to modern realities, clinging to traditional individualism when the times required organization. Therefore, rural life suffered from land speculation, poorly managed natural resources, inadequate roads, schools, and sanitation, labor shortages, and deplorable conditions for farm women. Many farmers doubtless never heard of the Country Life Commission, but others who did resented its condescension and its negative portrayal of rural Americans. A letter to the editor of a farm journal proclaimed that "the average farmer and his family" were "infinitely more blessed and happy . . . than the average city laborer of the same capital and income."[15]

In fact, many of the goals of the Country Life reformers threatened the cultural autonomy of rural people. At the turn of the century, parents controlled rural schools. Students attended numerous one-room schoolhouses governed by locally elected school committees which selected the teacher and determined the curriculum. In some places, school committees called parent meetings to elect new teachers. Students went to school when work obligations at home or the weather did not keep them away, and no central bureaucracy supervised teachers or school committees. Parents never hesitated to tell teachers what to teach and how to teach it.

Reformers for years had demanded centralized control of education to consolidate one-room schools, set standards for teachers, establish a common curriculum, and enforce attendance. A writer on school reform in 1915 complained of schools "controlled largely by rural people, who, too often, do not realize either their own needs or the possibilities of rural education."[16] Farmers resisted reformers' proposals. In Virginia, which had a vigorous school consolidation movement, one of every three schoolrooms in the state still stood in its own building in 1920. A Wisconsin school administrator concluded before World War I that two decades of effort had not consolidated a single school in his state. In much of rural America, and especially in the South, many rural parents ignored mandatory schooling laws where they existed. A 1917 survey in Kentucky concluded that in the rural areas of the state, the compulsory education statute amounted to a "virtually dead letter" which enforcement officials "winked at." Photographer Lewis Hine, campaigning against child labor in Georgia in 1911, saw petitions signed by thousands of mill workers opposing child labor restrictions. Legislators continually asked him, "Are you trying to do these things for these people that they *themselves* do not want?"[17]

Country Life reformers also sought to engage rural churches in addressing what they considered the backwardness of rural life. Rural folk remained deeply attached to their churches, however, and ministers and parishioners alike resisted reform. One pastor in 1916 denounced the Country Lifers' ideal of an activist church whose "chief concern is to make roads as 'a way of salvation,' 'to raise fat pigs for the glory of God,' to 'clean up dirty privies,' to turn the house of worship into a dance-hall and the preacher of the Gospel of Jesus Christ into the director of the dance."[18] In the South, rural traditionalists rejected mainline Baptists' and Methodists' emphasis on reason and reflection, and evangelical movements offered emotional prayer services. At Pentecostal prayer meetings, people spoke in tongues and proclaimed faith-healing miracles.

A man known as Brother Fisher told interviewers the story of his religious rebirth. Moving as a child from a farm in western North Carolina to a mill town, he remembered that "we sorta felt out of place in a city church with everybody dressed up in store-bought clothes," so they "started goin' to a tent revival that the Church of God was holdin'." The family felt "more at home and wasn't ashamed of our clothes," and found "*more power* in their meetin's." Fisher said he could "never forget the night I was saved." Jesus "was there that night as surely as there is a God. . . . I poured out my soul to Him . . . and my built-up emotions and feelin's came surgin' out as I sobbed and cried for the blood of Jesus and its cleansing power. It wasn't long before I felt that He was there, extendin' His holy hand and biddin' me to follow Him. Then I knew that the debt had been paid and my slate was clean as snow. . . . Oh, my, was I happy!"[19] Through this emotional and exuberant style of worship, many rural people asserted their cultural autonomy.

Businessmen, agriculture professors, and state and federal agriculture officials had no more success than Country Life reformers in persuading farmers to increase productivity by using the latest scientific techniques. By the turn of the century, most states and territories sponsored farmers' institutes while land grant universities established agricultural extension divisions. The Hatch Act of 1887 and the Adams Act of 1906 provided federal dollars for research to increase farm productivity.

Farmers gave these programs at best a lukewarm reception. Some welcomed technical advice, and Southerners sought help fighting the boll weevil. But many farmers denigrated "book farming." A Virginia institute instructor conceded in 1892 that "in almost every case" farmers had "shown a most disheartening appreciation for the efforts made to help them." In 1912, a farm publication complained that "the great body of farmers" continued to use "methods that prevailed fifty years ago." U.S. Secretary of Agriculture David Houston estimated in 1913 that only on one-eighth of the country's agricultural land did farmers achieve reasonably productive results. As late as 1917, a Nebraska farmer stated, "The average boy 10 or 12 years old on the farm knows what . . . will grow and what will not grow. If farmers had to depend on what these college boys preach they would be worse off than they are now."[20]

Farmers ignored scientific agriculture primarily because increased production threatened their economic security. In 1889 and 1890, L. L. Polk, president of the Farmers' Alliance, had argued that increased efficiency and greater yields would not solve farmers' problems. Rather, he argued, farmers must "again obtain control of the products of the farm and prevent them from passing into the hands of the corporations." One of the organizers of the Society of Equity, started by upper Midwest farmers seeking direct control of the marketing of their crops, reiterated the point in 1903, proclaiming that "what the farmer wants to produce is not crops, but money."[21] In 1915, a California farm woman rhetorically asked the U.S. Department of Agriculture what it sought to do for farmers. "Is it that you wish us to increase farm production, and are you contemplating sending us a lot of pamphlets to 'help' us make more butter, raise more vegetables, supply the markets with more eggs than we do now . . . ?" Continuing, she told USDA officials, "If that is what your 'service' to us would imply, I decline it with thanks."[22]

Corporate capitalists and government officials who supported scientific agriculture had other goals, however. Low food prices lessened pressure to increase the wages of industrial workers. High productivity increased overseas trade in farm commodities. Indeed, national farm income grew by 55 percent between 1900 and 1910 while productivity remained nearly flat. Gifford Pinchot, Theodore Roosevelt's conservationist and a member of the Country Life Commission, summed it up in 1918: "What the Government has done to help the farmer has been done still more to help the city man. . . . What the city man wanted was cheap food. Therefore, what was done for the farmer was directed almost without exception toward helping or inducing him to grow cheap food."[23]

It is hardly surprising, therefore, that farmers showed no great enthusiasm for the Smith-Lever Act of 1917, which provided federal funds to land grant colleges for "instruction and practical demonstration in agriculture and home economics." Farmers had long sought help from the government to loosen the currency, provide credit, and regulate railroad rates. In the early twentieth century, Equity leaders in Minnesota, the Dakotas, and elsewhere agitated for state-owned terminal grain elevators to bypass private grain traders. The Nonpartisan League, begun by radical farmers on the Great Plains in 1914, advocated direct government aid to farmers, stricter federal regulation of business, and higher business taxes. In North Dakota, the League elected its candidate for governor and a majority in the state legislature in 1916. President Woodrow Wilson had originally opposed a government credit program for farmers as special-interest legislation, but seeing the effectiveness of farmer activism in the West and facing a difficult reelection campaign, he endorsed the Federal Farm Loan Act and the Warehouse Act in 1916. These laws gave Southern and Western farmers low-interest loans for long periods, secured by the farmers' crops and land, the modest beginning of what later became an elaborate federal program to regulate crop levels and maintain prices. Through political organizing, by the time of the American entrance into World War I farmers had finally forced the government to act on their behalf.

Landownership in America had traditionally symbolized Jeffersonian yeomanry, and Progressive Era farmers still took pride in the autonomy that landownership seemed to confer. In the South, sharecroppers and tenants wanted desperately to own their own plots even though small owners lived almost as poorly as tenants. But recognizing that in the new era of global markets, farm ownership did not guarantee either autonomy or economic security, farmers continued their struggle for economic security through political agitation and cooperative organizations and by resisting the calls for increased productivity through scientific farming. They also resisted the efforts of reformers to reshape their way of life in accordance with middle-class urban ideals.

Rural people did not blindly oppose change. They responded to the world of corporate capitalism pragmatically and selectively. They welcomed such Country Life reforms as improved roads and rural free delivery and eagerly ordered goods from the Sears catalogue. They acquired labor-saving machines and grew new crops. At the same time, like workers in urban factories and mills, they held on to traditional values, resisted loss of control over local institutions like public schools and churches, and embraced change only when it served their economic and cultural goals.

5

AFRICAN-AMERICANS'
QUEST FOR FREEDOM

For African-Americans, the last decades of the nineteenth century and the first decades of the twentieth seemed in many respects the worst of times. The advance of industrial capitalism in the Progressive Era brought a mixture of pain and opportunity to most working-class Americans, but black people experienced mostly the pain. The overwhelming majority remained trapped in agricultural tenancy if not peonage, victimized by local landlords and furnishing merchants and by the market which mysteriously set the price of cotton and tobacco. Racism further circumscribed their economic opportunities; industrial employers, both North and South, largely excluded African-Americans from all but the most menial jobs.

But racism also demeaned African-Americans and robbed them of their political and civil rights. The federal government abandoned them, and white supremacists regained control of Southern state governments, barring black people from voting and imposing racial segregation and second-class citizenship. Southern whites demanded that African-Americans acknowledge their subservience by outward displays of deference. White mobs enforced the South's racial code by ever more frequent acts of violence. A half century after the end of slavery, most African-Americans lacked even the citizenship rights and meager economic opportunities which white workers and farmers enjoyed.

Sympathetic observers at the time readily concluded, as many historians would later, that black people had little choice but to accept their fate, but African-Americans never acquiesced in the status quo. They acquired and retained land, moved from place to place and job to job, and resisted the imposition of segregation, the loss of political rights, and white violence. Kin supported and cared for each other, and community members joined together to build schools, churches, mutual aid societies, and other institutions. They devised cultural strategies to cope with oppression and resist it simultaneously. Living in a world of drastically circumscribed opportunity and blatant injustice, African-Americans, like other working-class Americans, sought economic security and autonomy; but they also struggled for the civil and political rights others took for granted. They failed to secure the freedom so long denied them, but not for want of trying.

THE BURDEN OF RACISM

Before World War I, the majority of black people eked out a marginal existence as small landowners, agricultural wage laborers, or more commonly as sharecroppers in the South, where the lien system and the price of cotton kept them in perpetual poverty. The minority in Southern industrial or urban occupations rarely fared much better. By 1900, African-Americans made up about half the South's forest, sawmill, and mine workers. Black men in Southern cities loaded freight on the docks, collected garbage, paved roads, maintained sewers, and performed other unskilled labor. Women worked mostly as domestics and laundresses. Between 1870 and 1900, African-Americans made up at least 60 percent of all Southern domestics, and in some states as much as 90 percent. A modest number of African-Americans worked as bricklayers, blacksmiths, painters, carpenters, barbers, and in other skilled crafts; some held jobs with the railroads, a few as skilled firemen or brakemen but mostly as track laborers, baggage handlers, waiters, or porters.

African-Americans in Northern cities fared a bit better economically. Employers sometimes imported blacks from the South to break strikes, but otherwise managers seldom hired black people before World War I to work with machines, relegating them to common labor and service work. In 1900, nearly 40 percent of black men worked as janitors, servants, and waiters; and a staggering 80 percent of black women in Chicago worked as housekeepers, laundresses, servants, and waitresses.

During Reconstruction black men had voted and held political office in Southern states. When Southern whites regained political control in the 1870s and 1880s, they reestablished white dominance by imposing segregation in schools, libraries, streetcars, railroads, bathrooms, and even drinking fountains, reminding people continually of the inferior status they considered appropriate for blacks. They kept most African-Americans from the ballot box by giving local registrars broad authority to examine and exclude prospective voters, by passing laws permitting white-only primaries, by instituting poll taxes, by engaging in outright election fraud, and by assaulting and even murdering African-Americans who attempted to vote. The president of Mississippi's 1890 constitutional convention asserted quite forthrightly, "We came here to exclude the negro. Nothing short of this will answer."[1]

White Southerners also demanded absolute deference and humility from African-Americans. They might attack a black person for wearing good clothing on any day but Sunday, for example, or for smoking cigars in the presence of whites. Whites expected African-Americans to address them as "Mister" or "Miss," but used first names or simply "boy" or "girl" when addressing them. They demanded that black people approach their homes by the back door and step aside for a white person on the sidewalk. A black schoolteacher in Mississippi recalled that "the average Negro householder was afraid to paint his house and fix up his premises because of the attitude of some white man" who might consider him "uppity."[2]

Some white men used violence and the threat of violence to enforce subservience. Between 1880 and 1930, white mobs lynched approximately 3,220 African-Americans in the South for alleged physical attacks on whites, affronts to "white womanhood," and sometimes even for minor violations of racial etiquette. Lynch mobs commonly attacked men in jail awaiting trial or sentencing. Officials in Statesboro, Georgia, charged two illiterate black turpentine workers, Paul Reed and Will Cato, with brutally murdering a white landowner and his wife and daughter, and setting their house on fire in the summer of 1904, despite weak circumstantial evidence; they then sent them to Savannah for safekeeping until their trial. The jury quickly found both men guilty and sentenced them to hang, but a mob stormed the courthouse and dragged the two prisoners away unimpeded by law enforcement officials. A mile out of town, the mob surrounded the two men waist high with pine wood, doused it with twenty gallons of oil, paused to take photographs, and lit a fire to cheers from the crowd. Souvenir hunters later picked up charred bones. Then the mob randomly forced other African-Americans from their homes and assaulted them. Officials brought no charges against the killers of Reed and Cato, and the *Atlanta Journal* asked, "Where is the man who can wholly condemn those who on yesterday avenged the cruel murder of the Hodges family?"[3] In Hinds County, Mississippi, a white mob broke into an inquest of a black man accused of poisoning a well and hanged him before the inquest could be completed. Not satisfied, the mob came back for the man's wife, his mother-in-law, and two other black men, who had just been cleared of any responsibility by the coroner's jury, and lynched all four.

African-Americans who managed to rise a bit above poverty could face the wrath of poor whites envious of their success. In the southwestern counties of Mississippi, white farmers formed secret societies whose members whipped, killed, or burned the property of African-American landowners and independent renters. Local law enforcement officials did not interfere. One black Mississippi resident complained in 1913, "If we own a good farm or horse, or cow, or bird-dog, or yoke of oxen, we are harassed until we are bound to sell, give away, or run away, before we can have any peace in our lives."[4]

African-American women faced, in addition, the ever-present danger of sexual assault by white men, especially when these women worked as domestic servants. Odessa Minnie Barnes, who grew up in South Carolina, told historian Elizabeth Clark-Lewis that adults warned young black women about rape before the women went to their first job. "Nobody was sent out before you was told to be careful of the white man or his sons. They'd tell you the stories of rape . . . hard too! No lies. You was to be told true, so you'd not get raped." Barnes's neighbor, Weida Edwards, told Clark-Lewis, "You'd know how to run, or always not be in the house with the white man or big sons. Just everyone told you something to keep you from being raped, 'cause it happened, and they told you."[5]

In the North, black men voted throughout the Progressive Era. Streetcars, railroads, public bathrooms, and water fountains served black and white people together. Northern racism operated more by practice than by law. Unofficial segregation prevailed in parks and on beaches; YMCAs and social settlements had either a white or black clientele. Hotels, restaurants, and bars might or might not serve African-Americans, but they rarely posted signs indicating their practices.

As the black population in Northern cities grew, white prejudice and housing discrimination ghettoized African-Americans more completely than in Southern cities, and white residents physically assaulted African-Americans during race riots in New York (1900), Springfield, Illinois (1908), and elsewhere; but lynching remained a Southern institution.

ECONOMIC STRATEGIES

Like other poor people, African-Americans relied on a family economy in which nearly everyone worked. Isetta Peters, who grew up in York County, South Carolina, remembered that "by six you watch somebody all day, do some animal feeding and a little cleaning around the house" and "by seven or so, you'd be trained to do most of the things needed . . . minding children, farm field work, cooking, and . . . some parts of the wash."[6] City families likewise relied upon everyone's labor. They commonly took in boarders, and in some places the women sewed garments at home.

African-Americans, like immigrant and native-born industrial operatives, laborers, and farmers, moved frequently. Freedom to move, a prerogative denied to them as slaves, surely had special importance to African-Americans. Both black and white sharecroppers moved frequently at the conclusion of the fall harvest, looking for a better landlord. African-American men also commonly traveled to seasonal work at lumber camps, coal mines, railroads, sawmills, fertilizer plants, cotton gins, and cottonseed presses, and women sometimes did domestic work during the slack time in the cotton cultivation cycle. McCullom Cook of Alabama, who went to mine coal in Kentucky, remembered that his first pay envelope contained "more money than I had ever seen or money than I ever made."[7]

Some African-American farmers moved greater distances. In the 1870s and 1880s, many had gone to the western parts of Mississippi and Arkansas. Others, seeking autonomy as well as economic security, followed promoters to newly established all-black towns, founding thirty-two in Oklahoma alone between 1890 and 1910. The founders of Langston City (1891) hoped to stimulate a mass migration that would make Oklahoma an entirely African-American state. A Langston inhabitant remembered that in his native Texas he had to "bow down and grin to all the poor white folks" and "even had to call little poor white boys 'Mister,' " but in his new home "no matter how little you be here, you can still be a man."[8] Similar motives inspired others to organize towns in California, Illinois, Iowa, Kansas, Michigan, New Mexico, Alabama, Texas, Arkansas, Kentucky, and Tennessee.

The towns lured only small numbers because they could offer only limited economic opportunities in the age of corporate capitalism. Few succeeded. Many more black people moved to nearby Southern cities. Between 1900 and 1910, the African-American urban population in the South increased by almost 900,000. While Southern cities offered mostly menial jobs for African-Americans, segregated their public facilities, and gave no relief from white violence, they still had better schools and a wider range of black communal institutions; and former sharecroppers could at least free themselves from the hated lien system and the daily supervision of the landlord, receiving cash for their labor.

Migration North likewise opened no vast economic horizons. Although Northern cities boasted large numbers of industrial jobs, they also attracted new European immigrants every year, whom industrial employers hired ahead of black workers. Yet the North provided a greater range of job choices, relief from the Southern racial code, better schools than those in Southern cities, and, most important, higher wages. Only 88,000 African-Americans left the South in the 1880s, but 185,000 departed in the 1890s and 194,000 in the 1900s; about 2.5 percent of the South's black population went North between 1890 and 1910.

On a few occasions, Northern employers paid African-Americans' transportation costs to break strikes, but most migrated on their own. Many came from Southern cities, where they first experienced the wage economy. Migrants looking back on their decision to go North commonly explained that it offered a chance for greater economic security. Martha and Charlie Reynolds grew up in Promised Land, South Carolina, a community of African-American landowners, but their parents had no land to give them, so they became sharecroppers for a while, and then moved to Mississippi, where Martha had family. When a labor recruiter told them of opportunities in Chicago, they moved again. By 1910, Charlie and his older sons earned sufficient wages as unskilled laborers in the Windy City to buy a house.

Migrants also saw the move North as a way to resist the humiliation of Southern racism. Beulah Nelson, daughter of poor farmers in Maytonsburg, South Carolina, eagerly anticipated moving with her uncle to Washington, D.C. Three days before their planned departure, her mother sent her to work briefly as a domestic for a white family. "They didn't want no nigger to put they hand on their bread," she recalled. Her employer insisted that she bring the bread to the table only after grace, so it would stay hot. "Well, if she didn't want me to touch it, I couldn't touch it, I wasn't going to try not to touch it to carry it to the table to give it to them." So she refused to bring it when asked.

> And that's when she got mad, arguing with me so. She jumped up from table and she said to me, "Beulah, you fired." But she didn't fire me—I fired myself, 'cause I *intended* to do what I did. I said, "These two days I been in your house. You could've . . . done ate a lot of my spit. I could have done did anything I want to do to it, and you wouldn't have never known nothing about it. But just because you could see me if I touch it," I said. "No, if that's the way it's to be—not me!" I said. "For what? Six days a week for twenty-five cents? Not me!" You see, I didn't have to do it—I was leaving.[9]

Some African-American leaders sought to discourage this city-ward movement. In his Atlanta Exposition address in 1895, Booker T. Washington advised his people to "cast down your bucket where you are" and pursue farming, manual labor, business, and domestic service in the South. The leader of the Back-to-the-Farm Movement in Jefferson County, Tennessee, explained in 1913 that his group sought to "keep [our people] away from the cities."[10] But these admonitions, like those directed by European nationalist leaders to immigrants, had little effect on black people's eagerness to move in search of economic security and autonomy.

A few African-Americans even left the United States altogether. In the 1890s, over eight hundred went to Mexico to grow cotton. Between 1909 and 1911, several hundred from black towns in Oklahoma moved to Saskatchewan to take advantage of Canada's liberal homestead policy. And thousands enlisted in several plans to return to Africa, although only a few hundred actually got there.

Southern legislators, fearful of the loss of cheap black labor and undoubtedly recognizing that migration represented an assertion of autonomy, passed laws to restrict black movement. Enticement laws, enacted in most states before 1890, prohibited one employer from hiring an employee or sharecropper under contract to or in the employ of another. False-pretenses laws, passed in the first decade of the new century, classified failure to repay advances or work off one's debt to an employer as fraud for which a person could be imprisoned. In 1913, the U.S. Supreme Court overturned the Alabama false-pretenses statute as a violation of the Thirteenth Amendment and a federal antipeonage law, but Southern states ignored the ruling or found ways around it. Fearful of labor recruiters, states commonly imposed exorbitant license fees, $1,000 per county in North Carolina, for example, in counties with large African-American populations. Eight Southern states also passed stringent vagrancy laws between 1903 and 1909, under which African-Americans without jobs or sharecropping contracts could be jailed and then "leased" to an employer. Yet these efforts failed to stem the movement of African-Americans within the region and beyond.

Among the majority who stayed in their rural Southern communities, some black people pursued economic security and autonomy through organization and collective action, despite the hazards. The Colored Farmers' National Alliance, founded during the agrarian protests late in the nineteenth century, claimed 1,200,000 members by 1890, establishing cooperative exchanges in Norfolk, Charleston, Mobile, New Orleans, and Houston. In 1891, Colored Alliance leaders formed the Cotton Pickers League to spearhead strikes by laborers who harvested cotton, demanding a raise from fifty cents to a dollar a day. An East Texas planter summarily dismissed black laborers who went on strike. In Lee County, Arkansas, however, the strike looked like it might succeed. Then strikers on one plantation killed two nonunion men in a fight, and a white posse set out to capture the strike leader, Ben Patterson. Strikers burned a cotton gin, and the ensuing violence killed fifteen African-American men and one white plantation manager. Law enforcement officials sent six black strikers to jail. The white Alliance disassociated itself from the strike, and the Colored Alliance declined.

Some Southern white Populist leaders argued for a political alliance of black and white Southern farmers based on common economic interest, although they still opposed racial integration or social equality. But despite the economic grievances shared by poor white and black farmers, Southern Democrats effectively played on white racial hatred to defeat Southern Populism. Leaders like Georgia's Tom Watson, who during the agrarian crusade advocated a biracial coalition, in the new century engaged in virulent antiblack rhetoric.

After the defeat of the Alliance movement and Populism, some African-American farmers formed agricultural cooperatives to purchase goods, market their crops collectively, and acquire land by pooling their resources. In Georgia's Clarke County, for example, a successful cooperative helped its members purchase land, and it operated a sawmill, cotton gin, and thresher. Tennessee poultry producers established a Colored State Poultry Association in 1912. Such modest attempts at economic self-sufficiency could still arouse white hostility. In 1903, for example, someone blew up the boiler and later burned down the building housing a cotton gin owned by the Colored Joint Stock Company near Jackson, Tennessee.

Black industrial laborers faced even greater obstacles to collective action: a deeply conservative rural culture, a political system controlled by businessmen hostile to unions, employers who readily manipulated racial hatred, and white unions, most of which excluded African-Americans. Nonetheless, black industrial workers, most of whom still lived in the South, did unionize. As early as 1899, members of the black National League of Longshoremen in Norfolk refused to work with nonunion laborers. In 1899, 1905, and 1909, African-American dockworkers and steamboat hands went on strike for higher wages in Evansville, Indiana, but they received no support from white unions. However, when African-American workers constituted a large enough portion of the workforce, white union organizers could not ignore them, and black and white workers sometimes spanned the racial divide to pursue common economic interests. In 1902, the separate black and white dockworkers' unions in New Orleans agreed to divide all jobs equally, establishing a Dock and Cotton Council with equal representation from each race to coordinate collective action. In 1907, 10,000 longshoremen, screw men, yardmen, freight handlers, and other dockworkers of both races went on strike together for twenty days. Employers tried to split them by refusing to meet with African-American unionists, but white unionists refused to negotiate without their black fellow strikers. The biracial Council won all of its demands.

African-Americans also played a major role in the United Mine Workers (UMW) in Alabama and parts of Appalachia. By 1902, 65 percent of Alabama's 18,000 mine workers belonged to the UMW, more than half of them African-American. The Alabama union assigned its vice presidency and three of seven seats on its board to black union members and the other positions to whites, while union locals remained segregated. The union refused to meet in halls that barred black people, but during their assemblies whites and African-Americans sat separately, and afterward members ate at separate banquets. It held a single Labor Day parade followed by separate picnics. Black union leaders often acted independently. At the 1900 convention, for example, African-American delegates rejected a call by the Birmingham Trades Council for members to patronize only union workmen because the Council discriminated against African-Americans. In short, white and black miners united out of mutual economic interest without significantly challenging the Southern racial code.

Still, Alabama mine owners ultimately defeated the union by exploiting racial hatred. When the interracial union struck for recognition, the owners turned local citizens against the strike by arguing that the union mixed the races; a citizens' delegation told the union vice president, "No matter how much merit there may be in the miners' cause, you cannot change the opinion of the people in this country that you are violating one of the principles the South holds near and dear." Governor Braxton Bragg Comer, who ordered the strikers' tent camps demolished, told the president of the striking union, "You know what it means to have eight or nine thousand niggers idle in the State of Alabama, and I am not going to stand for it."[11]

In West Virginia, the UMW also organized a large number of black coal miners; and African-Americans served as union organizers and officials. In a bitter strike in Kanawha County in 1912 and 1913, African-American and white unionists fought against imported strikebreakers of both races and white private guards. Here, however, the owners' racial appeal did not work. A newly elected governor imposed a settlement, and black and white miners continued to work in West Virginia mines, jointly represented by the UMW.

Only the Industrial Workers of the World consistently refused to allow segregated unions, arguing that the class struggle required concerted action by all workers. In Philadelphia, the IWW's Marine Transport Workers Union, led by a black organizer, raised wages after 1913 from $1.25 to $4.00 a day for its largely African-American membership. And the Wobblies' Brotherhood of Timber Workers struggled for a decade, but without success, to organize black and white forest workers in the Piney Woods of Texas.

Given the obstacles to successful unionization, it is not surprising that most African-Americans, like other industrial workers, protested employment conditions only informally, by switching jobs frequently and limiting the pace of work. Black coal miners, for example, worked only as many days as suited them. A mine supervisor in Appalachia complained in 1911 that "a protracted meeting . . . of the colored people" had nearly shut down one shaft. Sometime later he reported that "our reason for falling down in our loading Saturday at Number 2 was on account of the color[e]d men

having a ball game." A month later, he expressed exasperation that
the "niggers . . . work one day and lye [sic] out the next," and later
apologized for still another delay "on account of a nigger wedding
and they all come out to attend it."¹²

African-American women who worked as servants engaged in
similar unorganized protests. They sometimes quit with little notice,
entered and left the job market as family demands required, and
looked constantly for a more compatible employer or better pay.
They also found ways to moderate the pace of work and protect
themselves from unending demands. Bernice Reeder, who began
working as a domestic in Washington, D.C., before World War I,
remembered that good servants "never are sitting when anybody
white is around. I mean the mistress or anybody. They'd keep moving, dusting, doing her errands. . . . They'd just be doing nothing,
but they made it seem so much to the whites. . . . When we were
around just us [the staff], we'd laugh. . . . We'd fool that woman
from dawn to dusk."¹³ Domestic workers also informally boycotted
mistresses who treated servants especially badly. In 1916, a Georgia Senate candidate accused Atlanta domestic workers of maintaining employer blacklists through their societies.

Like immigrant peddlers, domestics also sought autonomy by
seeking day work. Day workers could care for their families, attend
church on Sunday, and maintain their freedom of movement and
their privacy, even though their income was less certain and they
had to pay for their own rent and food. Live-in work seemed too
much like slavery. One woman who made the change explained,
"Nobody'd be looking over your shoulder, saying what you was to
do." "Working out you'd be able to pick homes, days, and kinds of
work you didn't do," stated another. And black women who began
day work almost always refused to wear a uniform, which employers
of live-ins required. "Wearing your own clothes—that's like you
being your own boss!" explained Virginia Lacey.¹⁴ In Southern cities, whites feared the very independence that domestic day workers
found appealing. In Atlanta, a progressive white physician running

for mayor on a platform of public health reform proposed a licensing bureau to maintain work records, conduct medical examinations, and provide "absolute control" of servants.

Indeed, Southern progressivism offered little help to African-Americans. They remained largely poor and dependent and few enjoyed either economic security or autonomy in the Progressive Era. But black people did not acquiesce in their condition, contesting it, as circumstances permitted, through formal organization, by moving, by restricting work output, and by making economic choices that maximized their control over their work. And they acted vigorously to provide for their own education.

SELF-EDUCATION

Southern whites had long sought to control their region's black population by denying it access to education. Most Southern states had made it a crime to teach slaves to read. When whites regained control in the states of the former Confederacy in the 1880s and 1890s, their state governments allocated only tiny sums to the nascent segregated black public schools. But as Southern states began to consolidate and reform their public school systems in the early twentieth century, some white educators argued that rudimentary schooling of African-Americans would strengthen white control. Willard F. Bond, Mississippi's Superintendent of Education, asserted that with the right kind of education an African-American "no longer pays any attention to false prophets of his own race who try to interest him in social equality, the franchise and other rot, but has turned to other leaders whose ideas coincide with those of Southern white people." University of Mississippi professor Thomas Pearce Bailey, on the other hand, when asked why "a few . . . grotesquely inefficient negro schools" disturbed whites, explained that "the white people want to 'keep the negro in his place' and educated people have a way of making their own places and their own terms."[15]

Indeed, African-Americans recognized that even if education alone could not change an economic and social system that confined them largely to marginal agriculture or unskilled labor, it still symbolized freedom and autonomy. A literate person could read a sharecropper contract, a letter, a job recruitment circular, and a newspaper, and could calculate the return on the crop and compute the amount of money owed. In the North and in some border states, literate African-Americans could vote. Bailey came closer to the truth than Bond. Although African-Americans might couch their appeal for education in customarily deferential terms, they understood that learning to read and compute contested white control.

Southern states provided only the most meager support for African-American schools. In Georgia, for example, counties with populations more than three-quarters black spent an average of $19.23 a year on each white schoolchild in 1910 and $1.61 on each black child. In 1900, only 22 percent of Southern black children between the ages of five and nine and about half those between ten and fourteen attended school, most for less than six months a year. Black secondary education barely existed. In 1916, only forty-seven black public schools in the South, almost all located in cities, offered four years of high school.

Denied common schools by state governments, African-Americans built their own, despite meager resources. Black towns like Mound Bayou often supported their own schools with little or no state money. A black woman who grew up on a farm in Anderson, South Carolina, recalled that "there was no school for ten miles in no direction," so her father built a "small log house" on his property to serve as a school. "My father and mother could not read or write, and my father said he wanted every one of his children to learn to be able to read and write."[16] By 1915, Georgia's county school boards owned only 208 school buildings for black pupils, but African-Americans in the state owned 1,544. More than 11,500 students attended black private schools in Georgia in 1913, some run by Northern whites but most by local African-Americans.

In 1914, Chicago philanthropist Julius Rosenwald began to support construction of African-American schools in the South, requiring that local communities or state governments share the costs. Between 1914 and 1916, black communities tapped Rosenwald money to build ninety-two schools, seventy-nine in Alabama under the direction of Booker T. Washington's Tuskegee Institute. Southern African-Americans raised almost half the total cost, Rosenwald contributed about a third, and the remainder came from public school authorities and local white donors. Since Southern states generally supported black schools only with tax revenues paid by African-Americans, the "state" contribution also came ultimately from African-Americans.

In 1915, a black school principal in Fayette County, Tennessee, and his wife, a schoolteacher, organized a fund-raising drive for a Rosenwald school, the first in the state. S. L. Smith, the State Agent for Negro Education in Tennessee, described attending a fund-raising rally for the school:

> I was notified that 1200 lodge members over the county had voted to give a dollar each and I was asked to be present at a county-wide meeting. Although it was a rainy day the committees of the lodges brought in and laid on the table 936 one-dollar bills and promised that the other lodges would report soon. Their interest grew in the project, their total contributions being more than $2,000.[17]

In the end, local black residents raised $2,200 of the $3,500 needed to build the school. In the next five years, the principal and his wife spearheaded a continuing campaign that built twenty Rosenwald schools in Fayette County. The black residents of Cleveland County, Arkansas, could not raise cash for a school, but a man who knew the lumber business obtained a blueprint for a Rosenwald school, got his neighbors to cut and dress the lumber, and together they built the school. And so it went in community after community.

Northern cities offered African-Americans substantially better educational opportunities. Children could get to their neighborhood schools easily, and state statutes mandated school attendance. Northern black children attended school at rates equal to and sometimes greater than whites. In 1911, the U.S. Immigration Commission found that at age fourteen, when many working-class youngsters left school to work full-time, 88 percent of black boys and 74 percent of girls attended school. In many Northern cities, African-American adults also acquired at night school the education denied them in the South.

Black schools with African-American teachers became ethnic community institutions, even if under the ultimate supervision of white state or county officials. Like immigrant parish and foreign-language schools, black schools fostered cultural autonomy. In supporting their schools, African-Americans contested vigorously the inferior status assigned to them in the prevailing racial order.

COMMUNAL INSTITUTIONS

Churches and other communal institutions also enabled African-Americans to assert group autonomy and resist the burdens of caste. After emancipation, former slaves established their own congregations and national denominations, worshipping in distinctive styles blending their African and American heritage. Although a few affluent city congregations built imposing edifices, most African-Americans attended small Southern rural churches which rarely could afford a full-time preacher. A social scientist writing in 1913 described the church as "the only institution which the Negro may call his own."

A new church may be built, a new pastor installed, new members received and all the machinery of the church set in motion without even consulting any white person. In a word, the church is the Negro's own institution, developing according to his own standards, and more nearly than anything else represents the real life of the race.[18]

In addition to meeting spiritual needs, churches provided social and recreational activities, mutual aid insurance, and other services. Their members gave charity to the poor and visited the sick and people in prison. In large urban congregations, such activities could be quite extensive. Philadelphia's Berean Presbyterian Church established a building and loan association, organized an industrial school with funds raised from white philanthropists, ran a kindergarten and a medical dispensary, and sponsored numerous social clubs.

Worshippers in Southern rural churches prayed in an emotional style, developed during slavery, that incorporated African folk practices into Christian prayer. This distinctive mode of worship offended many white missionaries and also some prominent and educated black people. Former black abolitionist William Wells Brown, for example, expressed disbelief at the intensity of public expression even in "refined congregations." At one Nashville church, he observed disapprovingly, "four or five sisters becoming exhausted, had fallen upon the floor and lay there, or had been removed by their friends." In another, the preacher held a "letter" in which he said were listed all the acts on which a person would be judged when he or she died:

> For fully ten minutes the preacher walked the pulpit, repeating in a loud, incoherent manner, "And the angel will read from this letter." This created the wildest excitement, and not less than ten or fifteen were shouting in different parts of the house, while four or five were going from seat to seat shaking hands with the occupants of the pews. "Let dat angel come right down now an' read dat letter," shouted a Sister, at the top of her voice. This was the signal for loud exclamations from various parts of the house. "Yes, yes, I want's to hear the letter." "Come, Jesus, come or send an angel to read the letter." "Lord, send us the power."[19]

The poorly paid and minimally educated rural ministers who presided at these services offered the kind of religious leadership that most poor African-Americans wanted. While intellectuals like Booker T. Washington and black poet Paul Laurence Dunbar, among others, openly criticized the poor education and low professional standards of much of the black clergy, ministers remained genuinely popular. An observer of African-American churches in Thomas County, Georgia, concluded in 1903, "The church which does not have its shouting, the church which does not measure the abilities of a preacher by the 'rousement' of his sermons, and indeed does not tacitly demand of its minister the shout-producing discourse, is an exception to the rule."[20] When rural African-Americans moved to cities, many rejected the formal black churches with decorous services which they found there. Instead, they attended more intimate Pentecostal and Holiness services, often in storefronts, and they went to emotional revival meetings. Despite admonitions from prominent black leaders, African-Americans continued to worship in the style which they found satisfying.

African-Americans also operated a host of mutual aid, burial, and social organizations. Ministers disapproved of the secret rituals and elaborate regalia which most of these groups embraced, undoubtedly recognizing that the heads of these organizations challenged their leadership and social status within their communities. In Georgia, the Masons had over 10,000 black male members before World War I, the Colored Knights of Pythias had 15,000 members, and the Grand United Order of Odd Fellows, the largest lodge order in the state, 33,000. Boasting a million dollars in assets, the Odd Fellows owned a large Atlanta office building with an auditorium, and maintained a $300,000 revolving loan fund to help members start businesses and buy homes.

These African-American lodges, like immigrant mutual aid societies, offered a small measure of economic protection to black people, many of whom lived on the margins. In Mississippi, African-American orders paid $16 million in burial and sickness benefits to members between 1870 and 1920. Pointing with pride to his order's financial assets, the Grand Master of the Mississippi Masons

declared that "Governor Vardaman and all the other devils this side
of Hades cannot stay this kind of progress."[21] But they could try.
Fearful that they could not control black secret societies, some
Georgia legislators advocated, unsuccessfully, a law requiring a
prohibitively high bond for all black fraternal organizations. And
bands of whites periodically burned or bombed African-American
lodge halls.

Middle-class African-Americans also owned numerous banks,
insurance companies, real estate agencies, funeral homes, barbershops, bars, groceries, and other enterprises serving the black population. They also created a variety of civic institutions. Hospitals,
like Provident in Chicago, offered medical care denied by white institutions, and black YMCAs and YWCAs offered recreational programs. Black newspapers, published in the larger cities, presented
community news excluded from the white daily press, provided a fo-
rum for discussion of the treatment of African-Americans, and provided information for those contemplating migration. Such activities
enhanced the social status of the middle-class people who led them.

Black voluntary organizations lessened dependence on white institutions. In 1905, twenty-two black women in Richmond, members of the largely female Order of Saint Luke, began a department
store, the Saint Luke Emporium, on Richmond's main shopping
street. White merchants, fearing the loss of black customers and
the threat which black enterprise posed to white supremacy, organized to crush, as they put it, "Negro merchants who are objectionable . . . because they compete with and get a few dollars which
would otherwise go to the white merchant."[22] When the order refused their offer to buy the emporium property at a substantial profit
to Saint Luke, white businessmen threatened to boycott wholesalers
who sold to the emporium. Nonetheless, it remained open for seven
years. This and other African-American institutions and businesses
fostered group self-reliance, enabling black people, indirectly and
in ways often imperceptible to outsiders, to contest white supremacy.

THE UPHILL BATTLE FOR CIVIL RIGHTS

Some African-Americans also fought overtly against white supremacy. Despite a formidable racist ideology, an inequitable legal and political system, and unending racial violence, black activists and intellectuals demanded civil rights through organized political actions, while at the grass roots many ordinary folk protested discrimination in spontaneous and informal ways.

During Reconstruction, black men eagerly exercised the franchise and participated in political life, retreating in the South only reluctantly and in many places under pain of death. In Northern and border cities, they stayed active in politics, and used the ballot to win city jobs, improve public services, limit discriminatory policies, and elect African-Americans to government positions. In Chicago, for example, the leaders of a black political machine built an alliance with white politicians, controlled substantial patronage, and elected an alderman, two state senators, and other officials before World War I.

Black elected officials might secure modest patronage for their constituents, but political machines could do little to advance civil rights in their own cities, let alone in the South. Some argued that the pursuit of legal equality by African-Americans would be a tactical error. Booker T. Washington, a former slave and the nation's best-known African-American, the founder in 1881 of the Tuskegee Institute in Alabama, gained national attention in 1895 for a speech in Atlanta urging African-American economic advancement while accepting Southern racial segregation and disenfranchisement. "In all things that are purely social we can be as separate as the fingers, yet one as the hand in all things essential to mutual progress," he explained. "The wisest among my race understand that the agitation of questions of social equality is the extremest folly, and that progress in the enjoyment of all privileges that will come to us must be the result of severe and constant struggle rather than of artificial forcing," he continued.[23] Through his political connections in the

Republican Party, his ties to philanthropists, his control of several black newspapers, and the National Negro Business League, which he founded in 1901, Washington exercised extraordinary influence until his death in 1915.

Not all African-American leaders accepted Washington's conservative approach, however. T. Thomas Fortune, editor of the *New York Age* from the mid-1880s to 1907, founded the Afro-American League in 1890, five years before Washington's famous address, to fight segregation and discrimination in any form. The National Equal Rights Council, formed in 1894, employed detectives and lawyers to investigate and seek legal action against those who led mob attacks on African-Americans. African-Americans in numerous communities formed local groups devoted to political and social equality.

Beginning in 1905, these local black civil rights activists met annually under the leadership of W. E. B. Du Bois to protest their second-class citizenship and consider strategies for change. Du Bois, who grew up in western Massachusetts, studied in Germany, received a Ph.D. in history from Harvard in 1895, and taught at Atlanta University, had publicly criticized Washington's philosophy in *The Souls of Black Folk* (1903), an eloquent collection of essays exploring the African-American experience. The first meeting, held in Niagara Falls, Canada, a major terminus of the Underground Railroad in the days of slavery, drew up a platform demanding elimination of all distinctions based on race. The group, which became known as the Niagara Movement, met subsequently at places associated with the fight against slavery—Harpers Ferry in 1906, Boston in 1907, and Oberlin, Ohio, in 1908. Speakers at these meetings did not mince words in describing the injustices heaped upon African-Americans. "In the past year, the work of the Negro hater has flourished in the land," proclaimed Du Bois in 1906. "The work of stealing the Black man's ballot has progressed and the fifty and more representatives of stolen votes sit still in the nation's capital."[24]

The Niagara Movement soon got some help from sympathetic

white reformers. William English Walling, a socialist labor activist and resident of University Settlement in New York, stunned by an ugly race riot in Springfield, Illinois, in 1908, joined with prominent New York settlement house residents, progressives, and African-American church leaders to issue a "Call to Discuss Means of Securing Political and Civic Equality for the Negro." The organizers invited the members of the Niagara Movement to attend. Meeting on Lincoln's birthday in 1909, they made plans for a permanent organization, the National Association for the Advancement of Colored People (NAACP), pledged to work toward the elimination of segregation, the enfranchisement of African-Americans, and the enforcement of the Fourteenth and Fifteenth amendments. When the NAACP began work the next year, Du Bois joined its staff as director of publicity and research, editing the group's magazine, *The Crisis*, whose circulation grew to 100,000 a month by 1918. Black author James Weldon Johnson joined the NAACP staff in 1916.

Even without a formal organization, however, black leaders across the country spoke up and acted against racial violence. Newspaper editors regularly decried lynching, sometimes facing white mobs themselves as a result, and community leaders beseeched white officials to intercede. In a number of cities, they sought to prevent performances of plays and showings of movies that might spark violence against them. In 1915, black leaders in Evansville persuaded the mayor to ban *The Nigger*, a film portraying a black man attacking a white girl, and whites retaliating by burning the man and brutalizing other black people. When theater owners and white business leaders objected, however, the mayor lifted the order. Elsewhere, black leaders sought to prevent the showing of D. W. Griffith's dramatic film *The Birth of a Nation*, which opened in 1915, depicting African-Americans and Northern white carpetbaggers degrading innocent Southern whites during Reconstruction. In San Francisco, black leaders convinced the city's mayor to require that objectionable scenes be removed. In most cities, however, Griffith's epic ran uncut.

When Southern states and cities segregated streetcars, African-

Americans protested en masse, boycotting trolleys in every state. In 1891, Georgia passed a law allowing cities to separate the races on streetcars. Trolley company officials stopped enforcing separate seating after black passengers boycotted segregated trolleys in Atlanta in 1892–93, in Augusta in 1898, and in Savannah in 1899. Segregationist pressure increased in the following decade, however. Although African-American boycotts in six cities succeeded at least temporarily, twenty-nine others, in every state of the former Confederacy, failed. Southern black newspapers supported the boycotts and urged participation. The *Savannah Tribune* told its readers, "Do not trample on our pride by being 'jim crowed.' Walk!"[25]

African-Americans participated in the boycotts in great numbers. The president of the Savannah Electric Company complained to the city council in 1908 that the boycott had cut business by 25 percent and cost the company $50,000. Blacks walked and organized private carriages to transport people; African-American hack owners lowered their price in Houston to five cents during the boycott there. In a few cities, boycott leaders successfully organized alternative transit companies, but none outlasted the protests. Some boycotts lasted only a few days, but others went on for two or three years.

Southern black people used the boycott in other situations as well. When a Savannah bank opened segregated deposit windows in 1903, most blacks withdrew their funds. They also boycotted the Beaufort-Savannah steamship line after it began segregating its ships in 1912. In 1917, African-Americans in Northumberland County, Virginia, refused to work for a white man who had recently led a lynch mob, even though the man offered to pay double. These actions demonstrated the breadth of African-American resistance to second-class citizenship at a time when more militant forms of protest in the South courted danger.

Still, if most African-Americans prudently avoided placing themselves in harm's way, some occasionally fought back directly and spontaneously despite the consequences. In 1899, a black crowd gathered in front of a jail in Darien, Georgia, to protect a prominent

African-American man falsely accused of raping a white woman. When the sheriff tried to remove the prisoner, the crowd stopped him; the sheriff called in the militia, and the crowd cheered when the militia commander placed the prisoner on a train to Savannah for protection until trial. A jury exonerated the prisoner, but a court convicted twenty-three people in the crowd of rioting in the "insurrection."

Black people could not always contain their rage. In 1892, a group of African-American businessmen opened the People's Grocery in Memphis, taking business away from a white-owned store across the street. When the owner of the rival store got officials to charge the People's Grocery with code violations, black patrons vowed to protect the store. As a group of white deputies approached the store after dark to serve arrest warrants, African-American defenders mistook them for vigilantes and opened fire. A white mob subsequently rounded up at least thirty black men and murdered three.

In 1900, New Orleans police attempting to arrest Robert Charles began clubbing him and a male companion. Charles pulled out a gun. The ensuing struggle with the police injured both Charles and a police officer and killed Charles's friend. Charles refused to surrender when the police returned, killing two police officers in the altercation. The mayor ordered Charles shot on sight, and offered a reward. A mob located him, and in the final battle Charles killed seven and injured eight of his pursuers before he died. Ida Wells-Barnett, who led the African-American crusade against lynching, described the Charles case in her pamphlet *Mob Rule in New Orleans*. A year before the incident, Charles had seen a white mob torture and burn alive an African-American accused of rape and murder. Stunned, Charles had told friends that "the time had come for every black man to prepare to defend himself."

Six years later, African-Americans in Wiggins, Mississippi, exchanged gunfire in a lengthy battle with white vigilantes to protect a black man from a lynching. Black residents of Wahalak, Mississippi, that same year armed themselves against a white mob and state militia members who invaded their neighborhood, according to one newspaper account, intent on striking "terror into the ne-groes, who had been getting defiant of late."[26] In two days of blood-shed, one white and sixteen black people died. In the coal-mining region of southern West Virginia, a black mob attacked a jail and freed two black men arrested in altercations with whites, killing the sheriff and two deputies. Law enforcement officials quickly cap-tured the escapees and many of those involved in the attack on the jail.

In urban race riots, African-Americans retaliated most dramati-cally against violent white attacks. Before World War I, the largest of these occurred in Atlanta. Incited by inflammatory newspaper headlines in 1906 alleging rapes by black men of young white women, one evening a white mob began randomly attacking and murdering African-Americans in the downtown area, pulling in-nocent people off streetcars and trashing black stores. When white mobs invaded black neighborhoods, residents fought back. In one area groups of African-Americans set up sniper stations, shot out streetlights, and repulsed white mobs entering the area with gunfire. As white police marched into the middle-class African-American neighborhood of Brownsville to arrest residents who had weapons, blacks ambushed them, killing the leader of the police unit. Al-though African-Americans suffered many more casualties in the Atlanta riot than whites, they showed that they would respond to mob violence in kind, whatever the risks. In retrospect, black peo-ple's resort to physical force and retaliatory violence seems limited in light of the violence and injustice heaped upon them; but when seen against the overwhelming power of whites, these instances of physical resistance by African-Americans appear remarkable.

THE GREAT MIGRATION

When war broke out in Europe in 1914, many African-Americans in the South seized the opportunities it created. Southern blacks had a long history of moving in search of economic opportunity and personal dignity, but the continuing flow of new European immigrants had limited the demand for their labor in the North. The war cut off immigration while Wilson's policy of war preparedness in 1916, followed by American entry into the war in 1917, increased jobs in Northern factories, coal mines, railroads, and shipyards.

Nearly a half million African-Americans left the South between 1910 and 1920, most of them in the second half of the decade. Before coming North, many of the migrants had worked in Southern cities or in wage jobs like logging, mining, and turpentine work. Another half million rural black people moved to Southern cities, replacing those who had left. Only the novel northward trek captured public attention, and the great industrial cities quickly felt its impact. Chicago's black population grew by 65,355 between 1910 and 1920, an increase of 148 percent. New York's expanded by 60,758, Philadelphia's by 49,770, Cleveland's by 35,000.

African-American migrants fled both economic and social oppression. In letters to relatives, friends, and prospective employers, migrants expressed their longing to profit from their labor, educate their children, and live free of discrimination and fear. A New Orleans woman sought "the great chance that a colored person has in Chicago of making a living with all the privilege that the whites have and it mak me the most ankious to go." "My children I wished to be educated in a different community than here. Where school facilities are better and less prejudice shown and in fact where advantages are better for our people in all respect," wrote a prospective migrant in Augusta. From Macon, another wrote, "We are down here where we have to be shot down like rabbits for every little orfence . . . it makes me want to leave the south worse than I ever did when such things happen right at my door." From Dapne, Alabama: "We work but cant get scarcely anything for it & they dont want us to go away & there is not much of anything here to do and nothing for it." Black editors and intellectuals echoed the theme. The NAACP's James Weldon Johnson called the northward movement "tantamount to a general strike."[27]

Many Southern whites assumed that contented African-Americans left only because of unscrupulous labor recruiters and radical agitators. In fact, the migration North developed spontaneously. Although labor recruiters furnished some railroad passes and promised jobs, few migrants needed to be convinced to leave. Like the European immigrants who preceded them, African-Americans followed chain migrations, moving where kin or neighbors could help them find housing and work. Clandestinely circulated Northern black newspapers like the *Chicago Defender* provided information, as did letters from those who had left. Money sent home and return visits from those who had succeeded in the North proved powerful stimuli for African-Americans, as they had been for immigrants. When John Wesley Rule's son returned to Mississippi in 1916 with an impressive amount of cash and explained that in the North he felt like a man, his father sold everything and went back with his son. Few people believed a poor woman from Meridian, Mississippi, who had written saying she earned $2.00 a day in the Chicago stockyards, until she returned with attractive clothes and substantial cash, sparking a new wave of interest in migration. In many places, people formed migration clubs to purchase discount group railroad tickets and provide mutual support for families headed for a common destination.

Contemporary observers commented frequently on the spontaneity of the migration and its lack of support from established Southern black leaders. George Haynes declared, "The movement is without organization or opportunities. The Negroes just quietly move away without taking their recognized leaders into their confidence any more than they do the white people about them." He explained that "a Negro minister may have all his deacons with him at the mid week meeting but by Sunday every church officer is likely to be in the North." An article in the *Dallas Express* put it this way: "The strangest thing, the real mystery about the exodus, is that in all the southland there has not been a single meeting or promoter to start the migration. Just simultaneously all over the South about a year ago, the Negro began to cross the Mason-Dixon line."[28]

Migrants left in spite of entreaties from their established leaders. In Jackson, Mississippi, lumber companies paid $3,000 to a prominent black man to encourage members of his race to stay put. Robert Moton, Washington's successor at Tuskegee, extolled the virtues of continued dedication to Southern agriculture. The migration threatened the social status and livelihood of many black professionals, ministers, and businessmen, who depended upon African-American patrons. The Negro Board of Trade in Jacksonville asked quite candidly, "Who will support the negro men of business and those in Professions" if blacks do not stop "running away"?[29]

White politicians and business leaders, who had already created elaborate laws to restrict black people's movement, feared losing the South's labor force and took additional steps to limit migration. Many Southern communities banned the sale of the *Chicago Defender* and confiscated copies from dealers. State legislatures tightened labor agent license laws and established exorbitant fees. Montgomery, Alabama, made it a crime to distribute any document written for the purpose of encouraging any laborer to leave the city for work elsewhere. Some Southern railroads refused to honor passes issued by Northern employers, and in a number of places police boarded trains and simply arrested African-Americans leaving town. In Summit, Mississippi, officials closed the train station and would not allow trains to stop. Some enlightened whites even suggested that instead of using coercion the South should improve its treatment of African-Americans to keep them from leaving, and wage levels did rise in many places.

White Southerners might stop a few individuals from leaving, but they could not control this grass-roots migration. Black people in the North endured prejudice, segregation, and violence, but they could earn relatively high wages, vote, send their children to better schools, and sit wherever they pleased on the streetcars. A black woman newly arrived in Chicago was stunned the first time she boarded a trolley and saw black people sitting next to whites. "I just held my breath, for I thought any minute they would start something. Then I saw nobody notices it, and I just thought this is a real place for Negroes."[30]

Whatever progress black people experienced in the Progressive Era came from migration, establishment of rural schools, and other grass-roots initiatives. In these years, African-Americans lost political and civil rights, faced tightening segregation, and suffered from pervasive poverty and continuous violence and terror. Nonetheless, African-Americans contested their condition and struggled to gain greater economic security and autonomy. They remained economically dependent and personally vulnerable, but they did not acquiesce in their condition.

6

White-Collar Workers
in Corporate America

In 1890, the U.S. Census Bureau classified the occupations and pay of workers in manufacturing firms in a new way. It created a single classification for proprietors, managers, and clerks and another that grouped skilled craftsmen and unskilled operatives together. Craftsmen often made more money and exercised more independent judgment on the job than clerks. But census officials still thought it critical to distinguish between white-collar workers who earned a fixed salary and blue-collar manual laborers who earned hourly or piecework wages. Ten years later, census officials decided that proprietors, who earned profits rather than salaries, and very highly paid corporate officers also belonged in different categories, but they continued to list clerks with general superintendents and managers.

The thinking of census officials mirrored that of white-collar workers themselves. Although they articulated grievances about their pay and working conditions, few white-collar workers showed much interest in unions. An organizer of women clerical workers complained of "pretentious office workers" wedded to "petty social distinctions."[1] The newspaper of the retail clerks' union told salesmen, "You should not look upon yourself as a superior being," and scolded, "You clerks are the hardest to reach . . . [because] your minds reflect the ideas of your employer."[2]

Although the conditions of industrial workers and their ongoing conflict with capital dominated public debate about the labor question in the Progressive Era, the number of white-collar workers increased much faster throughout the period than the number of manual laborers. In 1870, three-quarters of a million people held jobs as managers, salaried professionals, salespeople, and office workers, a mere 6 percent of the labor force. By 1910, one in five American workers held these jobs. A diverse group of men and women, they enjoyed none of the perquisites of business executives or independent professionals but only rarely displayed the militancy of industrial workers. Standing on an ambiguous middle ground in the occupational hierarchy, like other workers they sought economic security in an economy dominated by corporate capitalism. Their jobs required substantial schooling and refinement in dress, speech, and manner, and they prided themselves on having greater social status than those who worked with their hands. And although they worked mostly in large bureaucracies, some achieved considerable autonomy in performing their jobs.

OFFICE AND CLERICAL WORKERS

The advance of corporate capitalism created a tremendous demand for office workers to handle clerical, bookkeeping, and administrative tasks. Systematic management of large corporations demanded elaborate data collection and detailed reports and correspondence. Mail-order corporations employed thousands of clerks to process merchandise orders. Rapidly growing insurance companies and financial institutions relied upon an army of clerks, typists, and bookkeepers to maintain records, prepare correspondence, and make payments. Therefore, clerical work grew faster than any other major occupation in the country. In 1890, 381,000 Americans held clerical positions; by 1900, despite the depression of the previous decade, the number stood at 708,000. It jumped to 1,524,000 in 1910 and a staggering 2,838,000 workers by 1920. This clerical revolution engaged both men and women. In small antebellum offices, clerks had almost always been men; in 1870, a mere 2,000 women worked in offices, only 2 percent of all office employees, but by 1920 women held 45 percent of all clerical jobs, making this the most common middle-class female occupation.

Growth of such dimensions inevitably changed the nature of office work. A typical male clerk working for a small entrepreneur or a railroad in the mid-nineteenth century performed a wide variety of tasks, from copying documents to keeping accounts to delivering correspondence and packages. A clerkship introduced him to the practical workings of business, providing opportunities to move up or eventually start his own enterprise. As offices became larger, managers assigned more specialized tasks to their clerks, and opportunities to learn the entire business and move into management diminished. Then, in the early twentieth century, executives applied scientific management principles to office organization, further accelerating specialization and routinization, and further limiting internal mobility.

New technologies also spurred specialization. The typewriter, first patented in 1868, made correspondence quicker and neater when it came into common office use after 1880. Carbon paper appeared in 1869, dictating machines in the 1880s. The Census Bureau used the Hollerith machine to tabulate the 1890 census. Offices began purchasing adding machines shortly thereafter, and in the next few years acquired addressing, calculating, billing, check-writing, and other devices. In 1920, a management expert described office work as "simply production work of another kind. Indeed, it is 'light manufacturing,' and the principles are precisely the same."

He exaggerated. Office work certainly became more specialized. Stenographers, typists, and operators of tabulating machines repeated the same task, just like assembly-line operatives, but clerical work demanded much more skill, including mastery of written English and arithmetic. Other office workers performed tasks requiring initiative and judgment. Bookkeepers normally carried some responsibility for analyzing financial data and preparing reports. Although some clerks simply filed documents or kept routine records, others had diverse duties. Private secretaries organized their boss's schedule, screened telephone calls, greeted visitors, reviewed correspondence, and helped to prepare reports.

Supervisors usually hired women for the more routine work. As early as 1890, they constituted 64 percent of stenographers and typists, 92 percent by 1920. At the Metropolitan Life Insurance Company, only men worked in the mailroom, and only women worked in the insurance application numbering room or in the stenographic pool. In the actuarial room, female clerks filed cards with policy information while men used computing equipment for calculations. At Sears, Roebuck, women office workers, more than half of all Sears office employees by 1913, handled the company's billing, typing, and stenography. Men mostly conducted correspondence, which required more initiative. In many offices where men and women worked in close proximity, employers paid a gendered wage regardless of duties. Indeed, job titles provided poor guides to the work actually performed; lower-paid women sometimes performed the same tasks as better-paid men.

Who entered office work, and why? Office work required roughly a high school education and good command of the English language. Native-born Americans made up the overwhelming majority of office workers, but many of these were children of immigrants for whom office work offered an avenue of upward mobility. Most employers refused to hire the small number of African-Americans who had the requisite education for office jobs.

Young men continued to seek office jobs with the hope of advancement into management. In some cases men who failed as entrepreneurs sought secure jobs as clerks. Fred Dickerson completed two years of high school and two years in a Boston business college before securing his first job as a clerk in a small fruit and confectionery concern. He moved up to junior partner, but after the business faltered, Dickerson applied for a clerkship in the Census

Bureau. A. S. Taylor, who applied for a federal job in 1893, explained, "I had the misfortune to fail in business and lost all I made in ten years' hard work."[3]

Women seldom entered offices as failed entrepreneurs, but like the men, they worked to support themselves or their families. With fewer options, they welcomed the new opportunities for office jobs. While some late-nineteenth-century employers had reservations about hiring women, the supply of educated women grew as the need for office workers expanded. Office work quickly became a respectable occupation for middle-class females. Employers also accepted women as office workers because they assumed women would work for only a few years before getting married; therefore, they would not expect promotions and career advancement, and could be paid less than men. Henry Ford required his women office workers to be unmarried.

The federal government pioneered in employing large numbers of women clerks, and the first women to enter government service regularly stated that they needed to work in order to support their families. Josephine Waller, for example, the daughter of a prominent Philadelphia physician, went to work to support the family upon the death of her father. She took jobs as a teacher and a governess, finally gaining a position in the government in 1890. She married a few years later, but retained her government post because she supported her disabled husband and her sister.

Opening office jobs to women helped employers to keep salaries down, but office workers still generally earned more money than women who labored in factories. Women office workers earned more than female store clerks and sometimes more than teachers. Secretaries received higher salaries than bookkeepers or stenotypists, who received higher salaries than clerks. Men doing work similar to that of women generally earned about 50 percent more. But office workers had additional economic advantages. They worked a significantly shorter day than blue-collar workers or department store clerks, and they normally received a two-week paid vacation. Working more steadily than factory operatives, office employees normally did not lose pay for holidays or short illnesses.

Clerical workers certainly had grievances. Interviewers for a survey of Pennsylvania working women in 1894 heard complaints about discourteous treatment, rigid management, work strain, and especially inequitable pay. One bookkeeper told investigators, "I formerly taught school and had a high school certificate and had a great deal more experience in the work than a certain man . . . but because I was a woman I was obliged to take the job for ten dollars a month less salary."[4] Perhaps for this reason, young women clerical workers changed jobs frequently, seeking better pay and conditions.

Some office workers also complained about the limited opportunities for advancement. Men could move up more easily than women, but promotion became less certain than it had been for industrious male clerks in the mid-nineteenth century. Among Pittsburgh commercial students who had taken jobs at the turn of the century as clerks or bookkeepers, the vast majority, 70 percent, still held clerical or sales positions in 1915. Cleveland railroad managers routinely promoted office boys and male stenographers to the higher position of "clerk," according to a 1916 study, but only about seventy clerks in a thousand could expect promotion to supervisory or executive posts. The study's author interviewed an "unusually alert, intelligent youth of twenty-two," a graduate of an evening commercial school who had already received several promotions and could expect only three more in the next few years, at which time his salary would be $80 a month. "And there I will stick! There will be about four other fellows doing different work but all on the same level and we will all be waiting for the chief clerk to die off. If he does, then somebody will jump to $125—but any one of us has only one chance in five of being that person."[5]

If advancement to managerial positions remained difficult for men, it proved almost impossible for women. Many women worked only a few years before marriage, but those who stayed longer rarely rose very high in the office hierarchy. Jennie Peyton advanced in five years to a $1,400-a-year position in the federal government's General Land Office. Her responsibilities continued to increase, but she was not promoted further. Over a decade later, her supervisor unsuccessfully recommended her for a raise. A different supervisor tried again a few years after that. "The *character* of the work she is engaged upon . . . is entitled to the highest recognition by the employment upon it of a clerk of the highest grade," he pleaded, and explained that she did this work "in a masterful manner." Three years later he repeated his plea, explaining that she had not had a promotion in eighteen years "for the reason that she is a woman."[6] But to no avail.

In commercial offices, women seldom achieved a position higher than a private secretary to a business executive. Secretaries performed a wide range of tasks, exercised initiative, and received better pay than stenographers, clerks, and typists. In *The Ambitious Woman in Business* (1916), author Eleanor Gilbert conceded that "office work, taken as a whole, is usually overcrowded and underpaid," but she argued that secretarial work was different. To become a secretary, she advised a stenographer to "study the business as thoroughly and carefully as she could," to be "full of 'commercial curiosity,' eager to absorb every bit of available information," and to "become a veritable second mind to her employer."[7] Helen Gladwyn, secretary to a businessman, described how she learned to exercise initiative. "The weeks went on and I had been doing this secretarial work for about eight months, when Mr. Blank was hastily called away on a business trip." She explained that he gave her "practically no instructions" except to refer urgent mail to one of his assistants and hold the rest until he returned. She decided that "if I were a real secretary I ought to be able to handle that correspondence myself . . . and then I decided that I would . . ."

> In regard to the business material I asked advice occasionally, but on the whole I managed it myself. Visitors I likewise disposed of— graciously, I hope; with celerity, I know. The result was that when Mr.

Blank returned there were not three or four matters which actually required his personal attention. I showed him the rest of the material, together with the carbons of my replies, and explained how the various affairs stood.

"Why," he exclaimed with a pleasant smile, "it's very nice of you to have kept things up for me in this way! No one ever did it before."[8]

The next week, Mr. Blank raised Gladwyn's salary by ten dollars, but he apparently did not consider promoting her to a management position. Few women, however, even reached the secretarial level.

Despite limits on mobility and their complaints about working conditions and inequitable treatment, office workers generally took satisfaction in the relative economic security their jobs provided and the social status of doing white-collar work. Efforts to unionize office workers in the Progressive Era foundered more from the clerical workers' lack of enthusiasm than from employer resistance. In the late nineteenth century, some male and a few female clerical workers formed associations for mutual support and to improve wages. Early in the new century, the Women's Trade Union League, composed of middle- and upper-class women seeking to improve the lives of the women workers, organized a number of female unions for stenographers, bookkeepers, and typists. The Bookkeepers and Accountants Union No. 1 of New York, formed in 1908 with a charter from the American Federation of Labor, demanded shorter hours, better conditions and equal pay for women office workers. These efforts did not appeal to most clerical workers, who identified unions with blue-collar industrial employees.

Young people demonstrated the appeal of office work, whatever its drawbacks, by flocking to programs that would prepare them for these jobs. Initially, private commercial schools trained most office personnel, but when public high schools introduced commercial courses they proved enormously popular. In Pittsburgh, the number of girls entering the commercial department doubled in one year, when the schools introduced typing instruction in the mid-1890s.

Indeed, the opportunity to prepare for office employment caused public high school enrollments in cities with many office jobs to expand dramatically. In Cleveland, for example, the proportion of elementary school students who went on to graduate from the commercial high school went from 14 percent in 1903 to 45 percent in 1913. In Chicago, the enrollment in all public high schools increased 53 percent between 1913 and 1918, but enrollment in commercial programs went up 115 percent.

Commercial courses proved popular with boys and girls alike, and their parents. Many well-off skilled workers worried that technological and managerial changes would undermine their jobs in the long run, and apparently they concluded that office work presented better opportunities for their children. Progressive vocational educators discouraged these programs, believing that young men would have a better future by preparing for the skilled trades and that young women, who would soon be housewives and mothers should study home economics. But they could not deter young people from selecting commercial courses.

Some Progressive Era commentators feared that the ne white-collar employees lacked the independence, initiative, an manliness of antebellum entrepreneurs. Harking back to earl nineteenth-century ideals of free labor, Henry Stimpson, writing *The Atlantic Monthly* in 1904, worried that when men worked pe manently for others, they became "servants, in that their powe were obedient to the decisions of another." Although acknowledgi the necessity of large corporations, Stimpson bemoaned their li itations, of which "none is more serious than this radical one of effect upon the character of many employees, who, under forr conditions, would have been either managing their own busines or ambitious for the opportunity of doing so." He wondered out l what would "take the place of the old discipline, with its insis demand for those traits of character which have made the mercl and the manufacturer the sturdy, thoughtful, self-respecting they always have been."[9]

Others believed that the employment of middle-class women in commercial offices would undermine their traditional domestic role and weaken the American family. The president of Aetna Life Insurance Company, for example, insisted that an insurance firm was an inappropriate place for women, and maintained an all-male staff until 1908. Many employers, recognizing the need for female labor but concerned about the threat to women's virtue, separated men and women into different office areas to limit contact. At Metropolitan Life, where females constituted a majority of employees by the 1890s, men and women used different entrance doors until 1914, and different hallways, stairways, elevators, and cafeterias well after that. In deference to the presence of "the ladies," several companies prohibited men from spitting and chewing tobacco, and restricted smoking to specified areas. Men and women had to adhere to a strict dress code and rules of behavior. Women wore black skirts, white blouses and aprons, and had to keep their hair pinned up at all times. Men could walk outside the building during lunch; women had to stay within, but could walk on the roof.

Office workers themselves showed little concern about these supposed negative effects of salaried office work. Men valued the security of white-collar jobs over the independence of uncertain entrepreneurship. Women looked upon employment in a clean and middle-class workplace as respectable, at least prior to marriage. Developing personal and financial independence, and growing accustomed to traveling in the city without supervision, they challenged the exclusion of women from the public sphere. Men and women who had grown up with the Victorian ideal that the sexes should inhabit separate spheres and different physical spaces now readily defined a new heterosocial work culture and new gender roles.

The ideology of separate spheres surely did not disappear in the turn-of-the-century office, but the men and women who worked in offices redefined what it meant to be male and female. Men came to see competition for upward mobility in a large bureaucratic or-

ganization as masculine. Women viewed salaried work as fully compatible with female virtue; and they came to value the independence which work provided. Elizabeth Sears, writing in *Harper's* in 1917, explained that women took clerical jobs because they needed the money. She insisted that "it would never have struck me to apologize for the fact that I worked for my living. All the girls in my town expected to earn their own living." Sears went on to tell the "pathetic" story of a thirty-year-old unmarried female who had been forced to give up her club work when her father refused to pay her dues. "She was a victim of the old regime when every man was the overlord of his own household. . . . She regarded me rather dubiously when I told her I thought it served her right for expecting her father, at her age, to pay her club dues. . . . She is a slave to her job of being a daughter and a parasite upon her father's bounty."[10]

Few female office workers articulated Sears's position so starkly, but most undoubtedly took satisfaction in their independence and new freedom. A small number of their male co-workers who took office work after failing in small business may have bemoaned their loss of autonomy; but for most men, office work offered an economically and socially attractive alternative to the industrial or agricultural labor performed by their parents. Nostalgic writers might worry about the negative consequences of work in the modern office, but these fears did not trouble most of the men and women who worked there.

SALESMEN

Nor did it trouble the men who staffed the new corporate sales departments. In the early years of industrialization, manufacturers contracted with independent entrepreneurs to sell their goods in towns and cities across the country, but when giant corporations integrated vertically to strengthen their control of the market, salaried corporate salesmen became indispensable. International Harvester, for example, developed an elaborate sales department. Sales positions paid relatively well and offered opportunities for autonomy and social status. General sales agents made between $2,500 and $3,600 a year in 1910, and assistant agents between $2,000 and $2,500. Successful agents normally moved to larger communities as their careers progressed. These men hired additional sales workers in their respective offices, and became prominent members of their rural communities, participating actively in civic organizations. They educated farmers in the use of new machines and brought the farmers' technical suggestions back to the company, skillfully negotiating their primary relationships with their employer and their ties to the farmers they served.

C. E. Haynie, an agent for McCormick and its successor, International Harvester, in Lincoln, Nebraska, from 1898 to 1912, supervised nine people. A number of his employees had grown up on farms. Haynie joined the Union Commercial Club and the Chamber of Commerce, where he mingled with the city's business leaders. In remote Crawford, Nebraska, Harvester opened an office in 1909 headed by W. F. Acker, who had been a traveling salesman for McCormick for ten years and had worked as an assistant agent in the Omaha office. He supervised a staff of eight, joined the Knights of Pythias fraternal order, and won election to the city council, serving as its president and later as Crawford's mayor.

Du Pont managed its sales operation tightly through a centralized sales department with branch offices. Managers insisted that the salesmen dress neatly and conservatively. "You are well dressed when no one can remember anything you are wearing," the company instructed them. "You are not dressed for work until you put on a smile." The company expected salesmen to gather intelligence on competitors' products and prices. The department systematically evaluated them, awarded prizes to those who sold the most, and held contests for the best suggestion to improve sales. Salesmen regularly wrote about their experiences for the company magazine. Although they had far less autonomy than Harvester salesmen, they valued the social prestige of representing one of the country's largest corporations.

Salesmen for insurance companies commonly came from working-class families. Eager to sell inexpensive policies to immigrants, insurance companies often hired and promoted members of immigrant communities. By the late 1890s, Prudential employed approximately 10,000 agents, two-thirds of them immigrants. None had graduated from high school, and most had held factory jobs before starting to sell insurance. Agents sold policies costing between five and seventy cents a week, returning each week to collect the payment. A significant number of supervisors rose from the ranks of these salesmen.

For exceptional individuals, corporate employment could provide enormous opportunities. In 1909, a senior executive of Metropolitan Life employed Lee K. Frankel to organize a welfare program. Although educated as a chemist, Frankel had headed the United Hebrew Charities and joined the progressive crusade for government-sponsored social insurance. Frankel hired Louis Israel Dublin as his assistant. Dublin, an American-born child of Jewish immigrants from Lithuania, grew up in New York tenements, went to City College, and received a Ph.D. from Columbia University in biology in 1904 at the age of twenty-two. With close ties to the settlement movement, the Charity Organization Society, and reformist social scientists at Columbia, Frankel and Dublin developed a health insurance program, contracting with visiting nurse associations across the country to care for sick policyholders. They provided pamphlets to policyholders on health and safety; distributed disposable drinking cups to prevent the spread of tuberculosis; and set up "Health and Happiness" clubs for young people, which sponsored health-oriented field trips and essay contests. Frankel and Dublin argued that these activities saved the company money by helping people to live longer. In short, insurance salesmen from working-class backgrounds, like salesmen of agricultural machinery or chemicals, could earn substantial incomes and achieve considerable social status. Although they lacked the autonomy of independent entrepreneurs, many found in their work substantial opportunities for initiative and creativity.

SALESCLERKS

The big growth in sales employment occurred in retail sales jobs in shops and department stores, however, rather than in corporate sales and insurance. Consumption became an increasingly prominent part of Americans' lives as industrial capitalism produced an ever-expanding array of consumer goods and the modern department store emerged in cities in the late nineteenth century. In 1890, 615,000 Americans sold goods in stores; by 1920, 1,540,000 did so. Women held only 4 percent of these jobs in 1870, but 34 percent in 1920 and at least three-quarters of sales positions in big city department stores.

Native-born salesclerks predominated, as they did in office work. Department stores and downtown specialty stores sought salespeople who spoke English well, acted refined, and presented themselves as knowledgeable advisers to middle-class customers. Stores almost never knowingly hired African-American salesclerks, however, except in businesses that served a black clientele.

Many men took sales positions in stores hoping to learn the business and move into management. Male salesclerks in the early twentieth century identified with businessmen; in 1905 a union of sales workers estimated that 50 percent of salesclerks viewed their job as "transitional." Even the weak union of retail clerks, which urged salespeople to act as workers rather than as incipient businessmen, stated in its newspaper in 1909: "[S]alesmanship is really a science and a profession, and is fast becoming recognized as such. . . . The salesman—meaning also the saleswoman—is more and more the deciding factor in the success or failure of a retail store . . . this calling is being hailed as the fourth profession."[11]

Women, who had fewer options than men, welcomed sales work for its immediate advantages rather than as an avenue to a management job. The great department stores that developed in the mid-nineteenth century in the downtown areas of large cities became palaces of consumption, presenting a dazzling assortment of goods for sale and a wide variety of customer services, from art exhibits and musical performances to package delivery. Shopping downtown became a major activity for well-off women. It seemed natural, and therefore respectable, for middle-class women to sell consumer goods to other women. Leonora O'Reilly, the Irish labor organizer, noted with displeasure in 1899 that "department store women have a caste feeling about their work and think that persons working in a mercantile establishment are a little higher in society than the women who work in a factory."[12]

Sales work had a variety of other attractions. Store clerks did not need as much formal education as clerical workers. Department stores projected glamour, and work there appealed to women despite its physical strain. Sales work also attracted some married women because managers viewed favorably their maturity and experience as consumers and homemakers. Department and chain stores offered fairly steady employment, less vulnerable to business fluctuations than factory work. They also provided paid vacations, pensions, substantial discounts for merchandise, medical care, company-sponsored recreational programs, and other fringe benefits. Many stores paid bonuses or commissions to those who sold the most. Average salaries for salespeople varied considerably. Men earned significantly more than women. In general, salesmen earned less than skilled industrial workers. Women working in department stores earned more than those working in dime stores, who tended to be younger and less experienced. Department stores also employed a good number of part-time workers who earned lower pay and had less job security.

A few women rose to high positions as department store managers or buyers. Macy's hired Margaret Getchell as the first store superintendent in 1887, and from then on women occupied this post. In 1920 women constituted just under half of all department store buyers. Mary Tolman, who studied department stores, proclaimed in 1912 that "here more than anywhere else, equal pay and equal opportunities have been offered to those who show results whether they are men or women."[13] Bessie Harrison, for example, began work in 1905 as a duster in the china department of a department store in San Francisco to help her sick parents and six brothers and sisters. A half year later, she secured promotion to a sales position paying $8.00 a week. Within a decade, this ambitious woman had become a buyer, making twenty times her original salary. Only a tiny fraction of salespeople could become buyers, however.

To increase sales and service to customers and maintain the store's image, store officials imposed elaborate rules upon sales-clerks which restricted their autonomy. They could not sit while on duty, and managers docked their pay for lateness or errors at the cash register. Elaborate rule books defined proper conduct and pen-alties for misbehavior. Many stores imposed rigid dress require-ments. Salespeople often had to use different elevators and entrances than customers, and frequently remained at work after hours, without additional pay, to conclude a sale after the official closing, to arrange merchandise, or to move goods in the stockroom. Pennsylvania researchers in 1894 heard numerous complaints about long hours, especially on Saturday, from women store clerks. One clerk in Pittsburgh explained that Saturday evening work made it "almost impossible for us to get up in time for church on Sunday morning."[14]

Nonetheless, sales workers, particularly in department stores, ex-ercised a fair degree of autonomy. As department stores competed for customers, increased sales volume became indispensable. Sales workers had to be motivated to succeed at selling, and the art of selling could not readily be routinized. Salesclerks who had built a relationship with customers might leave the store, possibly taking their customers with them to a competitor. Working in a female-oriented institution, saleswomen created a supportive female work culture. They resisted punching time clocks, being searched for stolen goods, the dress code, and separate entrances. In some cases, managers changed these practices to motivate saleswomen and re-duce turnover.

Thus, like office workers, these agents of consumer culture showed little interest in unionization, despite modest wages and genuine workplace grievances. The Retail Clerks' National Protective Association, organized in 1890 and affiliated with the American Federation of Labor, had only about 15,000 members between 1909 and 1918. The union sought to limit store clerks' hours and had some success asking customers to boycott stores that stayed open evenings and Sundays. Otherwise it had little effect. Department store clerks, proud of their social status, modest economic security, and relative autonomy in a business that relied upon their ability and eagerness to sell, did not want to associate themselves with the industrial proletariat.

TELEPHONE OPERATORS

One group of white-collar workers did embrace unionization; telephone operators, mindful of the respectability associated with the job of connecting telephone customers and assisting subscribers in an all-female work setting, still embraced unionism in some cities to raise salaries and improve conditions.

Early telephone companies employed teenage boys to connect calls, but in the 1880s they replaced them with women and girls as daytime operators, believing that females would be more courteous to customers and more readily disciplined. Boys continued as nighttime operators until the first years of the twentieth century. Telephone operating soon became an occupation of unmarried, mostly native-born women. In the early twentieth century, the Bell Telephone System, a huge company with subsidiaries all across the country, became the largest employer of women in the United States.

At first, operators worked in a loosely structured environment. They served a discrete group of customers whom they came to know, taking messages and providing news and information about sporting events. Businesses using the telephone often gave operators cash gifts, sometimes as much as $50 a year, but by 1910 the phone companies prohibited gratuities to keep operators from favoring some customers over others.

As the telephone business grew and the volume of calls increased, companies, influenced by scientific management ideas, systematized the work of operators and imposed rigid performance standards. Between six and fifteen operators handled an exchange, supervised by a chief operator. The operators sat in front of the board, and the supervisor stood behind them. She observed and evaluated their work and assisted with problems. Managers promoted the most successful and experienced employees to "senior operators," who had roughly the same duties but somewhat higher pay, and they selected the chief operators, the highest position women could normally hold, from the ranks of the senior operators.

An operator's manual gave explicit instructions on how to handle every situation, the exact words to be used, and even the enunciation and voice inflection. The operators answered a call with the words "number please," and were told that ". . . '2' is to be spoken as 'TOO'—with a strong T and long OO. '3' is to be spoken as 'TH-R-R-EE' with a slightly rolling R and long E." When the requested line was in use, she replied "line busy" with "emphasis on the first syllable of the word 'busy' and with the same tone of sympathetic concern, as one would employ in saying 'I am *sorry*, Mr. Smith, but I cannot give you what you want.' " The rules prohibited operators from talking back to customers. If a customer complained about delay in connecting a call, she could only answer "number please" or, if necessary, connect the caller with the information desk. As the president of the telephone operators union unflatteringly described it:

> Inside the central office an operator is supervised, tested, observed, disciplined, almost to the breaking point. It is scarcely possible for her to obey any natural impulse without breaking a rule. She must not move her head to the left or to the right; she must not indulge in social conversation, by which may be construed her "hello" and "goodbye" to the adjacent operator; she must sit, even when not engaged in operating, if such a moment ever comes, with plug in hand ready to answer.

Supervisors pressed operators to answer calls as quickly as possible, and encouraged them to keep scrapbooks of materials on efficiency and work accuracy, giving prizes for the best.

Applicants for operator jobs had to be single women between the ages of seventeen and twenty-six, with at least a grammar school education and preferably two years of high school. "Telephone users are mostly the better educated, hence the necessity of these qualifications that she may cope with them on an equal plane," stated a Bell official.[15] Operators had to be in good physical health, have a pleasing voice and good diction, an arm stretch of at least five feet, and a height when seated of at least thirty-two inches. Companies sent "medical matrons" to inspect the homes of applicants for operator positions, ensuring that only those raised in middle-class environments would be hired. The New England Telephone Company did not hire Jewish or African-American women.

Vocational guidance counselors accepted the companies' definition of operators as white-collar workers, and considered these positions comparable to office workers and salesclerks. Telephone operators generally received better pay than saleswomen and factory workers, but lower than clerical workers. In 1913, Bell began providing sick pay beginning on the eighth day of illness for operators who had completed two years of service. Operators theoretically could also qualify for a pension, but few worked the requisite twenty years. Many operators agreed that their jobs constituted respectable, white-collar work. Even Julia O'Connor, a leader of their union, stated that telephone operators performed a "high calling" requiring "intelligence, devotion, and esprit de corps" and provided an "indispensable public service."

To maintain their image of respectability and attract women with middle-class speech and attitudes, companies established paternalistic working conditions for these unmarried female employees. The Chicago company assured women recruits that it provided "the parental care of a far-seeing monopoly" where young women worked secluded from the public in a "wholesome and refined" workplace.

Cafeterias served "nutritionally balanced" meals, and matrons supervised "retiring rooms" for rest periods, each equipped with a piano, magazines, and a record player.[16] The matrons advised the women on personal hygiene and cared for those who became sick at work. The company also sponsored athletic clubs, reading circles, and libraries, and in some places built dormitories so that evening and night operators would not have to go home after dark. In large cities, companies recruited operators through referrals from priests, high school officials, and the operators' families and friends, and did not normally advertise openings.

Despite their attachment to their occupation's white-collar status, telephone operators, unlike office workers and salesclerks, readily joined a union. The first telephone union struck successfully in Butte, Montana, a city with traditionally strong unions; a strike shortly thereafter by telephone operators in San Francisco in 1907, however, brought few gains. In 1913, Boston telephone operators organized a union, voted to strike, and with the help of the Women's Trade Union League of Boston, won pay raises and a process to hear grievances.

Why the appeal of unions? Office workers and salesclerks could move readily from one job to another, but operators worked for a single hegemonic employer committed to Taylorite efficiency and paternalistic control of its young female employees. Moreover, telephone operators lacked the relative autonomy in performing their daily jobs enjoyed by salesclerks and many office workers. Finally, Irish women, whose families and communities had extensive experience with unionization, held a large portion of operator jobs and most of the union's leadership positions. In embracing organized labor, these women drew upon their working-class experiences in seeking improved economic security, even as they clung to the idea that their jobs afforded them a higher social status than their mothers, aunts, and cousins achieved as domestic servants and factory laborers.

.   .   .

White-collar employees, the fastest-growing group of workers in the Progressive Era, stood on the cutting edge of social change in America. Occupying an ambiguous status between industrial workers and higher-status managers, entrepreneurs, and professionals, they performed the new jobs created by corporate management and a consumer society. They achieved greater economic security than most industrial workers, receiving moderately better pay and fringe benefits in jobs largely insulated from layoffs and the exigencies of the production process. Although most white-collar workers had to submit to the discipline of corporate bureaucracies, some, like corporate sales agents, personal secretaries, and department store clerks exercised a degree of autonomy. Others, like telephone operators and stenographers, worked under conditions similar to those on industrial assembly lines.

White-collar workers also helped to redefine the relationship between social status and gendered work in the Progressive Era. Nostalgic commentators bemoaned the threat to manly independence and virtuous womanhood in the new economic order created by corporate capitalism. But whatever the personal strains and disadvantages, middle-class men and women seized opportunities, albeit different and grossly inequitable ones, to enhance their economic security and social status through salaried white-collar employment.

7

THE COMPETITION FOR CONTROL
OF THE PROFESSIONS

In every profession, practitioners demanded the same thing. A physician, writing in the *Journal of the American Medical Association* in 1902 asked rhetorically, "Is it not about time that the professional mind began to dominate in control of [hospitals]?" The American Association of University Professors, writing about institutions of higher learning, asserted in its first statement on academic freedom in 1915 that a university professor, once appointed, "has professional responsibilities to perform in which the appointing authorities have neither competency nor moral right to intervene" because "the responsibility of the university teacher is primarily to the public itself, and to the judgment of his own profession."[1] Leading lawyers, engineers, teachers, social workers, and members of other professions said the same thing: expertise should confer autonomy, social status, and economic security on those who possessed it, and they alone should regulate and restrict the members of their calling.

In the mid-nineteenth century, most Americans would have dismissed such claims as preposterous. State legislatures during the Jacksonian era had abolished physician licensure as undemocratic and monopolistic, and nearly any white man who undertook a short apprenticeship "reading law" in an attorney's office could be admitted to the bar. But the rapid growth of scientific knowledge, the application of this knowledge to industry, law, government, education, social welfare, and other facets of American life, and the growing complexity of industrial society created an increasingly specialized set of occupations. Technological advances may have undermined the skills of iron puddlers or weavers, but the growth of scientific knowledge increased the expertise of physicians, lawyers, professors, engineers, and others with advanced education.

Indeed, of the traditional professions, only the ministry lost prestige in the Progressive Era, as many Americans looked to men of science rather than to men of faith for expertise on the great problems of the day. Some Protestant ministers left the pulpit for careers as sociologists or social workers. The best-educated clergymen now argued that spirituality must be undergirded by expertise and professionalism; many Protestant theological seminaries became more rigorous academically as modernizers steeped in secular learning fused science with traditional religious teachings through higher biblical criticism and pastoral sociology. But theological fundamentalists rejected this embrace of science, and rural and working-class Protestants, black, native white, and immigrant, often preferred less well-educated preachers who delivered the message of old-time or Old World religion. Religion in America, lacking state support, proved too democratic, and too diverse, for any one group of clergymen to establish a professional monopoly.

Similar dynamics occurred in American Catholicism and Judaism. Some leaders of the American Catholic Church at the turn of the century pressed for higher educational standards for priests. The "priesthood is preeminently one of the learned professions," Cardinal James Gibbons asserted in 1896. "Piety in a priest, though indispensable, can never be an adequate substitute for learning. . . . 'Knowledge is power' not only in the scientific and mechanical, but also in the social and religious world," he explained.[2] But modernists like Gibbons met resistance from conservative Irish priests and foreign-born priests who came to America to serve the spiritual needs of immigrants. Reformist, Americanized Jews founded Hebrew Union College in 1875 to train modern rabbis familiar with higher biblical criticism while traditionalists founded the Jewish Theological Seminary in 1886 to combine classical Jewish learning with modern thought. But the Eastern European rabbis who came over in the mass migration after 1881 rejected both versions of this modernized Judaism.

In other professions, however, the best-educated and most successful practitioners enhanced their prestige and economic rewards. They sought to restrict membership in the profession, often through state licensure authority not available to the clergy in a nation that barred state establishment of religion. They formed associations at the local, state, and national levels to gain power over the practice of their calling. And they gained public recognition for their expertise. These efforts to upgrade professional standards and membership pitted leading practitioners against those of humble origins and modest incomes. They also pitted men who believed that women in law or medicine lowered the profession's prestige against women practitioners in these fields.

Women gained numerical preponderance in teaching, nursing, social work, home economics, and librarianship, professions thought to be a natural extension of the female domestic sphere. In these fields, leading women professionals, like their counterparts in professions controlled by men, fought to restrict practice by those with limited education and simultaneously struggled with the men who controlled the schools, hospitals, and other institutions in which these women worked. In short, the dramatic growth in the number and power of the professions in the Progressive Era involved a vigorous contest for control between the most successful and the ordinary practitioners, between people of different social origins, and between men and women.

PHYSICIANS

At the turn of the century, leading physicians set out to transform the American medical profession. They succeeded spectacularly. Within a generation, they dramatically increased the rigor of medical education and the requirements for licensure, reduced the number of doctors while maintaining physicians' autonomy as self-employed entrepreneurs, and built a hospital system which physicians substantially controlled. The medical professionalizers so completely established physician autonomy, social status, income, and control of medical practice that they set the standard against which all others judged the "professionalization" of their occupations.

In the early nineteenth century, physicians, knowing relatively little about the causes of disease, held little public esteem. Medical schools provided an apprenticeship with an experienced physician; but a medical practitioner did not need to graduate from a medical school or, after the Jacksonian era, secure a license in most states. The rise of modern biology in the middle of the nineteenth century, and in particular the development of the germ theory in the 1870s, however, enabled scientifically trained doctors to claim genuine expertise and to convince legislatures to reinstitute physician licensing and to tighten requirements. Typically, state law first required a diploma from any medical school; then state officials certified the quality of those schools. Finally, states required that a licensed physician both have a diploma from an acceptable school and pass an examination. By 1901, twenty-five states and the District of Columbia required both an approved diploma and an examination; and every state had some licensure statute.

Despite these laws, new medical schools proliferated, enrollments more than doubled between 1880 and 1900, and the number of physicians increased steadily, driving down doctors' income. Many physicians complained about how little they earned. One New Orleans doctor asserted in 1898 that seven of every eight physicians in his city earned less than $1,000 a year; a doctor in New Paltz, New York, insisted that his patients refused to pay more than fifty cents for a house call and thirty-five cents for office treatment.[3] With fewer than one of every three physicians belonging to a local, state, or national medical society in the late nineteenth century, poorly organized physicians could not affect these conditions.

In 1900, however, the American Medical Association (AMA),

founded in 1846 by young physicians seeking to upgrade professional standards, began a concerted effort to organize the nation's
doctors in order to upgrade standards and restrict entry into the
profession. A revamped constitution made all county medical society members automatically members of their state society and the
national AMA. The AMA vigorously organized new county and state
societies; membership jumped from 8,000 in 1900 to 70,000 in
1910, 50 percent of the nation's doctors.

Now well organized, the leadership of the AMA set out to gain
control of the new state licensure boards. They secured statutes in
many states specifying that medical licensure board members be
selected from lists prepared by local medical societies. They got
the licensure boards to require that a physician hold a diploma from
an approved medical college and pass an examination. And they
pressed to upgrade medical education.

In 1893, the Johns Hopkins University opened its medical school
with some dramatic innovations, including a four-year curriculum,
a faculty active in medical research, and, in a radical departure,
admission limited only to those with undergraduate degrees. By
bringing together scientific study and research with clinical hospital
practice, Hopkins offered a model of what first-rate medical education could be. In 1904, the newly reorganized AMA established
a Council on Medical Education, which graded the nation's medical
schools, initially on how their students performed on licensure exams and then on their curricula, faculty, facilities, and standards
for admission. In 1906, its members visited and evaluated all 160
U.S. medical schools, categorizing 32 schools as inadequate. In the
next four years the number of medical schools declined to 131.

The Council on Medical Education soon asked the Carnegie
Foundation for the Advancement of Teaching to take up the work
of evaluating medical schools. Abraham Flexner, the young educator who conducted Carnegie's evaluation, visited every medical
school in the country, accompanied by a member of the AMA Council on Medical Education. His report, published in 1910, proposed
that many schools close and that most others improve substantially.

Flexner's report did not win universal acclaim within the medical profession. St. Louis College of Physicians and Surgeons filed a libel suit against Flexner and AMA leaders. The dean of Chattanooga Medical College complained of Flexner's arrogance and elite Eastern biases, asserting that "Mr. Flexner condemned our railroads as he arrived, our hotels as he tarried, and our medical colleges as he passed on." A well-known Chicago physician dubbed the AMA leaders who commissioned the Flexner report "impertinent porcine trust-monopolists."[4]

Flexner's report accelerated the reduction in the number of medical schools. In five years the number of graduates fell by a third, and by 1915 only 95 schools remained. In 1910, only 27 percent of the schools required at least one year of college for admission, but 80 percent did so by 1915. The census showed 173 physicians per 100,000 population in 1900, 164 in 1910, and 137 in 1920; as a result, the fees doctors could charge increased. AMA leaders also lobbied to restrict the free medical dispensaries run by medical schools. One Philadelphia physician stated bluntly in 1903, "When people in this land, except recent immigrants, are so poor that they cannot pay a moderate fee to some struggling physician, their poverty is a crime deserving punishment rather than encouragement."[5] AMA leaders objected as well to "contract" medicine, whereby a union, fraternal organization, or business contracted with a doctor to provide medical care as needed for its members for a fixed fee, but the practice remained popular throughout the Progressive Era.

Leading physicians also opposed providing treatment to youngsters in free school clinics, insisting that poor students diagnosed with an illness go to private physicians for treatment. Women physicians, facing obstacles to traditional forms of medical practice, often antagonized the male medical establishment by staffing public clinics. Josephine Baker, head of New York City's Bureau of Child Hygiene, recalled that after opening a public baby health station in the Brownsville section of Brooklyn "a petition was forwarded to my desk from the mayor's office, signed by 30-odd Brooklyn doctors, protesting bitterly against the Bureau of Child Hygiene because it was ruining medical practice by its results in keeping babies well, and demanding that it be abolished in the interests of the medical profession."[6] Likewise, Wisconsin medical practitioners criticized Dr. Dorothy Mendenhall for setting up that state's first public infant and maternal health center in 1915.

The successful campaign to upgrade the medical profession also made it more difficult for women, African-Americans, and people from working-class backgrounds to become physicians. Higher medical school tuition excluded some, and as the number of places in medical schools declined, schools readily rejected those from "less desirable" social backgrounds. A Minnesota physician, for example, complained in 1901 that too many American doctors came "from the toiling, laboring classes of people."[7]

At the end of the nineteenth century, eight medical schools served black students in the South, where white medical schools barred them entirely. Only two, Howard University and Meharry Medical School, survived the Flexner report. In Southern states, black physicians could not join the regular state or county medical societies; thus they were barred from membership in the AMA. In the North, most white hospitals would not grant black physicians operating and attending privileges.

The same thing happened to the much larger number of women's medical schools. In the late nineteenth century, significant numbers of women practiced medicine. Some women argued that the practice of medicine naturally extended women's domestic role in caring for the sick. Moreover, Victorian modesty justified having women physicians care for women patients. By 1910, women made up 6 percent of the country's doctors. Professionalization reduced the number of women in medicine. By 1903, fifteen of the nation's seventeen female medical schools had closed or merged with existing schools. As spaces for medical students dropped, many schools limited the number of women students on the grounds that a medical school spot would be "wasted" on someone who would likely marry, have children, and cease the practice of medicine.

The medical profession also gained substantial control over hospitals. Until late in the nineteenth century, most middle- and upper-class people avoided hospitals, receiving medical treatment and care at home. Hospitals served mostly indigents. The rise of antiseptic surgery after 1880 gave the old charitable hospitals a new mission. Hospitals started to rely on fees from wealthier patients undergoing surgery or short-term treatment for acute illnesses. Physicians disliked sending their patients to hospitals where they could not continue to provide treatment. One physician, reminding readers of the *Journal of the AMA* in 1906 that the industrial revolution had turned skilled craftsmen into "machine operators far removed from the people who furnish a market for the standardized product of their toil," warned fellow doctors, "If we wish to avoid the fate of the tool-less wage worker, we must control the hospital."[8] Hospitals, dependent on physician referrals, soon acquiesced, giving doctors sole responsibility for admitting and treating patients. In an age dominated by corporations and other corporate-like institutions, physicians secured the right to treat their patients in a complex institution, the hospital, without becoming employees.

Thus, leading physicians gained extraordinary control of medical practice during the Progressive Era, maintaining their personal autonomy as self-employed practitioners, enhancing their economic well-being, and establishing their status as experts on matters of life and death. These gains came at the expense of women, African-Americans, and those of modest means who found themselves excluded from the new medical schools. But this success at achieving a monopoly of established practitioners made medicine the ideal to which leaders in all other professions aspired.

LAWYERS

The most successful lawyers also organized new professional associations and began to upgrade legal education, but they could not rival the AMA's success in restricting entry into the profession. State legislatures, made up substantially of attorneys with limited formal legal education, would not grant the bar associations the monopoly of practice they gave to state medical associations. As in medicine, statutory standards for the practice of law had declined in the Jacksonian era. By 1860, only nine of thirty-nine states required any formal preparation, usually "reading law" in the office of an established attorney, and a number of state constitutions provided that any adult male of good character could practice law. This ease of entry produced attorneys from diverse social origins.

In the late nineteenth century, many of the wealthiest and most prominent lawyers, engaged increasingly in complex commercial transactions involving large corporations, expressed fear about the quality of the legal profession and the growing number of practitioners from working-class and immigrant families. Supreme Court Justice David Brewer asserted in 1895, "A growing multitude is crowding in who are not fit to be lawyers, who disgrace the profession after they are in it, who in a scramble after livelihood are debasing the noblest of professions into the meanest of avocations."[9] Reasserting their traditional role as the leaders of the legal profession, they founded nearly 600 state and local bar associations between 1880 and 1916, selective organizations of lawyers whose members had to be sponsored by another bar member and screened before admission.

A group of influential lawyers also founded the American Bar Association (ABA) in 1878 to upgrade and reform legal practice, seeking as members "leading men or those of high promise."[10] Made up of mostly of old-stock Protestants of social standing practicing in large cities, the ABA met each summer in Saratoga, New York, where these gentlemen lawyers could take the waters and discuss issues affecting the legal profession. In 1900, only 1.3 percent of American lawyers belonged. Early in the new century, the ABA began a campaign to recruit new members from the middle levels of the profession. By 1920, the ABA had enrolled 9.2 percent of the nation's lawyers. State and local bar associations remained independent of the ABA, however.

The ABA leaders sought to improve legal training so as to restrict the number of immigrants, Jews, African-Americans, and others of working-class origins in the profession. Elihu Root, who held key cabinet positions in the presidential administrations of William McKinley and Theodore Roosevelt and later served as ABA president, expressed concern about the impact on the legal system of "the huge numbers of immigrants from countries which differ fundamentally from the United States in conceptions of law and personal freedom."[11] In 1912, the ABA executive committee revoked the membership of three newly admitted attorneys after discovering that they were African-American. It was "a question of keeping pure the Anglo-Saxon race," explained the membership committee chairman.[12] When Morefield Storey, a past president of the ABA and the first president of the NAACP, protested, the ABA allowed the three black attorneys to retain their memberships. It announced, however, that in the future all applicants would have to identify themselves by race, and regularly denied membership to black attorneys thereafter. Root and six former presidents, Storey included, also opposed President Wilson's nomination of Louis Brandeis to the U.S. Supreme Court in 1916, arguing that his character made him unfit to serve. A Jew, Brandeis had also successfully litigated against the interests of large corporations.

Legal practice also remained almost entirely closed to women. Some law schools admitted small numbers of women, and pioneering women fought for admission to the bar. But by 1910, only 1,500 women practiced law in the United States, compared with 9,000 who practiced medicine. By 1920, women constituted a mere 1 percent of the legal profession.

The new members of the bar associations from the middle rungs of the profession undoubtedly shared these prejudices, but they had more basic concerns. The number of lawyers in the United States grew rapidly, nearly doubling between 1880 and 1900, and ordinary lawyers complained that competition drove down their incomes. The rise of real estate title companies and debt collection agencies in these years also eliminated much of the basic work traditionally handled by lawyers. One speaker at the 1911 meeting of the Baltimore Bar Association asserted that 70 percent of lawyers did not earn a decent income.

Upgrading legal education offered a way simultaneously to eliminate working-class attorneys and reduce the overall number of practitioners. Only one of every five lawyers admitted to the bar in 1890 had attended law school. In 1896, the ABA called for a high school diploma and two years of legal schooling as a prerequisite for legal practice; in 1897 it increased its recommendation to three years of study in a law school. However, the ABA could not convince state legislatures, made up substantially of lawyers with minimal formal training, to mandate these standards. By 1917, although thirty-six states required some period of formal training for admission to the bar, not a single state mandated that the training be in a school of law.

Still, many universities established law schools or legal departments toward the end of the century. The law grew more complex as corporations transformed economic life, and with typewriters and stenographers, law offices no longer needed young men to do routine work in exchange for the opportunity to "read law." Law school enrollments increased sixfold in the three decades after 1890; by 1910, according to one estimate, two-thirds of those admitted to the bar had graduated from a law school. In the cities, many law students attended proprietary schools at night.

The Association of American Law Schools (AALS), founded by the ABA in 1900, mandated that member schools require a high school diploma for admission, offer at least a two-year course of study, and give their students access to a law library. In 1907, it mandated a three-year program, and in 1912 restricted, but did not completely ban, night programs. But since admission to the practice of law did not require attendance at any law school, let alone an AALS member school, these new standards did not restrict membership in the legal profession as the AMA accreditation standards did for medicine. As the AALS expelled schools which did not meet its rising standards, the proportion of law students who attended its member schools dropped steadily.

Nor did the ABA leaders significantly restrict entrance into the profession through licensure exams, as the AMA had done. ABA leaders supported rigorous state bar examinations and formal study requirements to qualify to take the test. Between 1894 and 1906 twenty-eight states established boards of bar examiners. But professors at the top law schools split with the ABA leaders on the content of licensure exams, criticizing the exams for testing rote knowledge of state law instead of broader legal reasoning. A divided legal elite could not agree on how to use licensure exams to restrict professional membership.

Their failure to reduce the number of lawyers did not diminish the autonomy of leading attorneys, or their social status and incomes, however. To be sure, some top lawyers complained that they had lost their independence to all-powerful corporations. An attorney from an old Connecticut family of lawyers overstated the case when he insisted in 1914 that "many of the best equipped lawyers of the present day are to all intents and purposes owned by the great corporate and individual interests they represent, and while enormous fees result they are dearly earned by the surrender of individual independence."[13] In fact, the most successful lawyers maintained considerable autonomy and professional status and earned very high incomes by organizing law firms with several partners. As corporate and business law became increasingly complicated, lawyers in the firms became more specialized and law firms found it useful to take on additional attorneys. In the new specialized firms, the ability to negotiate complex business transactions and avoid litigation replaced traditional lawyerly skills of courtroom argumentation and advocacy. By organizing themselves into partnership firms, the senior lawyers maintained their autonomy as self-employed professionals, with corporate executives as clients rather than employers. Lawyers in these firms, a little over 1 percent of all attorneys in 1915, became the leaders of the ABA and the most influential state and city bar associations.

By the end of the Progressive Era, the best graduates of the best law schools from the best social backgrounds practiced specialized law in large law firms owned by the senior practitioners. They received hefty financial rewards for their efforts without becoming salaried employees of their corporate clients. They led their profession; but they could not dominate it. Law remained a socially diverse, stratified, and contested profession.

NEW PROFESSIONS:
ENGINEERS AND UNIVERSITY PROFESSORS

Industrialization also created entirely new professions like engineering and the academic disciplines. Unlike physicians and attorneys, both worked as employees, engineers in corporations and professors in large universities. They sought professional status and autonomy in contrasting ways.

The first engineers learned their craft entirely on the job, mostly designing canals and railroads. In 1816, there were perhaps 30 engineers in the entire country, but the number grew to 2,000 by 1850, when the U.S. Census first listed engineering as an occupation. Opportunities to apply science in industry increased after the Civil War, and the number of engineers reached 136,000 by 1920. Engineering colleges quickly replaced on-the-job training, enrolling 1,000 students in 1890 but 10,000 a decade later.

Like the AMA and the bar associations, engineering organizations sought to control professional standards. Some argued that engineers, like members of top law firms, should maintain professional independence from the corporations that employed them. Others insisted that, as the people most expert in the production process, they should see themselves as corporate managers. The American Institute of Mining Engineers, founded in 1871, placed no restrictions on membership. Owners and managers of businesses made up over half its members. The society's secretary explained, "The factory engineer is more and more a manager of men. . . . The engineer must be what he is often called, a businessman."[14] The American Society of Civil Engineers, founded in 1852, maintained high membership standards and sought to foster a strong sense of professionalism, but still it displayed great deference to business interests, ignoring in its publications issues like railroad mismanagement and dealing gingerly with industrial safety.

The American Institute of Electrical Engineers, founded in 1884, restricted full participation in the organization to professional electrical engineers in active practice, and commonly took positions against the interests of industrial corporations. Henry Gantt, a close associate of Frederick Taylor, in 1916 organized The New Machine, a group of fifty mechanical engineers who sought "political as well as economic power" to "take control of the huge and delicate apparatus of industry out of the hands of idlers and wastrels and deliver it over to those who understand its operations."[15] Morris Llewellyn Cooke, another Taylor disciple, served as Philadelphia's Director of Public Works, initiating a suit against the Philadelphia Electric Company to force it to lower its rates. Cooke denounced the cozy relationship between engineers and utility executives, criticizing leading members of his profession by name.

Engineers who sought independent professional status supported strict state licensure, but those who identified with management opposed it as an improper infringement on business. As a result, by 1921 only nineteen states had any kind of licensure, and these states rarely required formal education to receive a license. Licensure progressed slowly for another reason. In engineering, unlike law or medicine, no significant number of women, immigrants, African-Americans, or others from working-class backgrounds sought to enter the profession, and the old-stock Protestant men who dominated it did not need licensure to keep out people who threatened their social status. Those seeking an autonomous profession remained disappointed, but the majority in the profession readily

worked as corporate employees, enjoying, as their careers progressed, the monetary and status rewards of business managers.

Academicians, unlike engineers, gained substantial professional
autonomy and social status, exercising wide discretion over research and teaching, controlling the standards for entry and practice
in their respective disciplines, and playing an expanding role as
experts in public policy. Until the 1870s, higher education in the
United States consisted of small denominational colleges in which
four or five professors, usually ministers, tried to inculcate mental
discipline and morality in students through a fixed curriculum of
classical languages and philosophy. In the half century following
the Civil War, states established "land grant" universities with federal help, and industrialists endowed new private universities like
Cornell, Johns Hopkins, the University of Chicago, and Stanford.
Old liberal arts colleges like Harvard, Yale, and Columbia embraced research, graduate study, and the new academic disciplines.
With colleges offering preparation for a growing number of occupations, higher education enrollments reached 238,000 in 1900 and
598,000 in 1920. University scholars pursued specialized research,
founding the modern academic disciplines and professional societies to disseminate the latest developments in each field through
conferences and publications.

Like other professionals of the period, the new academicians
sought control of their professions. State licensure never became an
issue, because the Ph.D. degree, begun in Germany but quickly
developed in a small number of American universities, provided
more than adequate certification of professional competence and
social respectability. Professors faced a different problem. They
worked as employees of large, corporate-style institutions whose
presidents had formidable powers to hire and fire faculty and determine their salaries. Businessmen endowed private institutions
and served on their boards of trustees. Elected officials, sensitive
to political pressure, usually appointed state university trustees.

Faculty members did not enjoy tenure in the years before World
War I, and a small number of professors, particularly in the social

sciences, lost jobs because they expressed views unacceptable to their presidents and trustees. William Rainey Harper, the founding president of the University of Chicago, in 1895 dismissed economist Edward Bemis, a critic of laissez-faire determinist economics, after Bemis denounced the railroads during the Pullman strike. In 1894, the University of Wisconsin regents tried liberal economist Richard Ely on charges of favoring strikes and boycotts by labor unions, but ultimately dropped the charges and issued a strong statement affirming academic freedom. These and several other celebrated cases, although relatively rare, reminded professors of the dangers of unpopular public advocacy. In 1915, a group of academicians organized the American Association of University Professors (AAUP) to strengthen their professional autonomy. Arguing that only professors could evaluate the work of others in their discipline, and that unrestricted inquiry served the public good, the organization's declaration of principles on academic freedom asserted: "University teachers should be understood to be, with respect to the conclusions reached and expressed by them, no more subject to the control of the trustees, than are judges subject to the control of the President, with respect to their decisions."[16]

Although they lacked secure academic tenure, in most other ways professors quickly gained considerable control over their disciplines and most academic activities within their institutions. Professors remained free to determine the subjects and methods of their research. They also controlled academic appointments and the award of higher degrees. Overwhelmingly old-stock white Protestants, leading professors resisted the entrance of Jews and Catholics into fields like classics, literature, and history, but less so into sociology, anthropology, or law. They barred African-Americans, like the brilliant Harvard-trained historian and sociologist W. E. B. Du Bois, entirely from faculty positions except in separate black institutions. Catholic academicians taught primarily at one of several dozen Catholic institutions which catered largely to working-class children or grandchildren of immigrants.

They also kept women from faculty positions in the major disciplines. Given these obstacles, many women academicians welcomed the opportunity to teach at all-female colleges controlled by women. Other women forged academic careers by developing new female-oriented fields like home economics, also called sanitary or domestic science, which sought to develop scientific knowledge of nutrition and popularize it for homemakers. Ellen Swallow Richards, an 1870 graduate of Vassar College, founded the field in the 1880s and 1890s. The first woman admitted to graduate study in chemistry at the Massachusetts Institute of Technology (MIT), she argued for the application of science to women's domestic sphere. "Laboratory work, rightly carried out, makes women better housekeepers, better cooks, better wives, and mothers more fitted to care for the versatile American youth," she stated in 1880.[17] As an instructor in sanitary chemistry, Richards worked with MIT professors to analyze water samples and food composition. She wrote popular works on nutrition, organized the first national conference on home economics, and in 1908 became the founding president of the American Home Economics Association. In female-oriented fields like home economics, as in women's colleges, leading female academicians could enjoy the autonomy over admission of students, appointments, curricula, research, and publication that men exercised in the vast majority of universities and disciplines.

The leaders of the new academic professions, both men and women, also eagerly sought public recognition of their expertise. Social scientists at the University of Wisconsin developed close ties to progressive governor Robert M. La Follette, who held office from 1901 to 1906. La Follette organized a "lunch club" at which professors and legislators discussed state policy issues. He appointed professors to public bodies and relied heavily on the advice of one of Wisconsin's leading liberal economists, John R. Commons, whom he named to a commission on factory working conditions. Professors in private universities likewise used their expertise as leaders in numerous reform movements. Charles R. Henderson, a Baptist minister and sociologist at the University of Chicago, served as president of the citywide charity organization, played a key role in city government programs for the unemployed, and helped establish workmen's compensation. Political scientist Charles E. Merriam, Henderson's colleague at the University of Chicago and a pioneer in the study of city government and public administration, won election to the Chicago city council, becoming the central figure in progressive political reform in that city.

Academicians also dominated national progressive advocacy groups like the American Association for Labor Legislation (AALL), organized, according to one of its founders, to offer the "laboring classes . . . assistance and guidance . . . from the professional classes" to formulate and secure government policies that addressed workers' problems.[18] By applying their expertise to the social and economic problems of their society, professors, unlike engineers, enhanced their social status and bolstered their claim to professional autonomy.

SOCIAL WORK

Progressive reform, which divided engineers and enhanced professors' status as experts, also gave birth to professional social workers, who sought public recognition of their expertise on the problems of poor, handicapped, and socially deviant people. Largely controlled by women, this new field offered a rare opportunity for female professional autonomy.

Social work originated in the charity organization and settlement movements, which began quite differently. In the years after the Civil War, private charities in cities across the country, faced with growing poverty, banded together to make charity more "scientific." "Friendly visitors," volunteer women from well-to-do homes, visited the poor to determine if they were in genuine need and to assess the kind and amount of aid required. Specialized charities dispensed aid through a central charity organization, based upon the findings of the friendly visitor. Paid "caseworkers" soon replaced

friendly visitors. Idealistic young women and men opened the first
settlement houses in the late 1880s and early 1890s where residents
lived, and they worked among the poor in the immigrant slums of
large cities. The charity organization workers initially scoffed at social settlements, which they considered unscientific and indiscriminate.
The settlements thought the charities condescended to the poor and
failed to recognize that poverty came mostly from social conditions
rather than individual defects. But by the turn of the century, recognizing that they shared a common concern with the problems of
the urban poor, they began to exchange views at the annual gath-
ering of the charity workers, the National Conference of Charities
and Correction. Charity and settlement leaders moved closer together, finally renaming their organization the National Conference
of Social Work in 1917.

Women made up slightly more than half of all social workers in
1910 and 62 percent in 1920, and they held leadership positions
in the profession. Women controlled some settlement houses, including Hull House and the Henry Street Settlement, and men,
often graduates of Protestant theological seminaries, headed others,
such as Chicago Commons and Boston's South End House. Women
and men played roughly equal roles in executive and supervisory
positions in social agencies and in the upper reaches of the Russell
Sage Foundation, which provided much of the financial support for
the development of social work research and education in these
years.

As social work gained professional recognition, differences remained between leaders with roots in the charity organization movement, who thought social workers should concentrate on the direct
delivery of social services by caseworkers, and those tied to the
settlement movement, who believed that social work should focus
on social advocacy and the development and administration of social welfare policy. Differences emerged also between those who
wanted elaborate academic prerequisites for practice and those who
preferred practical training in social agencies.

In the first decade of the new century, social agencies in several cities established programs to train their employees in casework, charity administration, child welfare, organized recreation, and supervision of juvenile offenders. At the Chicago School of Civics and Philanthropy, Hull House residents Julia Lathrop, Sophonisba P. Breckinridge, and Edith Abbott headed a policy research program that studied the causes of poor housing, juvenile delinquency, and similar issues. In 1920, they wrested control of the Chicago social work school from Graham Taylor, head resident of Chicago Commons settlement, by bringing it into the University of Chicago. Breckenridge and Abbott transformed it from a vocational institute into a university graduate program in social welfare policy and administration whose students held baccalaureate degrees.

Samuel McCune Lindsay, a Columbia University political science professor, had similar goals for the New York School of Philanthropy, which he directed from 1907 to 1912, but leaders of New York's charity agencies resisted and ultimately forced Lindsay to resign. They argued that social work education should provide practical training for agency workers and opposed raising the academic requirements for professional practice. In a contest that mirrored those in law and engineering, social workers seeking the most selective standards for admission to and practice of the profession established only limited beachheads. Still, social work provided women, constrained in other professions, with a unique opportunity for career advancement, social status, and professional autonomy.

THE WOMEN'S PROFESSIONS: TEACHING, LIBRARIANSHIP, AND NURSING

Several other professional occupations seemed, like social work, uniquely appropriate for middle-class women's supposed domestic proclivities. By 1910, women made up 80 percent of the nation's teachers, 93 percent of nurses, and 79 percent of librarians. Leaders in each field aspired to the professional autonomy, social status, and economic rewards enjoyed by leading practitioners in other fields. But these leaders had only minimal success in raising the educational prerequisites for practice or in obtaining adequate pay for tasks seen as "women's work." And control of the institutions in which they worked remained largely in the hands of men, often men who were not even members of the profession.

States began establishing public school systems in the decades before the Civil War, and although men held most of the antebellum teaching positions, women avidly sought these jobs as men moved on to more lucrative opportunities. Some women college graduates also became teachers, particularly in the high schools, but grade school teaching required only a high school education or less. Normal schools, usually attached to high schools, provided training in pedagogy for new teachers.

As public schools expanded, the number of teachers tripled between 1870 and 1900, and women filled the new positions. Teaching paid poorly, and in many places law or custom prohibited married women from holding teaching positions. Young women from modest old-stock white families in rural areas and small towns filled most teaching jobs, although immigrants or children of immigrants, particularly among the Irish, made up about a quarter of all teachers by 1900. Black teachers in segregated schools held about 5 percent of all teaching jobs.

Female teachers enjoyed limited opportunities for career advancement beyond the classroom, but a few succeeded in moving into supervisory positions. Julia Richman, born in New York City in 1855 of well-off German-speaking Jewish immigrant parents, moved up by demonstrating leadership ability, introducing educational innovations, and working outside of school with influential German-Jewish reformers and philanthropists in programs to Americanize Jewish immigrants. Becoming a vice-principal in 1882 and a principal two years later, Richman became district superintendent for the schools of the Lower East Side in 1903. The first woman to hold this position in New York, she emerged as a leading figure in Lower East Side reform, establishing a settlement house for teachers in which she took up residence.

Ella Flagg Young, the most successful woman educator in the years before World War I, moved up steadily in the Chicago schools through her connections with progressive reformers like Jane Addams and academicians like John Dewey. Serving as a teacher and principal, she in turn became assistant superintendent, completed a Ph.D. in education under John Dewey at the University of Chicago, taught at the university, and then returned to the public schools as principal of Chicago Normal School in 1904. The Board of Education named her superintendent of schools in 1909, the first woman to head a large school system anywhere in the United States. In this position, she tried to raise teacher salaries and enhance teachers' professional autonomy by establishing teachers' councils. Young vigorously fought political interference in the hiring and promotion of teachers and in the selection of textbooks, antagonizing some members of the Board of Education. After six tumultuous years she resigned the superintendency when the board voted to ban membership in the Chicago Teachers Union.

Young's experiences illustrate some of the obstacles to professionalization of schoolteaching in the Progressive Era. Although a growing number of school systems began requiring a college education as a prerequisite for teaching, government officials, school board members, and administrators refused to grant significant autonomy and adequate pay to classroom teachers. Teachers did not always accept these conditions passively. Some left teaching for office work, which paid about the same. Female teachers in several urban school systems formed unions to seek improved salaries and working conditions, but school boards, as in Chicago, often dealt ruthlessly with them.

Women also dominated the growing public library field, holding nine-tenths of library jobs by 1920. Public libraries, underfunded and managed by politically appointed boards, gave librarians the lowest pay of all women professionals. Although university library schools taught librarians to organize, classify, and care for books, the average library worker had limited opportunities for independent work.

Women librarians often described their work as an extension of their traditional sphere as guardians of culture. During the Progressive Era, a university-educated elite among library workers in large cities, inspired by the settlement houses, began to concentrate their efforts on working-class and immigrant children. Libraries had traditionally barred children, fearing that an interest in fiction could distract them from schoolwork. However, settlement houses had already established small children's libraries, and soon thereafter public librarians opened children's rooms and organized clubs, classes, exhibits, and festivals. One librarian, acknowledging that "we cannot help an adult very much about his reading," enthused that "the child, we are certainly forming like clay in the hands of the potter."[19] Despite these efforts, most library workers remained poorly paid functionaries with little professional autonomy or status.

Nurses fared no better. As hospitals became important in American medical care after the Civil War, many started training programs for nurses, relying upon the labor of nursing students to care for patients. The number of graduates grew from 157 students in 1880 to 14,980 in 1920. The expansion of nurse-training programs glutted the market for private-duty nurses. Nurses educated in the best schools, who dominated the nursing professional associations, pushed to upgrade education and standards for admission to the profession, and sought independence from male physicians and hospital administrators, but with little success. The bulk of practicing nurses, many not even high school graduates, needed "respectable" remunerative employment and did not share the aspiration for higher professional standards and status. Despite their education and expertise, then, teachers, librarians, and nurses, the major female-dominated professions, secured only modest remuneration and little autonomy in the Progressive Era.

The growth in the size and prestige of expert professions, one of the major developments of the Progressive Era, profoundly reshaped America's social structure, its culture, and the way it provided services and solved problems. Professions like medicine, law, engineering, academe, and social work took their modern shape in these years. Others, like teaching, librarianship, and nursing, barely began the process of achieving professional autonomy and status. Yet in every field, professional elites committed to restricting entry and upgrading standards struggled against parochial and locally oriented practitioners, those having limited access to formal education, working-class people, immigrants, and African-Americans. Leaders of male-dominated professions worked to keep out women. Even professionals of the same social background, such as engineers, struggled over differing professional ideals.

Historians have shown that the new professionals of the Progressive Era formed a middle class that substantially created the modern bureaucratic culture of contemporary America. Yet whatever values these new middle-class professionals shared, they remained divided by social origin, ideology, and sex. Professionalization in the Progressive Era created competition for economic rewards, social status, and autonomy, producing losers as well as winners.

8

THE PROGRESSIVE DISCOURSE
IN AMERICAN POLITICS

Woodrow Wilson's words resonated with millions of Americans. Campaigning for President in 1912, he told voters that in the age of corporate capitalism "the individual has been submerged" and "individuality is swallowed up. . . . All over the Union," Wilson continued, "people are coming to feel they have no control over the course of their affairs."[1] Wilson's opponents—President William Howard Taft, former President Theodore Roosevelt, and socialist Eugene V. Debs—agreed, each in his own way. The assumption that the concentration of industrial wealth had robbed individual Americans of their autonomy and threatened the nation's democratic control over its destiny permeated America's political discourse.

In the Gilded Age, farmers, workers, and intellectuals who pointed to the erosion of autonomy and democratic government under corporate capitalism dissented from the era's dominant laissez-faire and social Darwinist ideology. Beginning in the 1890s, however, large numbers of reformers, social scientists, politicians, theolgians, and journalists systematically challenged these rigid ideas. For the first time in history, these intellectual insurgents argued, advances in scientific knowledge made it possible for people to control social evolution. An activist government and a properly organized society could re-empower individuals, invigorate American democracy, and allow Americans once again to shape their destiny. Early in the new century, these challengers of the prevailing orthodoxy captured the nation's political discourse. The central issue of politics became not whether government could restore individual autonomy and preserve democracy in an age of industrial concentration, but how.

Underlying hundreds of proposals and dozens of organized reform movements lay fundamentally new assumptions. First, humans were basically rational, so the citizenry of America, if properly informed and empowered, would insist that government eschew special interests to pursue the common good. Therefore, the machinery of government had to be altered to make it responsive to the popular will.

Second, the natural and social sciences could now discover the causes of the nation's social problems and offer solutions. Since the environment largely shaped people, most social ills could be cured by altering social conditions. Jane Addams argued in *Twenty Years at Hull House* (1910) that "the extraordinary pliability of human nature" made it "impossible to set any bounds to the moral capabilities which might unfold under ideal civic and educational conditions." Toledo's celebrated reform mayor, Samuel Jones, agreed. "Those who have studied the causes of poverty and social evils have discovered that nine-tenths of the world's misery is *preventible*," he proclaimed. "Science has countless treasures yet to be revealed."[2]

The activist government envisioned by reformers relied upon scientific experts to staff new, impartial administrative agencies. But toward what end? Undergirding progressives' technocratic faith in science and expertise lay a third assumption, a powerful if vaguely defined faith in Christian morality. "For the first time in religious history," wrote the activist Protestant theologian Walter Rauschenbusch in 1907, "religious energy" can be directed by "scientific knowledge" toward a "comprehensive and continuous reconstruction of social life in the name of God."[3] Inspired by a religious faith in inherent human goodness, reformers pursued their fight against society's ills with evangelical fervor.

Middle-class women, largely excluded from public life in mid-nineteenth-century America, played a substantial role in creating this new political discourse. Before the Civil War, the opinion makers of American society argued that women belonged in the home, nurturing their families and tending to the cultural and spiritual development of their children. Worldly matters of economics and politics belonged properly to men. In the late nineteenth century and through the Progressive Era, women organized a host of clubs and other female institutions for literary, cultural, and religious purposes and established private agencies to care for the sick, alcoholics, poor women, abused and neglected children, and others in need, arguing that their innate ability as nurturers qualified them uniquely for these tasks. They began to agitate for government services to the poor and dependent and for public policies to improve the home and family life, insisting that as mothers and nurturers they needed to vote to protect the domestic sphere. "Woman's place is in the Home," wrote suffragist Rheta Childe Dorr in 1910, "but Home is not contained within the four walls of an individual home. Home is the community."[4]

By 1912, writers and politicians routinely referred to this dramatic outpouring of reform energy as "progressivism" or "the progressive movement." Proponents of reforms lost at least as many battles as they won; conservative opponents of change remained powerful in many places. At the same time, many ordinary Americans, as we have seen, did not feel nearly so powerless as reformers portrayed them, or so deprived of an imagined individualism and autonomy now lost. Having never exercised significant political power, many workers, immigrants, and farmers had difficulty understanding the threat to democracy which reformers talked about with such passion. Southern African-Americans disenfranchised by politicians who called themselves progressives could hardly view reform as a struggle to re-empower American citizens. Others fought against reforms they found intrusive. Farmers ignored the entreaties of agricultural extension experts to increase production with scientific methods. Rural people rejected progressive school centralization, working-class men opposed temperance, and children resisted organized play.

Nonetheless, progressivism defined the language of political debate. "The trusts" and "the special interests" threatened "democracy" and "individual freedom." Laissez-faire government could not restore "competition" and bring about the social and economic "efficiency" that industrialism promised. The structures of government must be modified to respond to "the will of the people." An educated and informed citizenry would demand "justice" and do what was "morally right." Using such language, progressives captured the discourse of politics, defining the terms within which competing players argued their positions on corporate regulation, labor, conservation, welfare, women's rights, representative government and the other great issues of the day.

ASCENDANCE OF THE PROGRESSIVE DISCOURSE, 1900–1912

The depression of the 1890s had shaken middle-class faith in laissez-faire and heightened unease with the consequences of industrial capitalism. Recovery from the depression after 1897 did not diminish anxiety about economic concentration and American democracy, and the new wave of corporate consolidations between 1895 and 1904 exacerbated these fears. The dissenters who believed that an informed polity could use government to solve the problems caused by industrialism and economic concentration now moved to the center of American political debate.

The rise of investigative journalism in the first decade of the century, with sensational exposés of government corruption and corporate greed, both reflected and advanced the political mood. Earlier journalists had occasionally offered a detailed picture of some problem, as police reporter Jacob Riis did in his text and accompanying photographs on urban poverty, *How the Other Half Lives: Studies Among the Tenements of New York*, published in

1890. But the new investigative journalism did not limit itself to a single story.

S. S. McClure, who came to America as a young boy from Northern Ireland and grew up on farms in Indiana and Illinois, saw the potential for profit in mass-market public affairs journalism. In 1902, *McClure's* ran the first of a series of articles in which staff writer Ida Tarbell meticulously detailed how John D. Rockefeller crushed competitors in putting together the Standard Oil trust, and another series by Lincoln Steffens on municipal corruption. Steffens' seven articles described, for example, how the mayor of Minneapolis fired nearly half the members of the police force upon taking office and how some of those he retained on the force planned a burglary; or the way a firm owned by Pittsburgh's Democratic Party political boss received nearly all of the city's paving contracts at a grossly inflated cost. These articles caused a sensation, and the circulation of *McClure's* shot up.

Other exposés followed in both *McClure's* and other magazines that jumped on the investigative bandwagon. Journalist Ray Stannard Baker exposed exploitative labor conditions on railroads and in mines; David Graham Phillips depicted the "treason" of the U.S. Senate; Burton J. Hendrick revealed corruption in the life insurance industry. Many stories resulted in criminal prosecutions. These investigative magazine serials, often published afterward as books, reached millions of Americans.

The frenzy for journalistic revelations declined quickly after 1907, the public's interest in scandal seemingly sated. President Roosevelt condemned scandalmongers in April 1906, comparing them to a character John Bunyan created in *Pilgrim's Progress*, "the Man with the Muck-rake, who typifies the man who in this life constantly refuses to see aught that is lofty and fixes his eyes with solemn intentness only on that which is vile and debasing."[5] The pejorative term "muckraker" stuck.

Still, Roosevelt did not denigrate the importance of serious investigations and public dissemination. Indeed, meticulous research made accessible to the general public through magazines, books, and exhibits became a staple of progressive reform. Paul Kellogg, managing editor of the social work periodical *Charities and the Commons*, directed a massive study of the industrial and social conditions of Pittsburgh, begun in 1907 and published over the next several years in six volumes and thirty-five different articles. Kellogg described it as "in its origins a journalistic project."[6] The Pittsburgh Survey quickly inspired similar reform-oriented studies in other cities, and *Charities and the Commons* tellingly changed its name to *Survey* in 1909.

In this atmosphere, the pioneering urban civic and social reform of the 1890s expanded in the new century until reform proposals dominated city politics. In one metropolis after another, businessmen, lawyers, and other professionals sought revised charters giving city governments greater "home rule" authority to provide services and regulate urban life, developed new methods of budgeting, contracting, and administration, demanded lower rates and better service from traction and utility companies, and promoted party primaries for city offices or nonpartisan municipal elections to minimize political influence in city management. They also advocated the "short ballot," reducing the number of officials elected at one time so that voters could learn about the candidates. These reforms, they argued, would enable citizens to control their city government and the government to control the conditions of urban life.

The development of commission and city manager government illustrates the thrust of urban civic reform. Advocates of the commission system argued that dividing responsibility between legislative and executive branches ill suited cities, which existed to deliver a myriad of services. Commission government combined traditional executive and legislative responsibility in a small body whose members stood for election citywide. Each commissioner had direct administrative responsibility for certain city departments, the full commission enacting municipal ordinances and the budget.

The commission idea took hold after Galveston, Texas, adopted it to cope with massive devastation from a hurricane in 1901. Its success in rebuilding Galveston's infrastructure and reducing the city's debt drew attention to it. Houston adopted commission government in 1906, Des Moines and Dallas in 1907, and Memphis in 1909. By 1911, nineteen states had given their cities authority to opt for commission government, although almost none of the nation's largest cities did so. In 1913, Dayton, Ohio, went further, adopting a city manager system in which an elected city council employed an expert manager as the executive head of the government. The city manager system soon replaced the commission as the municipal reformers' preferred structure.

Commission and city manager government, the short ballot, and similar reforms appealed readily to business executives and professionals who valued systematic management and expertise and who despised political bosses and their patronage system. These plans replaced a fragmented and decentralized mode of urban service delivery, in which working-class neighborhoods had considerable influence, with a centralized government more readily controlled by leading citizens. Working-class people rarely supported these structural reforms.

Reformers simultaneously put forward a host of proposals aimed at the cities' social ills. Settlement residents, women's club members, clergymen, and social scientists provided numerous services to the poor and disadvantaged privately, at the same time pressing to expand government's scope. They called for kindergartens, vocational education and guidance programs, public health nurses, adult education classes, and recreational activities in public schools; neighborhood playgrounds and parks; agencies to protect newly arriving immigrants and to teach them English; sanitary improvements, inspection of milk sold in the city, and public baths; and elimination of commercialized prostitution in "vice districts." Many argued for municipal ownership of public utilities. Some in the North supported civil rights for African-Americans or helped to provide social services and education for rural black migrants from the South, but most accepted racial inequality and Southern black disenfranchisement. Overall, reformers brought about a significant expansion in the scope and responsibility of city government, and in some cases also greater intrusion of the state into the lives of lower-class families.

The movement to improve housing conditions in the crowded working-class areas of cities typified the thrust of urban social reform, and its limitations. Settlement house residents abhorred housing conditions in their neighborhoods. Lawrence Veiller, a resident of University Settlement in New York in the 1890s, prepared an exhibit in 1900 illustrating crowding, deterioration, and lack of air, light, and sanitation in working-class tenements. Theodore Roosevelt, then governor of New York, attended the exhibit and, duly horrified, established a State Tenement House Commission. Veiller, the commission's secretary, drafted a new housing code requiring ventilation, toilets, and running water in each apartment. The legislature passed it quickly, and reformers got the city government to establish a Tenement House Department to enforce the new code. Housing reformers elsewhere followed New York's lead, often consulting Veiller. Nonetheless, regulation could eliminate only the worst abuses. Developers did not build safe and decent low-income housing, because it did not pay. Although a few philanthropically oriented businessmen created model low-income tenements, Veiller and other housing reformers opposed government housing construction or subsidy, arguing that cities should regulate, but not build, rental housing.

In many cities, reformist mayors in the mold of Hazen Pingree and "Golden Rule" Jones established alliances with both structural and social reformers in the early years of the twentieth century, strengthening the executive power of the mayor and expanding the role of city government. The best-known included Brand Whitlock in Toledo, Mark Fagan in Jersey City, Seth Low in New York, Carter Harrison in Chicago, John Weaver in Philadelphia, Edward Dempsey in Cincinnati, and especially Tom Johnson in Cleveland. Johnson, a former congressman who had made a fortune running a streetcar company (which he sold before taking office), staffed his administration with men he described as combining "efficiency and a belief in the fundamental principles of democracy."[7] Johnson dramatically improved the police force and the water department and increased the number of city workers hired through the civil service at the same time that he forced down streetcar fares and gas and water rates. He altered the tax system to place a greater burden on corporations, took over garbage collection and street cleaning, built parks, recreation facilities, bathhouses, and a tuberculosis sanitarium, enforced the housing code strictly, and established city inspection of meat and milk. Lincoln Steffens, whose exposures of municipal corruption had created a sensation, called Johnson's Cleveland the best-governed city in the United States.

Many reform mayors did battle with traditional big-city machines, but as urban reform gained ground, traditional party bosses discovered advantages to alliances with middle-class reformers. Stronger executive authority enhanced bosses' power and ability to govern. Moreover, the machine's working-class supporters benefited from many progressive social reforms. Charles Murphy, the head of Tammany Hall, New York's Democratic organization, selected candidates with interests in social reform who nonetheless remained loyal to the machine, young politicians like Al Smith and Robert Wagner.

Smith, the child of Irish parents, grew up poor on New York's East Side; Robert F. Wagner, who had emigrated to America with his family at age nine, grew up in a predominantly German section of Manhattan, where his father, a displaced craftsman, worked as a janitor, his mother took in laundry, and his five older brothers and sisters left school early to help support the family. Wagner and Smith supported many of the efforts of settlement house residents and other reformers to address the economic problems of New York's poor.

Faced with a revolt against Tammany by upstate clean government reformers, Murphy selected Smith and Wagner to lead the Democratic-controlled Assembly and Senate in Albany in 1911, just as a tragic fire at the Triangle Shirtwaist Factory pushed issues of factory safety, working conditions, and wages to the fore. One hundred and forty-six women died in the fire, many trampled to death or falling from upper-story windows, the only way out. When preliminary investigations revealed that the factory blatantly violated building and fire code standards, Smith and Wagner joined with settlement house residents like Henry and Belle Moskowitz and Frances Perkins to win support for extensive social welfare and labor legislation. The progressive political program, originally espoused by a segment of the middle class, now bridged class and cultural differences in New York and elsewhere.

Progressive reform also captured many state governments in the early twentieth century. Concerned about corruption and the power of the trusts over elected officials, reformers called for primary elections, laws prohibiting corrupt practices, campaign expenditure limits, strengthened voter registration systems to minimize voter fraud, the short ballot, initiative and referendum in which voters could bypass the legislature to enact or repeal laws, and recall procedures whereby citizens could require an elected official to face the voters prior to the normally scheduled election. Most state-level progressives also favored granting women the right to vote. Southern progressives worked vigorously to disenfranchise African-Americans, whom they considered unqualified to vote.

These democratic reforms, progressive publicists like Benjamin Parke De Witt argued, gave "to the people direct and continuous control over all the branches of government" so that they could "direct their attention more profitably to the problems connected with the prevention and relief of social and economic distress."[8] Progressives joined organized labor and business groups to win passage of workmen's compensation laws in most states, providing payments to injured or disabled workers without resort to lengthy litigation, and increased state regulation of safety in factories and

mines. Following the success of Hull House in Illinois, they established juvenile courts with probation officers in twenty-two states
by 1912, pressed to outlaw child labor, and secured widow's pension programs in twenty states by 1913 so dependent mothers could
stay home with their children. They also helped create state commissions to regulate railroads, utilities, and insurance companies.

The state-level campaigns initiated by female settlement house
residents and clubwomen to regulate the conditions of women working in industry highlighted again their political skill at engaging
government in the welfare of working-class families. Inspired by
the Illinois factory law of 1893, which limited employment of
women to eight hours a day, reformers in several other states secured women's protective laws; simultaneously, women in a number
of cities created leagues which boycotted "unethical" manufacturers and businesses, coming together in 1899 to form the National
Consumers' League (NCL). Under Florence Kelley's leadership, the
NCL led the campaign to regulate female and child labor.

When, in 1906, a laundryman named Curt Muller challenged
Oregon's ten-hour statute for women, Kelley persuaded Louis Brandeis to defend the law before the U.S. Supreme Court. The ground-
breaking "Brandeis brief" contained two pages of legal argument
and over a hundred pages of sociological data and expert opinion
which Kelley and NCL staffer Josephine Goldmark (Brandeis'
sister-in-law) assembled from the state leagues and associates
across the country. Brandeis used this evidence to prove that over-
work had damaged the health of mothers and potential mothers.
Therefore, he argued, the state had a compelling need to regulate
women's labor. Kelley believed that the state should regulate all
labor, but she knew from previous rulings that the courts would
reject that principle. The Court, in a landmark decision, upheld the
Oregon law. Following their victory in Muller v. Oregon, the Consumers' League, organized labor, the General Federation of
Women's Clubs, and other women's groups won restrictive legislation in state after state.

Seeing the support these well-organized movements for reform attracted, many state politicians embraced reform programs. Robert M. La Follette of Wisconsin led the way. Born on a farm in Dane County, left fatherless in his first year of life, La Follette moved with his mother to nearby Madison in the 1870s and attended the University of Wisconsin while working to help support his family. After graduation, he read law, attended the university law school, and began legal practice. A superb orator, he decided to run for district attorney, upsetting the candidate backed by Dane County's Republican boss. Elected to Congress before the age of thirty, the independent-minded La Follette embraced the increasingly vigorous civic reform movements in his state in the early 1890s in a bid to become Wisconsin's governor. In 1900, after two unsuccessful tries, he won the Republican nomination and the general election on a platform that called for direct primaries for state and national offices, and equitable taxation and state regulation of railroads.

La Follette made Wisconsin the model for state-level progressive reform. His administration readily won changes in the tax laws, establishing an inheritance tax and forcing railroads to pay the same rates as farms and businesses. He fought a bitter and protracted battle to establish party primaries, ultimately winning when the matter went before the voters in a 1904 referendum. Over much opposition, he got the legislature to give the state Railroad Commission authority to overturn rates and to conduct investigations. He secured initiative, referendum, and recall, a bill restricting lobbying, and a merit system for minor state offices. He built up the University of Wisconsin and relied on its liberal economists. Elected to the U.S. Senate in 1906, La Follette left behind a progressive Republican Party that ruled the state continuously until World War I, expanding state regulation of business and embracing labor, social welfare, and child labor reforms, natural resource conservation, public health programs, and food inspection. "The Wisconsin Idea" spread to other states, pursued with varying degrees of success by such governors as Charles Evans Hughes in New

York, Woodrow Wilson in New Jersey, Albert B. Cummings in Iowa, William U'Ren in Oregon, Hiram Johnson in California, Joseph Folk in Missouri, and many others.

In the South, women's clubs and others pushed for expanded educational opportunities, school consolidation, public health programs, child labor restrictions, and laws against consumption of alcohol. A new breed of politicians there combined virulent hatred of African-Americans with programs to regulate corporations and extend social reform. Having removed African-Americans from the polity, many Southern politicians and reformers felt they could address the issues of democratic governance (for whites) and corporate power that dominated the nation's politics elsewhere. James K. Vardaman, for example, a flamboyant orator who had agitated for party primaries, won Mississippi's governorship in 1903, the first time the state's voters selected the Democratic gubernatorial nominee. An effective grass-roots campaigner known popularly as the "White Chief" for the color of his suits and for his racial views, Vardaman appealed to poor white voters by attacking African-Americans, corporations, and rich Mississippi delta planters. Once elected, he expanded social and educational services for whites, tightened state regulation of corporations, and eliminated convict leasing.

The political changes reshaping state and local politics in the first decade of the new century soon reverberated in Washington. On September 6, 1901, an anarchist named Leon Czolgosz approached President McKinley from a receiving line at an exposition in Buffalo; his bandaged hand concealed a gun, and Czolgosz shot the President twice in the stomach. McKinley lingered eight days before succumbing to internal bleeding and infection. Vice President Theodore Roosevelt, forty-two years old, became the youngest man to serve as President.

Born in New York to a well-to-do merchant family of Dutch ancestry, Roosevelt grew up privileged, traveling widely and developing a love of strenuous outdoor activities and hunting despite boyhood illnesses. Earning a Phi Beta Kappa key at Harvard University, Roosevelt displayed a passion for politics uncharacteristic of Eastern aristocrats. He served in the New York State legislature, as a member of New York City's Police Commission, and ran unsuccessfully for mayor. Spending time as a rancher in the Dakota Territory in the 1880s, "TR" also read voraciously and wrote ten books before becoming President, including five works of history. Roosevelt glorified masculine physical strength and fighting ability, and when President McKinley declared war on Spain in 1898, TR raised his own cavalry unit and rushed it to Cuba, where he led his Rough Riders up San Juan Hill in a battle that made him a national hero. He readily won election as governor of New York, and McKinley selected him as his running mate in 1900 partly as a favor to New York's Republican political boss, Thomas C. Platt, who worried about tentative proposals Roosevelt had floated to increase corporate regulation and taxation. After McKinley's unexpected death, McKinley's campaign manager and close adviser Mark Hanna exclaimed bitterly that "that damned cowboy" had become President.

Although basically conservative in outlook, Roosevelt feared the excessive power of corporate wealth and the danger of working-class radicalism and class conflict. "The unscrupulous rich man who seeks to exploit and oppress those who are less well off is in spirit not opposed to, but identical with, the unscrupulous poor man who desires to plunder and oppress those who are better off," he told an audience in Syracuse in 1903.[9] Egotistical, moralistic, intelligent, driven to lead, Roosevelt used his "bully pulpit" to expound on the evils of irresponsible trusts and the need for aggressive federal policy. Skilled at cultivating and using the press, he enhanced his popularity by publicizing his personal exploits to an admiring public. He won extensive press coverage for becoming the first President to ride in an automobile, fly in an airplane, or go underwater in a submarine. The story of this great outdoorsman protecting a bear cub inspired a toy manufacturer to market a small stuffed "Teddy bear."

Roosevelt's unexpected elevation to the presidency placed the issues of corporate power and American democracy at the center of national politics at the same time that these issues dominated state and local politics in much of the country. Roosevelt made only modest changes in the role of the federal government, but he significantly reshaped public opinion about economic concentration and the role of government, dramatically altering the orthodoxies of late-nineteenth-century political thought.

Keenly aware that he had not been elected, Roosevelt proceeded cautiously in his first term. He gained a reputation as a "trustbuster" largely on the strength of his administration's prosecutions of a few large conglomerates, most notably the Northern Securities Company, a holding company put together by J. P. Morgan combining nearly all the long-distance railroads west of Chicago. In fact, Roosevelt did not oppose industrial combinations per se, only those that in his opinion did not serve the public interest. In 1902, he intervened with much fanfare to end a strike by anthracite coal miners seeking pay raises, shorter hours, and improved safety. Roosevelt spoke out publicly about the need for a fair settlement, sponsored negotiations in the White House, and got J. P. Morgan to twist the arms of intransigent mine owners. Securing a settlement, Roosevelt won acclaim for his sympathy for working men far beyond what he deserved.

The President also sponsored legislation enlarging the administrative capacity of the federal government. The Expedition Act added staff to the Justice Department to expand antitrust litigation, the Elkins Act prohibited corporations from demanding rebate payments from railroads, and the establishment of the Department of Commerce provided for a Bureau of Corporations to investigate firms involved in interstate commerce. Some corporate leaders opposed the bureau, but many others believed regulation could serve corporate interests. George Perkins of J. P. Morgan & Company mobilized business support even as Roosevelt publicly attacked John D. Rockefeller for sending telegrams to key senators demanding that this "antitrust legislation" be stopped.

In his first term, Roosevelt also embraced the nascent movement for conservation of natural resources. He rejected the position of the Sierra Club, founded in 1892, which urged that wilderness areas be protected from any human exploitation. But he also opposed the demands of Eastern lumber, mining, and industrial interests for unimpeded access to the land. Instead, he supported a utilitarian approach which balanced development and long-term preservation of forest and water resources. He backed passage of legislation proposed by Democratic senator Francis Newlands of Nevada to dedicate proceeds from the sale of public lands to irrigation and land reclamation projects, adding thirty million acres to the nation's forest reserves during his first term.

By the time of the 1904 election, Roosevelt had won broad personal popularity and established a reputation for vigorous assertion of government authority to control excessive corporate power. Facing an unbeatable opponent, the Democrats passed over William Jennings Bryan in favor of a lackluster judge from New York, Alton Parker. Roosevelt triumphed in a landslide.

Having won election in his own right, the President now moved less cautiously. He quickly got Congress to transfer authority over the greatly expanded forest reserves to the newly created U.S. Forest Service, headed by the flamboyant forester Gifford Pinchot. In 1906, TR secured passage of the Hepburn Act giving the Interstate Commerce Commission authority to set maximum railroad rates and review railroads' finances. Roosevelt also capitalized on the publication of *The Jungle*, Upton Sinclair's socialist novel exposing conditions in Chicago's stockyards. The President won passage of legislation creating the Food and Drug Administration and authorizing the Agriculture Department to inspect meat. In his last two years, Roosevelt also undertook several new antitrust prosecutions against such corporate giants as American Tobacco, Standard Oil, and Du Pont, and supported laws establishing employer liability for injuries and accidents and prohibiting child labor in the District of Columbia.

Overall, in his two terms Roosevelt strengthened the federal government's capacity to regulate railroads, food and drugs, and other corporations and to manage forest preserves and promote conservation. This enormously popular President magnified these modest achievements by mobilizing public opinion, making Americans more fully aware of the power, and danger, of unchecked economic concentration, and by projecting himself as a personal symbol of activist government. He recast the terms of political debate so that the role of government in economic life became the central issue of national politics.

As Roosevelt neared the end of his second term, political support for bolder federal action increased. Organized movements for child labor restriction, worker legislation, conservation, woman suffrage, and many other issues demanded federal action, and progressive Republican state politicians like La Follette grew restive at the slow pace of change. The Democratic Party, returning to Bryan as its 1908 nominee, adopted a broad progressive platform embracing stronger antitrust policy and railroad regulation, protection of unions from antistrike injunctions, the eight-hour day for government workers, and employer liability laws. With Republicans the nation's majority party, Taft, wearing the mantle of Teddy Roosevelt, who had handpicked him as his successor, won readily, but he polled far behind Roosevelt's showing in 1904.

Taft proved unable to mediate between the demand for more aggressive federal policy and powerful conservative resistance to it. A distinguished lawyer and experienced administrator from a prominent Cincinnati family, Taft had served as Solicitor General in the early 1890s, as a federal judge, as governor of the Philippines after the Spanish-American War, and as Roosevelt's Secretary of War. Trying to continue Roosevelt's policies, Taft's administration undertook many more antitrust prosecutions in four years than Roosevelt did in eight and put more land into federal forest reserves. The new President won legislation expanding the ICC's railroad regulatory authority and bringing telephones and the telegraph under federal regulation for the first time. Taft also cooperated with settlement house residents and social welfare progressives in supporting factory safety legislation and in establishing the U.S. Children's Bureau.

In 1903, Lillian Wald and Florence Kelley proposed a federal bureau to collect data on child welfare. They built support for the bureau through their national network of women's organizations. Just before leaving office, Theodore Roosevelt called a White House Conference on the Care of Dependent Children, in part to increase pressure on Congress to pass the Children's Bureau bill. Taft also supported the bill, and signed it into law when it finally passed in 1912.

A few years earlier, Taft's accomplishments might have been recognized as substantial progressive achievements, but the national political discourse had changed dramatically under Roosevelt, and, unlike his predecessor, Taft could not project a progressive image. Taft gave reluctant support to a resolution for a constitutional amendment permitting a federal income tax, which Democrats and insurgent Republicans pushed through Congress in 1909. (The Sixteenth Amendment won ratification in 1913.) He opposed progressive proposals for recall of federal judges and remained cool to an amendment for direct election of senators, passed by Congress in 1912 and ratified the following year. Taft also made political mistakes. He supported, albeit uneasily, an upward revision of tariffs pushed by business-oriented Republicans in Congress. In a complex bureaucratic struggle within his administration, Taft fired Gifford Pinchot, head of the U.S. Forest Service, antagonizing conservationists and Roosevelt. And in an important antitrust case, Taft's Justice Department implicitly criticized the former President for having approved the acquisition of the Tennessee Coal and Iron Company by U.S. Steel. Further complicating Taft's situation, progressive Republicans had defeated conservatives in several state primaries in 1910 at the same moment that the Democrats, now firmly committed to reform, took control of the House of Representatives for the first time in fifteen years. National politics moved too quickly for this cautious lawyer from Ohio.

1912: TRIUMPH OF THE PROGRESSIVE DISCOURSE

During the unfolding political events of 1912, the progressive political discourse fully displaced the limited government/social Darwinist discourse of the late nineteenth century. The writings of scholars, journalists, and theologians in the half dozen years before the 1912 election offered a systematic rationale for the now-dominant reform spirit. University of Wisconsin sociologist E. A. Ross, in his popular tract *Sin and Society* (1907), argued that society must "establish righteousness" through an activist government. Theologian Walter Rauschenbusch asserted that the Christian church had failed to establish God's kingdom on earth because it had concerned itself only with individual righteousness. "We . . . are in the midst of a vast historical movement," he wrote in *Christianity and the Social Crisis* (1907), which "if rightly directed . . . will shape humanity for good more than huge labor when the iron is cold." A better future "will have to be planned and constructed rather than fulfilled of its own momentum," wrote political theorist Herbert Croly in *The Promise of American Life* (1909), the most systematic political treatise of American progressivism. Columbia University historian James Harvey Robinson explained in *The New History* (1912) that only at the start of the twentieth century had humans learned that they could "cooperate with and direct [the] innate forces of change."[10]

In this intellectual and political environment, insurgent Republicans, who for some years had called themselves "progressives," organized the Progressive Republican League in 1911 to oppose Taft's renomination. La Follette announced plans to challenge Taft. To his consternation, Theodore Roosevelt decided in January 1912 to seek the Republican nomination himself, and most progressives in the party lined up behind the former President. Taft controlled the party machinery, however. Facing an inevitable rift, Taft fully expected to lose the election to the Democrats, but determined to protect the Republicans from what he saw as the radicalism of their insurgents and to position the party to return to power four years hence. The party's nominating convention in Chicago in early June seated Taft delegates in nearly every challenge, giving the Roosevelt forces a pretext to walk out and reassemble in an adjacent hall where the former President attacked the "treason" perpetrated by a "corrupt alliance between crooked business and crooked politics."[11]

The Democrats convened later that month in Baltimore. On the forty-third ballot, the party nominated Woodrow Wilson, a former professor of history and political science and president of Princeton University, who had won election as a progressive reformer to the governorship of New Jersey in 1910. Born in Staunton, Virginia, this son of a Presbyterian minister and seminary professor grew up in Georgia and South Carolina. He attended Princeton, studied law at the University of Virginia, and earned a Ph.D. at Johns Hopkins in 1886, teaching at Bryn Mawr and Wesleyan before returning to Princeton in 1890. Twelve years later Princeton named him president. Wilson shared Roosevelt's intellectuality, his passion for strong leadership, and his self-righteous moralism. A shrewd political tactician, he too recognized the growing importance of the press and public opinion in contemporary politics. Like Roosevelt, Wilson feared radicalism and class conflict, and wanted to direct the powerful national sentiment for reform in safe directions. But Wilson lacked Roosevelt's personal charisma. Nor did he share his militarism or his love of strenuous physical exertion.

In August, Roosevelt's supporters returned to Chicago to found the Progressive Party and nominate the former President, attracting prominent progressive writers and reformers as well as disgruntled Republicans to its banner. Herbert Croly and Walter Lippmann, intellectuals who argued for vigorous government action to control economic concentration and direct national life, advised Roosevelt on campaign issues. Many settlement house residents and social welfare reformers also supported Roosevelt.

The party's platform read like a catalogue of reform proposals of the preceding three decades: direct primaries, direct election of U.S. senators, the short ballot, initiative, referendum, and recall, campaign finance disclosure and regulation, restrictions on the power of the courts to overturn legislation and to issue injunctions against labor unions, industrial health and safety legislation, prohibition of child labor, regulation of women's hours, wages, and conditions in industry, a six-day workweek for all laborers, workmen's compensation, industrial education in public schools, government health, old-age and unemployment insurance, and strong federal regulation of corporations.

And it endorsed woman suffrage. Women reformers, heavily represented at the convention, played key roles in the campaign. Jane Addams seconded Roosevelt's nomination, although she opposed Roosevelt's decision to deny seating to black delegates from the South and to include in the party platform construction of two new battleships annually. A "Jane Addams chorus" sang "Onward, Christian Soldiers" and "The Battle Hymn of the Republic." Frances Kellor, head of the New York State Commission of Industries and Immigration and a former Hull House resident, helped to manage Roosevelt's campaign.

Election debate magnified subtle differences between the leading candidates, Roosevelt and Wilson, obscuring broad consensus on activist regulatory government. Although the Democratic Party platform did not mirror the Progressives' expansive proposals, Wilson and Roosevelt agreed on most progressive positions, differing mostly on woman suffrage and the tariff. Wilson argued against a suffrage amendment on the grounds that suffrage issues belonged to the states. Roosevelt did not support the Democrats' traditional call for a low tariff. But the heart of the campaign centered on the "trust issue," around which the candidates debated the role of an activist federal government.

Roosevelt's reputation as a "trustbuster" had never been deserved. He had preferred to prosecute trusts selectively, not for bigness itself but for bad behavior, judging goodness and badness himself. Reflecting Croly's influence, Roosevelt now called for a "New Nationalism" in which government aggressively regulated inevitable economic concentration in the public interest. In his acceptance speech at Chicago, he told the party's delegates that a "scientific solution of the mighty industrial problem which now confronts this nation" required concentration, cooperation, and control. "Through co-operation we may limit the wastes of the competitive system," he explained. "Through control by commission, we may secure freedom for fair competition, elimination of unfair practices, conservation of our natural resources, fair wages, good social conditions, and reasonable prices." The concentration of economic power required "control in order to protect the people."[12]

Wilson, attached to traditional Jeffersonian ideals of individualism and limited government, criticized Roosevelt for his eagerness to accept economic concentration and for his support of protectionist tariffs. Democrats pointed out that corporate figures, like George Perkins of U.S. Steel and J. P. Morgan & Company, supported the Progressive Party. But Wilson accepted the necessity of activist government to regulate and restrain corporate concentration. Relying on advice from Louis Brandeis, the brilliant progressive lawyer and critic of big business, Wilson suggested that regulation of trusts and elimination of protectionist tariffs could stimulate greater economic competition. He argued that activist regulatory government must maximize individual freedom and avoid paternalism. "Freedom today is something more than being left alone," he explained during the campaign. Government must "be positive, not negative merely." But "when it is proposed to set up guardians over [the] people and to take care of them by a process of tutelage and supervision, in which they play no part, I utter my absolute objection." On a campaign swing through the West in October, Wilson called on Democrats to "organize the forces of liberty in our time to make conquest of a new freedom for America."[13]

The Roosevelt-Wilson debate revealed a tension in the now dominant progressive ideology. Some progressives highlighted the ways that economic concentration robbed individual Americans of their autonomy, while others emphasized how it denied the democratic polity collective control of the nation's destiny. By 1912, both types of progressives had united behind a broad program to reform the mechanisms of democracy, regulate corporations for the public good, and protect human welfare. Both agreed on the need for activist government. They differed not so much on their specific programs as on their visions of the good society. Because Roosevelt and Wilson agreed on so much, the campaign forced them to highlight these differences in their values. Roosevelt envisioned a society of efficient large-scale enterprises directed toward national interests by a strong administrative government responsible to the democratic polity. Wilson envisioned a society in which government regulated large-scale enterprises to maximize individual autonomy.

Taft, resigned to defeat and temperamentally uncomfortable with appeals to the public, hardly campaigned. Roosevelt and Wilson largely ignored him. But the record of this conservative standard-bearer showed how profoundly the political discourse had changed since the days of Cleveland and McKinley. Although ideologically uncomfortable with activist government, Taft as President had expanded administrative agencies, vigorously prosecuted antitrust violators, pursued federal land reclamation, and supported the creation of a federal bureau to promote child welfare. The foremost conservative spokesman of 1912 asked not for laissez-faire but for judicious use of government's regulatory power, with due respect for property rights and strict adherence to court rulings.

If Taft demonstrated how far conservatives had moved away from rigid adherence to laissez-faire since the 1890s, the campaign of Eugene V. Debs, jailed by Cleveland in the railroad strike of 1894, showed that the socialist program of government in the interests of the working class and public ownership of railroads and utilities had gained respectability. The Socialist Party, founded in 1901, had polled 424,000 votes in the 1908 presidential election with Debs as its standard-bearer. By 1911, Socialist candidates had won eighteen mayoral elections, including Buffalo, Schenectady, and Milwaukee, seats in the New York and Rhode Island legislatures, and a seat in Congress; in all, Socialists held 1,150 offices in thirty-six states. Debs, running for President again in 1912, attracted large crowds to his campaign rallies.

With the Republican Party split, few doubted the election's outcome. Wilson carried forty states, outpolling Roosevelt by 2,200,000 votes. Roosevelt carried six states, and Taft two, the President running 700,000 votes behind Roosevelt. The Democrats also took control of the Senate and enlarged their majority in the House. Debs polled nearly 900,000 votes, 6 percent of the total cast in the presidential balloting and the highest number the Socialists would ever receive.

PROGRESSIVISM AT HIGH TIDE, 1913–1916

Although no candidate won a majority of the popular vote, the 1912 election provided a mandate for activist government. Wilson, whose party won majorities in the House and Senate, seized the mandate. Despite his campaign rhetoric, his policies largely built upon and extended the course charted by Roosevelt, regulating corporations rather than trying to break them up. Wilson proved a skilled legislative tactician, securing significant new laws expanding the role and apparatus of the national government. He broke a precedent set by Thomas Jefferson and followed by every subsequent President by delivering in person special messages and his annual report on "the state of the Union" in speeches before joint sessions of Congress. He also cultivated public opinion through the press, holding weekly press conferences during the first two years of his presidency.

Wilson turned immediately to three aspects of economic policy: taxation, banking and currency, and corporate regulation. House

Democrats moved speedily to reduce the tariff, but when it seemed that protectionist interests would amend the tariff legislation to death in the Senate, Wilson denounced the tariff lobby as "insidious" people spending huge sums to advance their narrow self-interest over the public good. Senator La Follette began an investigation of tariff lobbying and senators' financial stake in the tariff law, and the opposition crumbled. Wilson secured from Congress a reduction of tariff rates of about 25 percent, offsetting the revenue loss with a tax on the incomes of the wealthiest Americans authorized by the Sixteenth Amendment, ratified in February 1913. (The Supreme Court had struck down a federal income tax contained in the Wilson-Gorman tariff bill of 1894, making the income tax amendment necessary.)

Many different constituencies wanted banking and currency reform. Repeated bank failures, the shortage of credit in the South and West, and big business's continuing concern for sound money all argued for change. But different interests had different goals. Eastern bankers favored a centralized system, Westerners and Southerners a decentralized one. Some argued for a privately owned central bank over which the government would exercise little control; others wanted the government to own and operate the nation's central bank. Wilson allowed different parties to articulate their concerns as legislation progressed, then brokered the compromise legislation. The new Federal Reserve System contained a centralized and publicly appointed Federal Reserve Board in Washington supervising regional reserve banks, whose private member banks would appoint some of the regional bank directors.

To regulate corporations, Wilson backed the Clayton Antitrust Act, which outlawed specific business practices deemed to restrain trade, like price discrimination or combinations for the purpose of controlling the market for a particular product, and specified penalties for violation. Corporate leaders favored it because it clarified the antitrust laws. Organized labor welcomed its provision restricting the ability of the courts to issue injunctions for restraint of trade against striking unions. Wilson also pushed to create the Federal Trade Commission to hear complaints against unfair corporate practices without resort to antitrust prosecutions. This approach, consistent with Roosevelt's New Nationalism, drew criticism from some anticorporate progressives, who cited Wilson's own campaign rhetoric in arguing against the act. But Wilson secured passage in 1914.

Except for the modest protection afforded unions in the Clayton Act, Wilson's legislative successes in 1913 and 1914 ignored the concerns of social welfare progressives. And Wilson also deeply disappointed African-American leaders and the few white progressives who cared about civil rights when he initiated segregation in government offices where it had not existed previously and reduced the number of African-Americans appointed to government positions. But the political status of African-Americans, at most a minor concern of progressive reformers, did not hurt Wilson politically.

Democrats and Progressive Party candidates did poorly in the 1914 congressional elections, in part because of a downturn in the economy that year, worsened in the short run by international trade dislocations caused by the outbreak of war in Europe. Still, Wilson sought to expand his progressive record in the next two years, hoping to tap growing agrarian discontent in the traditionally Republican West and to win support of members of the Progressive Party. Even before the 1914 congressional elections, he had backed an act to protect the safety and regulate the conditions of merchant seamen offered by Senator La Follette, which passed Congress in February 1915. When Congress adjourned in 1916, Wilson could point to the Rural Credits Act for farmers, a federal law prohibiting child labor on products sold in interstate commerce (later struck down by the Supreme Court), a substantial increase in the income tax for the wealthy coupled with a federal inheritance tax, a program providing federal money to the states for highway construction, the Adamson Act mandating an eight-hour day for railroad workers, and the successful nomination of Louis Brandeis to the Supreme

Court over conservative opposition. He could also point to the extension of the regulatory initiatives of his first two years: a Tariff Commission to bring administrative expertise to the establishment of import duties and a Shipping Board extending federal regulation to merchant marine passenger and freight rates.

In the two years after the 1914 congressional elections, however, Wilson devoted more of his time to foreign affairs, and especially to the war in Europe. The President announced a policy of strict neutrality in the conflict, and attempted to use U.S. diplomatic pressure on Germany to protect American shipping and American passengers on British ships. In 1916, he also initiated a military preparedness program, expanding the limited fighting capacity of American armed forces.

Wilson could thus run for reelection on a progressive legislative record and as the President whose steady leadership kept the nation out of war. Theodore Roosevelt abandoned the Progressive Party and supported Charles Evans Hughes, nominated by a reunited Republican Party. Hughes, a moderately progressive former governor of New York, went to the U.S. Supreme Court in 1910, in time to avoid completely the political divisions in his party in 1912. During the campaign, Hughes and the Republicans attacked Wilson on the income tax and the Adamson Act; Roosevelt denounced the latter as class legislation. But Hughes did not call for an abandonment of activist government.

Wilson highlighted his progressive record, frequently referring to his party as the "Progressive Democrats," and endorsed woman suffrage for the first time. With the Republicans, still the nation's majority party, now reunited, the race proved close. Wilson, attracting support from Westerners, workers in industrial states, and Republican Progressives, won a narrow victory by carrying traditional Republican states like Ohio and New Hampshire, most of the states west of the Mississippi River, and the Democratic stronghold in the South. The Progressive Party nominated no candidate, and with Debs now retired the Socialist vote declined by a third. Wilson outpolled Hughes by about 600,000 popular votes, winning 277 electoral votes against Hughes's 254. Democrats retained small margins in both houses of Congress. Progressive reform organizations remained active throughout the country during Wilson's first term. Julia Lathrop, who became head of the Children's Bureau in Taft's final year as President, for example, cultivated the support of women's clubs throughout the country to expand the federal role on behalf of children. Clubs collected data in their communities on birth registration and infant mortality, sending it to Washington for analysis. Women's groups lobbied for uniform birth-reporting laws, improved sewage systems, milk inspection, and other policies to combat infant and child mortality. They also asked their representatives in Congress to support larger appropriations for the Children's Bureau. In 1914, when the House Appropriations Committee rejected Lathrop's request for increased funds, she used the women's network to get articles of support published in major magazines and letters written to congressmen from districts across the country. The tactic worked, and the full House overwhelmingly voted for the larger appropriation. With this kind of constituency, the bureau grew rapidly. Starting in 1912 with an appropriation of $25,640 and a staff of fifteen, by 1915 seventy-six people worked for the bureau, which had a budget of $164,640.

The academicians of the American Association for Labor Legislation likewise began a campaign during the Wilson administration to persuade states to enact "social insurance," old-age pensions, unemployment compensation, and health care. In 1916, the AALL released, with much fanfare, a model state bill providing for compulsory health insurance for industrial workers earning less than $1,200 annually, paid by employer and employee contributions and direct state government appropriations. Organized labor objected to mandatory employee contributions, and many members of the American Medical Association feared that health insurance would bring government intrusion into doctors' private practices.

America's entrance into World War I soon put the issue on hold, however.

Woman suffrage also made substantial progress during the Wilson administration, as organized women became an increasingly significant political force. In 1890, Wyoming joined the Union with woman suffrage. Colorado amended its constitution to give women voting rights in 1893, and Idaho and Utah in 1896. After that, however, the movement stalled.

Then, between 1911 and 1914, California, Oregon, Kansas, Arizona, Montana, and Nevada adopted woman suffrage, Illinois gave women the right to vote in presidential elections, and the Progressive Party platform endorsed suffrage. In 1915, Carrie Chapman Catt, a skilled organizer and strategist, took over leadership of the main suffrage organization, the National American Woman Suffrage Association (NAWSA), and within two years the NAWSA had over two million members. Wilson endorsed suffrage in 1916, but American entrance into World War I postponed the impending suffragist victory.

Progressive intellectuals, meanwhile, undergirded the reform movements and the political accomplishments of the Wilson administration with a bold vision of what purposeful government could accomplish. Walter Lippmann, a brilliant young journalist, offered the most forceful statement of what government must do to control the nation's destiny. An only child, Lippmann grew up in the sheltered world of New York's affluent German Jews, attending the Americanized Temple Emanu-El and a predominantly Jewish private school. Lippmann went to Harvard in 1906, where he studied philosophy and plunged into radical politics. Strongly influenced by a seminar taught by the British Fabian socialist Graham Wallas, Lippmann embraced the Fabian idea that an intellectual elite should put aside its own interests and use the state to foster economic equality.

Upon graduation in 1910, Lippmann wrote for two months for the reformist paper *Boston Common* before landing a better position helping Lincoln Steffens to research a series on the banking industry. When Steffens finished, Lippmann went to work for the new socialist mayor of Schenectady, Reverend George Lunn, in January 1912. Finding Lunn weak and indecisive, Lippmann resigned in less than six months and denounced his former boss in the *Call* for "timidity of action, the lack of a bold plan, a kind of aimlessness."[14] Lippmann, now twenty-two, eighteen months out of college, decided to return to New York and write a book about politics. In nine crisp chapters entitled *A Preface to Politics*, the iconoclastic Lippmann criticized American government and progressive reform for their lack of clear purpose and their failure to understand human nature. He dismissed nineteenth-century Victorian morality. He called the U.S. Constitution a mechanistic document unsuited to mediating human social relations. Writing in the midst of the 1912 presidential campaign, Lippmann declared Teddy Roosevelt "the working model" of the ideal politician.

Human nature, Lippmann argued, could be developed in positive ways by government. He pleaded for statesmen who believed that "at last men were to be the masters of their own history, instead of its victims," who would turn statesmanship from routine administration and preservation of order "to the invention of new political forms, the provision of social wants, and the preparation for new economic growths." Arguing that Americans could control the forces of change, he insisted that "the dynamics for a splendid human civilization are all about us. They need to be used."[15]

A Preface to Politics had drawn heavily upon Croly's *The Promise of American Life*, which opposed Jeffersonian individualism and called for systematic government direction of economic life. Willard and Dorothy Straight, a wealthy activist couple who had read Croly's book, decided to underwrite a national magazine of political opinion edited by Croly. In October 1913, Croly invited Lippmann to lunch, and although they had never met before, asked him to join the editorial staff, along with progressive journalist Walter Weyl. Lippmann was delighted. The magazine, *The New Republic*, quickly became an influential organ of political opinion.

Meanwhile, Lippmann was completing another book, which he

published just as *The New Republic* appeared in 1914. *Drift and Mastery* spelled out systematically a social philosophy of human control. Even more than in *A Preface to Politics*, Lippmann looked askance at the aimlessness of American government, insisting, however, that science and human intelligence pointed to a way out. Attacking the profit motive in business as outdated, Lippmann echoed Frederick Taylor's argument that professional managers should replace old-style merchants and industrialists. Industrial efficiency could provide ample wages and dignified conditions to all workers. The task before America, Lippmann believed, went beyond economic efficiency and just distribution. Modern society's complex organizations had changed every aspect of life. Mastery, concluded Lippmann, meant embracing science and harnessing it to shape human life. "The scientific spirit is the discipline of democracy, the escape from drift, the outlook of a free man."[16]

Lippmann and his colleagues at *The New Republic*, longtime admirers of Theodore Roosevelt, found much to approve in Woodrow Wilson's presidential leadership, and endorsed his reelection in 1916. When America declared war in 1917, Lippmann went to work for the Wilson administration. In the 1920s, Lippmann disavowed his progressive faith in an informed citizenry and in the ability of activist government to control the future, becoming a prominent critic of American liberalism. In 1914, however, *Drift and Mastery* offered perhaps the single most eloquent statement of the dominant progressive political ideal.

The changes in government accomplished by the time America entered World War I substantially altered the American political system. The executive branch gained strength at the expense of legislative bodies in cities, states, and the federal government. Political parties came under public supervision, and voter loyalty to parties declined. Administrative and regulatory agencies, which barely existed before the Progressive Era, now virtually constituted a new branch of government.

The weakening of close citizen identification with parties coincided with the beginnings of a century-long decline in voter participation in elections. Stricter voter registration laws, designed to prevent corruption, made it more difficult for Americans, especially from working-class and immigrant backgrounds, to vote, while Southern progressivism disenfranchised African-American voters completely. Although woman suffrage expanded the size of the electorate, until late in the century women voted at lower rates than men, and their choices generally mirrored those of men from the same social backgrounds.

It is ironic that a movement designed to restore to the democratic polity power to pursue the common good magnified instead the power of well-organized interest groups. In the nineteenth century, many Americans felt a personal relationship with local political party officials at a time when government itself had limited functions. Progressive reform urged centralization of city and county services to create efficiency and limit corruption, undermining locally based patronage which had tied city services closely to those who lived in an urban neighborhood or had placed control of rural schools in the hands of local citizen committees. Administrative and regulatory agencies and strong executive government further encouraged the proliferation of special-interest lobbies. Industries regulated by the new commissions had little difficulty influencing expert commissioners and staff members. Bureaucrats in new government departments became adept at using their constituencies to secure political support and increased appropriations. At the same time, the progressives' reliance on public education and publicity coupled with reforms like initiative, referendum, and recall helped shift power to those organized interest groups capable of influencing public opinion.

The new system was not inherently less democratic than the old. The wealthy had a great deal of political power and the poor very little in both. In the new American democracy, conflicting interests competed to influence bureaucrats and regulatory officials and to shape public opinion through the press and the mass media as much as they competed to influence elections. Ironically a movement that boldly promised to empower enlightened citizens to pursue the national interest ultimately reduced ordinary citizens' direct participation in government. And it magnified the importance of the organized interests whose power it had set out to restrain. Woodrow Wilson warned in 1912 that Americans "are coming to feel they have no control over the course of their affairs." At the end of the twentieth century, when the progressives' reforms had become standard features of the nation's government, Americans still felt that way.

9

THE GREAT WAR AND
THE COMPETITION FOR CONTROL

War accelerates history and changes it. For two generations, the quest for control—of one's own life, of production and the market, and of society—had pitted people and groups against each other, as industrialism and corporate capitalism transformed the nation. Now war intensified the competition.

On April 6, 1917, Congress formally declared war against Germany, acting on a request from President Wilson, who had campaigned for reelection as the leader who had "kept us out of war." The administration launched a frantic mobilization. Federal agencies coordinated industrial production so that the nation's factories could efficiently turn out goods needed to fight the Germans, encouraged farmers to increase food production, and asked consumers to observe "meatless" and "wheatless" days. The military quickly raised and trained an army of over four million, mostly through conscription, and sent the American Expeditionary Force to fight in France. Elaborate government propaganda campaigns built support for the war while law enforcement officials suppressed antiwar dissent. President Wilson called on Americans to put aside individual and group interests to fight the common enemy.

Yet despite outward displays of patriotism and commitment to the mobilization effort, American entrance into the European war escalated long-standing conflicts and social strains. Adapting to the changes caused by economic concentration and industrial capitalism, Americans of the Progressive Era had struggled for economic security, autonomy, and social status, making choices about where to live, for whom to work, how hard to toil, how to raise their children, which organizations to join, whether to engage in collective action, and how to respond to injustice. Economic circumstances, residence, education, race, national origin, and sex circumscribed the choices, often severely so. But industrial and white-collar workers, small entrepreneurs, farmers, immigrants, African-Americans, and Indians rarely accepted the effects of corporate capitalism passively. At the same time, leaders in many professions tried to restrict entry and upgrade standards while giant corporations looked for better ways to control the market. Against this backdrop, reformers and intellectuals fought to expand the role of government and argued over the ways in which it could restore individual autonomy and empower citizens to direct the nation's future.

For nineteen months, the social struggles and conflicts of a generation appeared in bold relief.

WORKERS AND INDUSTRIALISTS

The war gave both industrialists and workers unusual opportunities to prosper. President Wilson, although fearing excessive government entanglement with business, recognized that federal officials had to allocate the nation's resources and its productive capacity to win the war. After continuing attempts to coordinate the country's railroads failed miserably, a federal agency took over direct management early in 1918. But this was the exception. Mostly the government sought to induce business to cooperate by offering high profits and simultaneously threatening prosecution or government takeover if voluntary cooperation failed.

Initially, Wilson vested responsibility for industrial coordination in the Council of National Defense (CND), consisting of six cabinet members, assisted by a National Defense Advisory Commission (NDAC) of businessmen, professionals, and labor leaders. The CND also established "cooperative committees" for each major industry, made up of corporate executives who remained on their company's payroll, dubbed "dollar-a-year men" in Washington parlance. The CND and its advisory groups had great difficulty allocating resources, setting production quotas, and getting businesses to accept the prices it fixed for each product. Moreover, the dollar-a-year men drew criticism from Congress for steering lucrative contracts to their own companies.

Looking for a better mechanism, Wilson approved establishment of the War Industries Board (WIB) in July 1917 to supervise all war-related industrial production. It was initially under the CND, but the President soon placed it directly under himself, naming Bernard M. Baruch, a millionaire speculator from South Carolina, as its chairman. Baruch, an exceptionally persuasive man well connected in American industry and backed strongly by Wilson, achieved substantial industrial coordination. He replaced the "cooperative committees" with Commodity Committees staffed by military officials and dollar-a-year men which negotiated production targets and prices with over three thousand War Service Committees, basically trade associations of the leading manufacturers or producers in each industry.

Some businessmen resisted such overt government intrusion, but many leaders of the largest corporations welcomed the opportunity to use government authority to bring order and stability to the market, something they had been unable to achieve on their own. A majority of the dollar-a-year men, and those with the greatest influence, came from the largest corporations. Howard E. Coffin, vice president of the Hudson Motor Car Company and president of the Society of Automotive Engineers, who served with the CND, expressed his "hope that we may lay the foundation for that closely knit structure, industrial, civil, and military, which every thinking American has come to realize is vital to the future life of this country."[1]

This close cooperation between industry and government, coupled with massive purchases of arms and equipment by the military, caused corporate profits to soar. An official of the McKinney Steel Company admitted, "We are all making more money out of this war than the average human being ought to."[2] Indeed, U.S. Steel's annual profit went from $76 million before the war to $478 million in 1917. Total business profit in the United States climbed from less than $4 billion to over $10 billion between 1914 and 1917.

If corporate managers gained greater control of the market, they lost some of their customary control over their employees. Few European immigrants, the traditional supply of unskilled labor, could get to America after 1914. Wartime production demanded more workers just as several million men left work for military service. Placing 4.8 million workers in the military amounted to reducing the labor force by 16 percent. Southern black migrants, new immigrants from Mexico, Puerto Rican laborers, and women met some of the need, but the labor shortage remained acute throughout the war.

Government propaganda campaigns beseeched workers to increase production; and many labor leaders, led by Samuel Gompers, endorsed the war, participating in government mobilization efforts. The leader of the United Mine Workers opposed American entry, claiming that there existed "little sentiment among the working people in favor of this terrible war."[3] The government jailed Debs, Milwaukee's Socialist congressman Victor Berger, labor organizer Kate Richards O'Hare, and nearly a third of the Socialist Party's national executive committee for opposing the war. Federal agents arrested 113 leaders of the IWW, effectively destroying the organization. In all, the Justice Department initiated 2,200 prosecutions of radicals and socialists and secured 1,055 convictions. Despite the repression, the Socialist Party still had substantial support in some places. In New York City, for example, Socialist candidates won ten seats in the state legislature and seven on the board of aldermen in the election of 1917, and the Socialist candidate for mayor received 22 percent of the vote. The government responded to workers' quest for control during the war not only with the carrot of union recognition and mediation but with the stick of suppression of radicals.

Whatever their views of the war itself, workers did not express their patriotism through higher production and pliant behavior. Instead, they used the war to increase their economic security and their autonomy. With so many jobs available, workers changed positions even more frequently than before. Some employers reported labor turnover as high as 100 percent a week during the war. In Philadelphia, the manager of a General Electric plant said that in one week he had to hire 125 women to fill twenty-five operative positions, because the newly hired workers did not show up or left after their first day or two.

Employers expressed frustration. One Missouri manager suggested that "if . . . we can distribute the thousands of men that are hanging around our moving picture shows at 11 o'clock in the morning waiting to get in" it would help solve "some of our labor shortage problems."[4] An executive at Westinghouse estimated that during the war, workers, confident that they would not be fired, reduced their "effort" at his plant 20 to 30 percent.

Companies responded to the labor shortage by raising wages, expanding welfare programs, providing the means to address worker grievances, and developing more elaborate personnel departments. The Chicago packinghouses jointly established the Stockyards Community Clearing House to run community welfare and charity programs, athletic activities, children's social events, and a nursery. Crown Cotton Mills in Dalton, Georgia, faced with a severe regional labor shortage, introduced employee life and disability insurance, the amount of coverage increasing with each year of service.

Businesses also added or expanded personnel departments to improve the training, placement, motivation, and supervision of workers. In 1915, only about 5 percent of American firms with more than 250 workers maintained personnel departments; by 1920, 25 percent did. A wartime management study at General Electric argued that the company should hire "specialized human nature engineers to keep its human machinery frictionless." Corporate executives also expressed support for "industrial democracy" through "representation plans" in which the company initiated and managed the selection of worker representatives to advise management and present grievances, an idea endorsed by federal officials. The leading corporate advocate of representation plans, John D. Rockefeller, Jr., explained, "On the battlefields of France this nation poured out its blood freely in order that democracy might be maintained at home. . . . Surely it is not consistent for us as Americans to demand democracy in government and practice autocracy in industry."[5]

Most workers preferred their own unions, however, and they now pressed the government to recognize their right to organize and bargain collectively. President Wilson rewarded Gompers' support for the war with a seat on the NDAC, which encouraged government mediation to prevent strikes and lockouts. Wilson established a Mediation Commission directed by a progressive Harvard law professor, Felix Frankfurter, whose members toured factories across the country, concluding that labor unrest stemmed mostly from "the autocratic conduct" of industrial managers who refused to participate in collective bargaining.[6] The President also created the National War Labor Board (NWLB), a kind of Supreme Court for labor disputes, which encouraged the eight-hour day and a "living wage." General Order 13 of the Office of the Chief of Ordnance, written by liberal Taylorite Morris L. Cooke and social worker Mary Van Kleeck, set out guidelines for hours, overtime, holidays, workroom standards, and wages for women and children. The Department of Labor created a Women in Industry Service, later renamed the U.S. Women's Bureau, and a Working Conditions Service. When the government took over the railroads in 1918, it cooperated with the railroad brotherhood and expanded unionization of unskilled railroad workers.

Workers nonetheless struck in record numbers, ignoring an NDAC admonition against taking advantage of wartime conditions.

At a union meeting in western Pennsylvania, a Polish steelworker made a passionate plea linking the eight-hour day to America's war aims. "Just like a horse and wagon, work all day," he complained. "Take horse out of wagon—put in stable. Take horse out of stable, put in wagon. Same way like mills," he continued. "Come home— go sleep. Get up—go work in mills—come home. . . . For why this war? For why we buy Liberty bonds?" he asked rhetorically, answering emphatically, "For freedom and America—for everybody. No more horse and wagon. For eight hour day."[7]

In 1917, over a million workers struck against 4,200 different employers, three-quarters of these after the declaration of war. The nineteen months of war witnessed more than 6,000 strikes. Overall, union membership doubled from 2,607,000 in 1915 to 5,110,000 in 1920. Before the war, railroad brotherhoods represented only 20 percent of the workforce. When the federal government returned the railroads to private operation early in 1920, unions had signed up 90 percent of train service workers and 80 percent of all others. In Chicago's stockyards, management initially resisted recognizing the union, but eventually agreed to federal arbitration; workers gained an eight-hour day and a guaranteed forty-eight-hour week with time and a half for overtime, and paid holidays. Despite soaring wartime inflation, the average real wages of manual workers expanded by almost 20 percent during the war period. Between 1910 and 1919, the percentage of Americans who worked a forty-eight-hour week jumped from 8 to 48.

One million additional women, mostly unmarried, took jobs during the war. Working women seized the wartime opportunities for better-paying positions, including some previously reserved for men. More women entered industry, and fewer did domestic work. One and a quarter million women worked in munitions plants and other war-related manufacturing jobs. More than half the workers who made artillery shells were women.

A number of unions actively organized women workers, particularly in the textile, clothing, and shoe industries. By 1920,

397,000 women belonged to unions. But men often saw women as low-paid competitors. The railroad brotherhood made no effort to organize the 5,600 women who worked as car sweepers and cleaners during the war, or the black women who worked as common laborers on scrap docks, supply depots, and freight transfer stations. The International Association of Machinists, worried about wartime training programs that taught women laborers a single industrial task like welding without an extended apprenticeship in machine shop production, decided to organize women machinists. Nonetheless, in some shops men discouraged women from joining the machinists' union, and in one case they refused to enroll women and asked the foreman to fire them. In Baltimore, women welders told federal officials that male co-workers harassed and intimidated them. The International Molders' and Foundry Workers' Union joined with advocates of protective legislation to lobby for state prohibitions on women in heavy industrial jobs, and miners in Lehigh, Pennsylvania, secured a state ban on the employment of women in aboveground coal-producing operations. Twelve cities hired women as streetcar conductors. In several they worked without incident. But in others, male conductors, worried about the competition, went on strike in protest, arguing that the work exposed women to physical danger and immoral influences.

The momentary advantage enjoyed by male and female workers alike ended abruptly with the armistice. Wilson quickly dismantled the government agencies of production and labor coordination, and employers initiated a new campaign to roll back wartime wages. Elbert Gary, the head of U.S. Steel, told his subordinates two months after the armistice that "the employers, the capitalists, those having the highest education, the greatest power and influence" must see that "the workmen and their families are appropriately and effectively cared for," at the same time "keeping the whole affair in [their] own hands."[8] To diffuse tensions, many employers now embraced representation plans and expanded their welfare programs. Only twenty corporations had representation plans by the end of 1917, but the number grew to 225 by 1919. These plans did not eclipse workers' enthusiasm for unionization and collective bargaining, however, and strikes, numerous during the war, skyrocketed afterward. Raymond Fosdick, who had headed a committee concerned with providing recreation for soldiers during the war and now worked for John D. Rockefeller, Jr., concluded:

> There is a psychological appeal in labor unionism . . . It seems to give the men a sense not only of power but of dignity and self-respect. They feel that only through labor unions can they deal with employers on an equal plane. They seem to regard the representation plan as a sort of counterfeit, largely, perhaps, because the machinery of such plans is too often managed by the employers. They want something which they themselves have created and not something which is handed down to them by those who will pay their wages.[9]

Indeed, workers struck everywhere after the armistice, as management sought to roll back not only wages but wartime union gains. When the AFL attempted to organize the steel industry in 1919, U.S. Steel refused to negotiate, sparking a long, bitter, and ultimately unsuccessful strike. The same year, 450,000 miners walked off the job, and when the union accepted a government order to return to work, many miners refused to obey. A walkout by Seattle shipyard workers escalated into a general strike. In all, 1919 witnessed 3,300 strikes involving four million workers, one of every five. At the same time, government law enforcement officials, led by Attorney General A. Mitchell Palmer, tightened their repression of political radicals, arresting and often deporting alleged revolutionaries in what became known as the "Red Scare."

Workers succeeded in some of the 1919 strikes, but most wartime economic gains and the autonomy workers had achieved on the job proved transitory. Corporate leaders, on the other hand, retained many of the advantages of an activist government of and by businessmen in the programs Herbert Hoover initiated as Secretary of

Commerce in the 1920s, without the wartime coercion and without pressure from government to bargain collectively with workers. In the wartime competition for control of the industrial workplace, corporate managers emerged the big winners.

OFFICE WORKERS

The war expanded office employment permanently. Growing businesses generated more paperwork, and government contracts required detailed records. Government bureaucracy also expanded. Whatever resistance remained before 1917 to the employment of women in offices dissipated immediately after American entrance into the war. According to a Census Bureau study, office clerks, stenographers, typists, bookkeepers, and cashiers accounted for most of the permanent growth in women's employment in the years between 1910 and 1920, over 800,000 jobs.

An official of Guarantee Trust in New York explained during the war that "due to the demand upon our men for Government Service, opportunities for bookkeeping and clerical work . . . , Private Secretaryships and other junior clerical positions, formerly held by men, are now being filled by women." Banks employed women to operate bookkeeping machines. An advertisement for adding machines read: "Uncle Sam took my experienced clerks. In their place I have willing workers but *inexperienced*. So I must have simple office machines . . . inexperienced operators soon become lightening [sic] fast on the 10-key *Dalton* [which will] substitute womanpower for man-power." Like other workers, women office employees switched jobs regularly to improve pay and conditions, and informally regulated the pace of work. A young woman with a business college education told an interviewer, "You could get a job anywhere . . . Another girl and I, we'd take a job in the morning, and if we didn't like it we'd quit at noontime and take another one in the afternoon."[10]

Female clerks still harbored substantial grievances. Employers limited women mostly to sex-segregated jobs, and promotions remained hard to come by. The clerk in charge of a railroad accounting office told interviewers that he preferred to hire young women because they did not mind doing monotonous work for a short time between school and marriage. Some women complained that the men they worked with treated them condescendingly, and some told an investigator that male co-workers constantly touched them, lifted up their skirts, and pinched their breasts.

Nonetheless, some women achieved promotions to coveted supervisory positions during the war. For example, Adrianna Fass, who supported her disabled husband, worked for the Wabash Railroad for thirteen years. Supervisors told her that she could not rise above her position as head comptometer operator. But during the war, they promoted her to station remittance clerk. During the federal takeover of the railroads, a female "acting" chief clerk who for years had been paid the salary of an assistant clerk finally won her promotion and the higher salary. Since office employment did not contract after the war as industrial employment did, women who advanced in the office hierarchy tended to keep their jobs. Although their opportunities remained circumscribed after the armistice, women office workers had used the wartime demand to solidify their presence in offices and to push upward, if ever so slightly, the limits on the positions they could hold.

WAR AND AGRICULTURE

With the outbreak of war in Europe the British bought large quantities of American wheat and other foodstuffs, causing prices to soar. When the United States entered the war, mobilization planners placed a high priority on expanding food production, particularly wheat, to feed American troops and the Allied countries. Wilson assigned the task to the U.S. Food Administration led by millionaire businessman and engineer Herbert Hoover, who in the 1920s would serve as Secretary of Commerce and win election to the presidency. Agricultural experts seized the war-time opportunity to pursue their long-standing goal of getting American farmers to embrace scientific farming. One early war pamphlet declared, "Our food production has not kept pace with the growth of our population. This fact caused anxiety to agricultural experts even before the outbreak of the war. Now, when we must supply food not only to ourselves but to our allies, it is the gravest aspect of a grave situation."[11]

The number of county agricultural extension agents multiplied. In June 1917, agents served only half the nation's counties, but by the end of the war they worked in nearly every county. Virtually the only federal bureaucrats in most rural areas, they provided expert assistance in increasing crop yields. They could also help cooperative farmers to acquire scarce fuel, fertilizer, and equipment, which the government distributed on the basis of mobilization priorities. Country Life reformers likewise welcomed this golden opportunity finally to bring modern economic and social organization to rural America. Officials of the Bureau of Indian Affairs encouraged Native Americans to increase the acreage they cultivated on reservations, and leased large amounts of reservation land to big commercial farmers.

The government fixed the price of wheat at $2.20 per bushel, angering farmers who believed an open market could bring much more; farmers switched acreage from wheat to corn or held wheat off the market. When the $2.20 price proved profitable, however, farmers planted additional wheat in 1918, harvesting 44.7 percent more than the year before. However, some farmers still refused to embrace the agents. A congressman from Illinois complained, "You do not have to hire some shoemaker or corn doctor to go on a farm and demonstrate to a farmer the need for raising crops, he knows how to do that himself."[12]

Farmers also used the war to seek redress for traditional grievances. The Grange and other farmers' organizations called for programs to eliminate middlemen and local merchants from the sale and distribution of agricultural produce and for postwar controls on production. A Wisconsin farmer admitted in 1917 that farmers "have not been as active to participate in Food Conservation, Red Cross Work or Liberty Bond sales . . . as might be expected," because the war mobilization agencies were run "by the same class of people who have incurred [farmers'] ill will in former times, the bankers, lawyers, professional politicians, representatives of a business system . . . who now under guise of Patriotism are trying to ram down the farmers' throats things they hardly dared before."

The rural reformers and agricultural extension specialists claimed great wartime success. Farmers brought new land under cultivation and increased their purchase of farm equipment. The value of farm produce more than doubled between 1914 and 1918 despite a 10 percent decline in the number of farmworkers, although the increase probably stemmed more from higher commodity prices than from government encouragement. An Assistant Secretary of Agriculture claimed just after the war, "If these farmers were left to their own individual initiative, aloof as they are from one another and from the common currents of national information, we would have had a breakdown in agriculture."[13]

Wartime agents succeeded in building farm bureaus, organizations of rural bankers, businessmen, and the most prosperous farmers in each county. The first bureau began in 1911, but the bureau movement made rapid strides during the war, backed by the county agents. Government agricultural officials saw the bureaus as a bulwark against the agrarian radicalism of the Farmers' Union, the Grange, the Nonpartisan League, and similar groups. After the war, local bureaus formed the American Farm Bureau Federation, which significantly influenced government agricultural policy in the 1920s.

Small and poor farmers benefited little from the farm bureaus or the extension movement, however. Although farm income increased during the war years, so did farm debt, and when farm commodity prices dropped precipitously after 1919, small owners, tenants, and sharecroppers faced continuing hardships. Like industrial workers, most farmers seized the opportunities the war afforded to enhance their economic security and autonomy, but they could no more sustain their gains than workers could.

AFRICAN-AMERICANS

African-American workers and farmers also made the most of the opportunities the war provided. Southern city dwellers went North and rural Southerners moved to cities in the South in ever-greater numbers after American entrance into the conflict. In the North, African-Americans secured industrial work, men in steel mills, in meatpacking plants, and on automobile assembly lines, women in the metal, leather, paper products, clothing, textile, and meatpacking industries, and as common laborers for the railroads. The numbers remained small, however. Most black women in the North still worked as domestic servants in jobs vacated by white women moving into factory jobs. Although female employment in domestic service declined nationally during the war, the number of black domestic servants in the North grew by 17.4 percent between 1910 and 1920.

Women valued the greater autonomy over their lives offered by factory work's regular hours, comparing it favorably with the continuous demands on live-in servants. One African-American woman exclaimed, "I'll never work in nobody's kitchen but my own any more. No indeed! That's the one thing that makes me stick to this [factory] job. You . . . have some time to call your own." Another, who got work as a common laborer for a railroad, explained, "All the colored women like this work and want to keep it. We are making more money at this than any work we can get, and we do not have to work as hard as at housework which requires us to be on duty from six o'clock in the morning until nine or ten at night."[14]

African-Americans, like other workers, changed jobs frequently to capitalize on the wartime labor shortage, and undertook numerous strikes and job actions. In the North, many women moved between domestic and factory jobs, and employers complained bitterly about their high rates of absenteeism. In the South, blacks employed in twelve-hour shifts in tobacco, guano, and cottonseed factories regularly disappeared on Saturdays and Mondays. In hosiery knitting mills, frustrated employers offered bonuses to black workers who showed up every day. In Rocky Mill, black women struck to force the removal of a white manager who had cursed at them, and in several other plants they successfully demanded supervision by black forewomen. Laundresses and domestic workers in several Southern cities organized to demand higher wages and better conditions.

In the most successful black union effort of the war years, the Transport Workers Association, representing the black stevedores and longshoremen in Norfolk who filled 90 percent of these jobs, negotiated a contract in 1917 that improved salaries, guaranteed a minimum wage, provided time and a half for overtime, and required that workers be paid for time spent waiting for an assignment. The transport union also supported strikes by black tobacco stemmers, domestic workers, and oyster shuckers, but these did not meet with the same success. In 1918, African-American railroad track laborers outside New Orleans and building trade workers in St. Petersburg struck for higher wages. Sharecroppers and agricultural laborers likewise demanded and often secured better terms from their landlords, as their neighbors left for the cities. A fivefold increase in the price of cotton helped landowners, independent renters, and sharecroppers alike.

Most African-American leaders supported the war. A conflict to make the world safe for democracy would raise American consciousness about the denial of democracy to African-Americans, they reasoned, and demonstrations of loyalty during the war would bring rewards once peace arrived. The socialist newspaper editor

A. Philip Randolph opposed the war and went to jail; but most African-American leaders joined W. E. B. Du Bois, who urged his people to "forget our special grievances and close our ranks shoulder to shoulder with our own white fellow citizens." Roscoe Conkling Simmons, a nephew of Booker T. Washington, told a rally in Memphis in 1917, "You may burn me, but you cannot burn away my record of undying loyalty," but he announced that after the war "we will make the United States safe for the Negroes."[15] Although Southern whites opposed the very idea of armed black men in uniform, black leaders demanded that African-Americans be allowed to serve as soldiers, see combat, and gain commissions as officers. The NAACP used prowar rhetoric to push (unsuccessfully) for an antilynching law, arguing that lynching undermined war morale and violated the war's democratic principles.

Ordinary black people seemed to accept these arguments grudgingly at best. Although African-Americans volunteered for military service out of proportion to their numbers and subscribed heavily to Liberty bonds, thousands also protested lynching and discrimination in a march down New York's Fifth Avenue, carrying signs that read: "Make America Safe for Democracy," "Taxation Without Representation Is Tyranny," and "Mother, Do Lynchers Go to Heaven?" African-American newspaper publishers shared their ambivalence. Emmett Scott of Tuskegee, appointed special assistant to the Secretary of War to deal with African-American issues, met secretly with African-American editors to discuss accounts of the mistreatment of black soldiers. The editors, although agreeing to cooperate with the government, wrote to President Wilson that "the apparent indifference of our own Government" to the legitimate grievances of black people "may be dangerous."[16] Censors held up distribution of African-American periodicals for stories critical of government policy, including an issue of *The Crisis* which detailed discrimination in the army.

The war did little to change white attitudes toward black people, but African-Americans' own actions sometimes caused whites to change their rhetoric if not their minds. Fear over black exodus from the South caused some white Southerners to acknowledge abuse of African-Americans. Georgia governor Hugh Dorsey expressed alarm in 1917 at the departure of 50,000 black people from his state in the previous year, calling successfully for more state support of African-American schools. The *Tifton Gazette* in Georgia complained that "whites have allowed Negroes to be lynched, five at a time, on nothing stronger than suspicion," and the Negro "has no assured right to live, to own property, or to expect justice in Georgia."[17] At interracial meetings, white leaders pledged to improve conditions for African-Americans; and the Georgia Federation of Women's Clubs condemned lynching.

Repression of African-Americans continued unabated, however. All-white draft boards called up African-Americans in proportionately greater numbers than whites. The federal government offered financial rewards for apprehending "slackers," men who avoided the draft, and an investigation by the army concluded that in five Georgia counties sheriffs "have reaped a harvest by fraudulently arresting colored men and turning them over to the local boards as slackers, for the sole purpose of getting the reward of $50 offered by the government." In 1918, the government issued a "work or fight" order, requiring men in nonessential work to find war-related employment or face immediate induction. Southern whites used the order as a pretext to remove African-Americans from more desirable occupations. The Memphis police commissioner ordered all African-American bootblack and pressing stands closed, calling them "unnecessary from a business standpoint" and demanding that they "get out and go to work in a legitimate calling."[18] A law enforcement official in Pelham, Georgia, arrested the head of a black insurance agency on the grounds that insurance was not an essential war activity for a black man.

Some officials tried to use the "work or fight" order to coerce black women into domestic service. When African-American women organized for higher pay and a six-day week, employers threatened to fire these women and turn them in for violation of the order. A white group in Macon declared that patriotism demanded that black women not "sit at home and hold their hands, refusing to do the labor for which they are specially trained and otherwise adapted," labor which freed white women "from the routine of housework in order that they may do the work which negro women cannot do."[19] Blacks in Atlanta successfully lobbied the governor to veto a state "work or fight" bill, arguing that it would accelerate out-migration.

Despite the kind words and conciliatory gestures from a few leading white citizens, lynchings increased from thirty-eight in 1917 to fifty-eight in 1918 and seventy in 1919; ten victims were soldiers in uniform. A particularly horrific episode occurred in Houston, where black soldiers, many from outside the South, refused to honor local Jim Crow laws in streetcars and theaters, would not drink from separate water barrels, and tore down Jim Crow signs. On August 23, 1917, an African-American soldier intervened as a police officer beat a black woman. Local police then beat and arrested the soldier. Rumors spread that the police had killed a black corporal visiting the arrested soldier. (They had beaten but not seriously injured him.) According to the official account, black soldiers stole ammunition from a supply tent, marched to town, where they met armed white police and civilians, and exchanged shots. Two African-Americans and seventeen whites died. The army swiftly tried 156 black soldiers for mutiny, sentencing thirteen to death and forty-one to life imprisonment. One African-American, moved to write to the condemned men, pronounced it better to die protecting black women than to fight in a supposed war for democracy which the United States itself denied to African-Americans.

More ominous still, a spate of race riots shattered Southern and especially Northern cities during and immediately after the war, as black urban migrants competed with white workers for housing and jobs. When employers imported African-Americans to break strikes in Chicago and other cities, racial tensions increased. Conflicts erupted in more than a half dozen cities in 1917, most viciously in East St. Louis, Illinois. On May 28, someone announced at a white union meeting that African-Americans had just killed a white man. A mob formed quickly and for two days randomly attacked black people. Then, on the night of July 1, a car occupied by whites drove through an African-American area shooting randomly, and a group of African-Americans shot back at another car filled with whites, killing two of the passengers. Enraged bands of whites rampaged through the city, assaulting black people, burning their homes, and shooting at residents as they fled. The National Guard, called in to quell the riot, did almost nothing to stop these attacks. In all, eight whites and at least thirty-nine African-Americans died in the violence.

The East St. Louis riot foreshadowed the two-sided violence that erupted in dozens of cities in 1919. In Washington, D.C., a mob of white sailors, inflamed by newspaper headlines, indiscriminately beat African-American men and women as they searched for two men accused of harassing a white woman. Armed black men fought back. In Chicago, which witnessed the worst of these conflicts, white youths stoned to death a black boy swimming near a lakefront beach unofficially restricted to whites while a police officer stood by. An African-American mob attacked the police officer, bands of whites attacked the ghetto, and African-Americans responded in kind. In five gruesome days, thirty-eight people died and over 500 were injured. And so it went, in city after city: Knoxville, Omaha, Philadelphia, Norfolk, New Orleans, Syracuse, Baltimore, Wilmington (Delaware), and many others.

By the end of 1919, African-Americans recognized that white hostility would not lessen and that the great migration had made antiblack violence a national rather than just a Southern manifestation of racism. Still, many African-Americans mingled bitterness with satisfaction at having resisted violence with violence. Black poet Claude McKay wrote in July 1919:

If we must die, let it not be like hogs
Hunted and penned in an inglorious spot.
Like men we'll face the murderous, cowardly pack.
Pressed to the wall, dying, but—fighting back!

One African-American woman eloquently bared her soul, explaining her emotional response to the riot in the nation's capital:

> The Washington riots gave me the thrill that comes once in a lifetime. I was alone when I read between the lines of the morning paper that at last our men had stood like men, struck back, were no longer dumb, driven cattle. When I could no longer read for my streaming tears, I stood up, alone in my room, held both hands high over my head and exclaimed, "Oh, I thank God, thank God!" When I remember anything after this, I was prone on my bed, beating the pillow with both fists, laughing and crying, whimpering like a whipped child, for sheer gladness and madness. The pent-up humiliation, grief and horror of a lifetime—half a century—was being stripped from me.[20]

Participation in the war, even in segregated units and in menial jobs, and physical resistance to white violence, however unequal, had enhanced African-Americans' self-respect; and in the 1920s, social commentators proclaimed an assertive "New Negro." Although African-Americans could not collect on the promise of freedom after America's victory in the war for democracy, migrants to the North and to Southern cities, women who left live-in domestic jobs for factory work, and others exploited the circumstances of the war to increase, however marginally, their economic security and autonomy. Moreover, in their guarded and contingent support for the war itself, and in their forcible resistance to white violence, many African-Americans strengthened their psychic autonomy from the dominant white society, enhancing group consciousness for the struggles lying ahead.

IMMIGRANTS AND NATIVIST HYSTERIA

The wartime government and much of the public demanded absolute loyalty to the United States, adding new urgency to the national debate over Americanization. When war broke out in 1914, and immigrants in America lined up on one side or the other of the European conflict, social worker Frances Kellor and other Americanization activists got the Interior Department to develop educational programs for immigrants, establishing a new Division of Immigrant Education within the U.S. Bureau of Education. When the United States entered the war, a CND advisory committee on foreigners within the United States called for concerted national action to oversee and educate the millions of immigrants who lived "in colonies, camps, and quarters isolated from American control," warning of the potential for "the control of industries by aliens."[21]

Kellor headed the government's wartime Americanization program, producing educational materials, working with public schools, and encouraging patriotic ceremonies. The government's main war propaganda agency, the Committee on Public Information, established a Division of Work with the Foreign-Born, which placed announcements of Red Cross drives and Liberty bond sales in foreign-language newspapers, and pressed immigrant leaders to speak in favor of the war.

Americanization programs provided the "carrot" and repression the "stick" in this campaign to ensure immigrant loyalty. The Postmaster General required foreign-language newspapers to submit translations for review by government censors. The Justice Department paid a private, quasi-vigilante group, the American Protective Association, to monitor the activities and meetings of suspect foreigners, especially Germans. Nebraska, which a few years earlier had encouraged public schools to teach German and other immigrant languages, now forbade the teaching of any subject in a language other than English at public or private schools in the state. (The law actually outlawed the teaching of Latin!) Several other states imposed similar restrictions, especially on the teaching of German. South Dakota banned the use of German on the telephone or in gatherings of three or more people. Montana removed all German-language books from its libraries.

As early as 1915, President Wilson decried hyphenated Americanism, telling newly naturalized citizens that "you cannot become thorough Americans if you think of yourselves in groups. . . . A man who thinks of himself as belonging to a particular national group in America has not yet become an American." On another occasion that year, he complained that some naturalized citizens "have poured the poison of disloyalty into the very arteries of our national life."[22] This environment encouraged ultrapatriots to attack German-Americans, their churches, and other buildings. On April 5, 1918, a drunken mob lynched a German-born coal miner, Robert Praeger, in Collinsville, Illinois, on a false suspicion of his being a German spy. Shortly thereafter, a mob in Pensacola, Florida, severely flogged a man of German descent and forced him to shout, "To hell with the Kaiser, hurrah for Wilson." In Aoca, Pennsylvania, ultrapatriots hoisted an Austrian-American thirty feet in the air and turned a fire hose on him because they thought he had criticized the Red Cross. An Oakland mob hanged a German-American tailor, then tied his body to a tree. In Corpus Christi, irate patriots whipped a Lutheran preacher for giving a sermon in German. By the summer of 1918, such episodes were almost daily occurrences, particularly in the Midwest, where most German-Americans lived.

The climate of intolerance caused a crisis for German-Americans, the largest European ethnic group in America. German-language newspapers conspicuously endorsed the American cause and ran a stream of patriotic articles. To avoid the censors' burdensome translation requirements, some converted entirely to English. Nearly half of the country's 522 German-language publications ceased by war's end and the combined circulation of German-language dailies fell by two-thirds. The National German-

American Alliance, the most prominent of the group's nationalist institutions, regularly repeated its strong support for the United States; after its leaders testified before the U.S. Senate, the organization disbanded, donating its assets to the Red Cross. Some state federations followed suit, others had their charters revoked by state governments, and still others held no meetings and did nothing to attract attention. The Cincinnati German-American Alliance changed its name to the American Citizens League; the Kaiser-Kuhn grocery of St. Louis became the Pioneer Grocery Company.

Individual German-Americans coped as best they could. Some sought to protect themselves by joining ultrapatriotic organizations like the National Patriotic Council of German Americans or the Friends of German Democracy, urging fellow Germans to support the war, and criticizing German culture. Others panicked. In Perry County, Missouri, church members hid German Bibles and destroyed German textbooks used in their school. Many German parents stopped speaking their native tongue at home or changed names such as Schmidt to Smith.

In a few instances, German-Americans resisted violence with force. Members of a German Lutheran congregation in Steeleville, Illinois, used guns to protect their church from a mob attack. In Havana, Illinois, fifteen German-Americans held off a mob seeking to tar-and-feather a young German-American. Still, the virulent campaign proved sadly effective. Demoralized, defensive about their national origin, German-Americans dismantled their elaborate ethnic communal institutions. Anti-German hysteria destroyed their long-standing cultural autonomy in America.

The war did not take the same toll on most other nationalities. Immigrant leaders asserted their loyalty to America, linking their group's values with America's. On July 4, 1918, leaders of thirty-three different immigrant groups sailed with President and Mrs. Wilson from the capital to George Washington's Mount Vernon plantation, a richly symbolic gesture of national unity. Many immigrant leaders tried to persuade Wilson to support self-determination for their respective European brethren. Irish-Americans, in particular, held large rallies in support of Irish independence, but with no effect on the President. American Jews, however, won Wilson's support for Britain's Balfour Declaration favoring the establishment of a Jewish homeland in Palestine, and Polish-Americans for an independent Poland.

Despite these few achievements, the lesson of the German experience, and of the Americanization campaign generally, could not have been clearer. America tolerated ethnic group life that did not conflict with larger national purposes, but did not welcome it. Hostility toward "hyphenated Americans" made ethnic identification a liability. Within a few years of the war's end, nativists won passage of a racist law restricting immigration through national origins quotas. It reduced immigration from Southern and Eastern Europe to a trickle, extended Chinese exclusion, and formalized the exclusion of the Japanese. Liberals and immigrants themselves concluded that the best thing to say about ethnic differences was as little as possible, dampening immigrant leaders' prewar assertions of cultural autonomy and their calls for American pluralism.

PROFESSIONS IN WARTIME

Leaders in many professions sought to win public favor by demonstrating their value to society in the wartime emergency. The leaders of the American Bar Association vigorously defended the government's blatant violations of civil liberties in suppressing antiwar sentiment and capitalized on the nativist mood to argue for a more selective and socially homogeneous bar. An American Bar Association committee, chaired by Elihu Root, urged that law schools require two years of college for admission as a way of excluding immigrants. One member from West Virginia declared that foreigners formed "an uneducated mass of men who have no conception of our constitutional government." Root argued that by attending college for two years, prospective lawyers "will be taking in through the pores of [their] skin American life and American thought and feeling." One New York delegate to an ABA meeting declared it "absolutely necessary" that lawyers be "able to read, write and talk the English language—not Bohemian, not Gaelic, not Yiddish, but English."[23] The ABA endorsed the Root committee proposals in 1921, the same year Congress enacted the first overall immigration restriction law.

Other professionals used the war to demonstrate in positive ways their value to society. Psychiatrists welcomed the opportunity to win recognition by treating victims of shell shock with some success. Engineers played a major role in industrial mobilization. Engineers predominated on the staff of the CND. A Naval Consulting Board of engineers screened suggestions for military inventions. By 1918, one-third of the scientific management experts of the Taylor Society had become reserve officers in the Army Ordnance production division.

The American Library Association provided reading material to soldiers, raising $5 million and distributing 10 million books and magazines. One librarian described the war as "the opportunity for which we have been waiting . . . to demonstrate to the MEN of America . . . that library work is a profession."[24] Leaders in the nursing profession urged the military to employ only trained nurses, but the Red Cross opposed them, favoring extensive use of volunteer aides. Three months before the armistice, the War Department authorized establishment of an Army Nursing School to train nurses for military service.

Although prominent social workers had opposed American participation in the war before 1917, and a few like Jane Addams maintained their opposition throughout, most jumped on the war mobilization bandwagon. The Red Cross expanded greatly, and three-quarters of its new employees came from charity organization societies. *Survey* editor Paul Kellogg ended his opposition to American participation in the war after U.S. entry, and went to work for the Red Cross, calling the war "the opportunity of a generation."

Edward Devine described the war in 1917 as "a vast laboratory for the demonstration of the truths in which social work is based."[25]

The war also expanded opportunities for women in male-dominated professions. With so many prospective medical students serving in the army, Yale, Columbia, and eleven other medical schools opened their doors to women for the first time. Hospitals short of staff physicians accepted women interns. Women established a number of military hospitals in Europe, and the army hired fifty-five women as contract surgeons but refused to commission women physicians. In New York, twenty women lawyers received appointments as temporary judges to meet the wartime shortage.

University teachers went to exceptional lengths to win public favor during the war, even abandoning their commitment to academic freedom. The AAUP, which before the war asserted that professors' responsibilities to society required "absolute freedom of thought, of inquiry, of discussion and of teaching," now decreed that professors could be dismissed because of their "attitude or conduct in relation to the war." The AAUP took no action on numerous violations of academic freedom, and did not even protest Columbia University's dismissal of psychologist James McKeen Cattell, one of the organization's founders, for writing to members of Congress urging that American troops not be permitted to fight in Europe.

Professors, seeing the war as a singular opportunity to enhance the status of their disciplines, eagerly joined the mobilization. Prominent scientists created the National Research Council (NRC) to link their disciplines to war needs—"the first time in history," boasted physicist J. S. Ames, that men of science could prove "their worth to their country." After the armistice, the NRC became a permanent agency funding basic research in physics and chemistry. Historians established the National Board for Historical Service (NBHS) for similar purposes. Carl Russell Fish, one of its members, explained that the war offered historians a rare chance to reform the teaching of history in public schools, "an opportunity for the greatest usefulness and for a corresponding increase in public estimation."[26] Historians and social scientists also joined in the work of the government's war propaganda agency, the Committee on Public Information, preparing pamphlets, curricula, and other materials to explain the war to the public.

The president of the American Psychological Association, Robert Yerkes, a pioneer in mental testing, outdid all others in capitalizing on the wartime draft. He got the association to establish twelve committees to look at different uses of psychology in the war. Yerkes won government approval for an ambitious plan to administer intelligence tests to every recruit in the army in order to place each man in the task for which he was best suited, supervising examiners who administered 1,750,000 tests. A Committee on Classification of Personnel, headed by Walter Dill Scott, like Yerkes a university psychologist, designed procedures to use the results of Yerkes' test in making assignments. Military officers resented having outside "experts" tell them how to deploy their men, and the elaborate testing program had no significant impact on the army. It provided data on millions of men for scholars of human intelligence, however, thereby facilitating the expansion of the field. Like lawyers, engineers, librarians, and social workers, members of the academic professions used the war to enhance public perceptions of their value to society, strengthening their autonomy and social status.

PROGRESSIVE REFORMERS AND THE WAR

Most progressive reformers and intellectuals embraced and even welcomed American entry into the war as an opportunity to demonstrate at last how society could be controlled and directed for the common good. John Dewey, in an article in *The New Republic*, "What America Will Fight For," proclaimed that American participation would lead to "the beginnings of a public control which crosses nationalistic boundaries and interests." Walter Lippmann, who spent the war years in Washington as an assistant to Secretary of War Newton D. Baker and helped a group of experts known as "the Inquiry" analyze issues for the postwar peace conference, believed that the war would finally replace "routineers" with "inventors" and social engineers. He predicted at the start of the war that the country would "turn with fresh interest to our own tyrannies—to our Colorado mines, our autocratic steel industries, our sweatshops and our slums." William Allen White declared in his progressive *Emporia Gazette* in June 1917 that government coordination of the economy had broken "the back of the profit system." John R. Commons predicted that "American labor will come out of this war with as much power to fix its own wages by its own representatives as employers have."[27]

A few progressives dissented. California senator Hiram Johnson feared that the war would drain energy from reform. Writer Randolph Bourne charged that progressive intellectuals had been mesmerized by the opportunity to work within the war government. "If the war is too strong for you to prevent, how is it going to be weak enough for you to control and mold to your liberal purposes?" he wrote.[28] Most progressives ignored these warnings.

On the surface the reformers' optimism seemed warranted. The government set out to manage the economy and arbitrate labor disputes. Reformers convinced Congress to provide death and disability insurance to all soldiers and their families, a plan designed by Julia Lathrop and progressive Judge Julian Mack of the Cook County Juvenile Court. In 1918, when the Supreme Court struck down a federal law prohibiting child labor, Congress placed a heavy tax on goods produced by children, and federal officials inserted child labor restrictions into federal contracts.

The CND's Housing Committee urged the federal government to build decent and affordable homes for war workers, the U.S. Shipping Board Emergency Fleet Corporation broke ground for thirty thousand units, and in May 1918 Congress established the U.S. Housing Corporation to undertake civilian housing construction. One housing reformer explained that Congress "would not for a moment have dreamed of considering favorably this project of the government going into the housing business, which some of them term 'state socialism,' except as a means of winning the war."[29] Progressives employed by the Railway Administration, Army Ordnance, and the Labor Department worked to protect wage-earning women and ensure enforcement of state protective statutes. Several states also passed new laws establishing a minimum wage, maximum hours, and workmen's compensation, protecting women and children, and providing widows' pensions. Leaders of the National American Woman Suffrage Association, eager to increase public support for voting rights, set up departments to promote food production and conservation, Americanization, and women's service. The CND created a Women's Committee, dominated by NAWSA members and chaired by former NAWSA president Anna Howard Shaw.

Social purity, temperance, and recreation reformers proved unusually successful in using war patriotism to advance their agendas. They persuaded the military to ban alcohol in army camps, close nearby brothels and saloons, and establish a Commission on Training Camp Activities to provide wholesome sports and entertainment for the draftees. The Social Hygiene Association, the leader of the progressive fight against venereal disease, assisted the commission, and its director raved about "the wonderful opportunity which came to the Association with the outbreak of the war." By war's end, most red-light districts in the country had been shut down in the name of patriotism. Meanwhile, recreation specialists from the progressive Russell Sage Foundation and the YMCA organized the doughboys' leisure time.

The Committee on Public Information (CPI), headed by Wilson loyalist George Creel, built support for the war using the methods for arousing public opinion which progressives had developed to a high art. Creel, a prototypical reformer, edited several Western newspapers, served as Denver's police commissioner, and in 1916 directed publicity for Wilson's reelection campaign. He brought to his task a progressive's faith in the rationality of an informed citizenry. "I feel that public opinion has its source in the minds of people, that it has its base in reason," Creel wrote in 1918. He thought that the war would accelerate the movement toward social justice. Under his leadership, the CPI turned out great quantities of books, pamphlets, posters, advertisements, and instructional guides and sent speakers to every corner of the country.

Creel's CPI attracted all sorts of progressives. Playwright Henry O'Higgins, head of one division, had worked previously with Judge Ben Lindsay of the Denver Juvenile Court. Robert Maisel, a former socialist and writer for the *Call*, worked for the Labor Publications Division. John R. Commons wrote tracts for the CPI. Josephine Roche, who directed the Division of Work with the Foreign-Born, had been active in the Progressive Party and the National Consumers' League. Moderate socialists like Algie Martin Simons, John Spargo, and Upton Sinclair also worked for the CPI, as did more than two hundred historians and other scholars, including the eminent progressive historian Carl Becker. Professor Charles E. Merriam, a leading figure in Chicago's progressive reform movement, worked for the CPI office in Italy, and Judge Ben Lindsay toured Europe for the CPI in 1918. One of Creel's congressional critics described CPI workers as "socialistic, muckraking misfits."[30]

Immediately after the armistice, many progressives remained optimistic. Grosvenor B. Clarkson, secretary of the CND, declared, "Out of the turmoil and the sacrifice will come discipline and orderly living and thinking." The irrepressible Edward Devine declared that the country now would pursue "a social order in which all shall have income enough to live on, education enough to know how to live, and health enough to enjoy life."[31]

To be sure, progressives soon achieved a few long-standing goals. Wilson linked suffrage for women to the war's aims in a speech in 1918, stating, "We have made women partners in the war; shall we admit them only to a partnership of suffering and sacrifice and toil and not to a partnership of privilege and right?"[32] The House passed the suffrage amendment in 1918, the Senate early the following year, and the required thirty-six states ratified it in time for women to vote in the 1920 elections. Some progressives had long favored an outright ban on alcoholic beverages, and in 1917 Congress temporarily banned brewing and distilling to conserve grain and fuel. The WCTU, the Anti-Saloon League, and their allies then secured passage of a prohibition amendment in Congress, ratified by the states in 1919. When Congress returned the railroads to private management in 1920, it greatly expanded the powers of the ICC. In 1921, Congress passed the Sheppard-Towner Act, giving the Children's Bureau vast new responsibilities to provide infant and maternal health services, especially in rural areas. The war permanently expanded the size of the federal budget and established the principle of progressive taxation. For the first time taxes on income, profits, and estates rather than tariffs and other consumption taxes accounted for most of the government's revenue.

Nonetheless, postwar politics turned decisively against progressive social engineering. Wilson quickly dismantled the government agencies of economic coordination and control. Strikes increased, workers lost ground, repression of radicals reached new heights, and racial violence flared in the bloody summer of 1919. The bold new world of justice and efficiency was stillborn.

Some progressives recognized their failure sooner than others. Just after the armistice, John Dewey conceded that the war had brought out the worst in human nature, had failed to instill a larger common purpose, and had encouraged a "cult of irrationality" which contradicted progressives' faith in the reasonableness of an intelligent citizenry. In a 1926 symposium on postwar America in *Survey*, Ida Tarbell acknowledged with hindsight that "the pre-war radical . . . knew little about human beings, and what as individuals and herds they can be counted on to do under certain circumstances."[33]

If progressives proved overly optimistic about human rationality, they also failed to see how readily the powers of the administrative state, in which they vested so much hope, could be captured by the very trusts they were designed to regulate. Frederic Howe wrote in 1919 that he had "seen the government at close range, with its mask off; it existed for itself and for hidden men behind it. It was frankly doing the bidding of business." Nor did progressives acknowledge to themselves their own stake in the reforms they advocated. Ray Stannard Baker, looking back self-critically, conceded, "We were more interested in bossing our neighbors into our own little plans for goodness, or efficiency, or justice."[34] Progressives, as Baker implied, failed to recognize that, just like corporate capitalists, industrial workers, farmers, small business owners, immigrants, African-Americans, and other groups, reformers also sought autonomy, social status, and economic security.

For, like other Americans, progressive reformers and intellectuals tried to control their lives in "a very different age." However decent their motives and genuine their intentions, in seeking expert solutions to the problems of society, implemented through an activist government, they inevitably competed for power with other social groups. Unable to reflect on their stake in the policies they advocated, genuinely convinced that their proposals served the common good and not their own interests, they could never fully understand how other groups of Americans adapted to modern society. In the end, progressives, like other Americans, joined a contest for control under rules set by industrial capitalism.

NOTES

INTRODUCTION

1. Quoted in John Whiteclay Chambers II, *The Tyranny of Change*, 2nd ed. (New York, 1992), p. 2.
2. Benjamin Parke De Witt, *The Progressive Movement* (New York, 1915), p. 14.

PROLOGUE: CRISIS IN THE 1890S

1. Quoted in Stephen Brier et al., *Who Built America?*, Vol. 2 (New York, 1992), p. 147.
2. Quoted in Gene Clanton, *Populism: The Humane Preference in America, 1890–1900* (Boston, 1991), p. 23.
3. Jane Addams, *Twenty Years at Hull House* (New York, 1910), pp. 98–100.

1. OWNERS, MANAGERS, AND CORPORATE CAPITALISM

1. Woodrow Wilson, *The New Freedom* (New York, 1913), p. 27.
2. Quoted in James R. Beniger, *The Control Revolution* (Cambridge, 1986), p. 240.
3. Quoted in Alfred D. Chandler, Jr., *Strategy and Structure* (Cambridge, 1962), p. 55.
4. Quoted in Daniel Nelson, *Managers and Workers* (Madison, WI, 1975), p. 40.
5. Quoted in Sanford M. Jacoby, *Employing Bureaucracy* (New York, 1985), p. 17.
6. Quoted in JoAnne Yates, *Control Through Communication* (Baltimore, 1989), pp. 150, 152.

7. Quoted in Jacoby, *Employing Bureaucracy*, p. 44, and Dan Clawson, *Bureaucracy and the Labor Process* (New York, 1980), p. 128.

8. Frederick Winslow Taylor, *The Principles of Scientific Management* (New York, 1911), pp. 47, 7, 142–43.

9. Ibid., p. 7.

10. Quoted in Stuart D. Brandes, *American Welfare Capitalism* (Chicago, 1976), pp. 30, 32.

11. Quoted in Nelson, *Managers and Workers*, p. 151, and Olivier Zunz, *Making America Corporate* (Chicago, 1990), p. 135.

12. Quoted in James H. Soltow, *Origins of Small Business* (Philadelphia, 1965), p. 18.

13. Quoted in Philip Scranton, *Figured Tapestry* (Cambridge, 1989), pp. 136, 242.

14. Quoted in Beniger, *Control Revolution*, p. 347.

15. Quoted in Zunz, *Making America Corporate*, p. 31.

16. Quoted in Beniger, *Control Revolution*, p. 339, and Roy Alden Atwood, "Routes of Rural Discontent: Cultural Contradictions of Rural Free Delivery in Southeastern Iowa, 1899–1917," *Annals of Iowa* 48 (Summer–Fall 1987), pp. 270, 272.

17. Quoted in Glenn Porter, *The Rise of Big Business*, 2nd ed. (Wheeling, IL, 1992), p. 95.

18. Quoted in Robert H. Wiebe, *Businessmen and Reform* (Cambridge, 1962), p. 14.

2. INDUSTRIAL WORKERS' STRUGGLE FOR CONTROL

1. Quoted in David Brody, *Workers in Industrial America*, 2nd ed. (New York, 1993), pp. 3–4.

2. Quoted in ibid., p. 7.

3. Quoted in David Montgomery, *The Fall of the House of Labor* (Cambridge, 1987), pp. 39, 41.

4. Taylor, *Principles*, pp. 49–50.

5. Quoted in Montgomery, *Fall*, p. 248.

6. Quoted in ibid., p. 113.

7. Quoted in I. A. Newby, *Plain Folk in the New South* (Baton Rouge, 1989), p. 183.

8. Quoted in Alice Kessler-Harris, *Out to Work* (Oxford, 1982), p. 144.
9. Quoted in James R. Barrett, *Work and Community in the Jungle* (Urbana, 1987), p. 27.
10. Quoted in Montgomery, *Fall*, p. 234.
11. Tamara K. Hareven, *Family Time and Industrial Time* (Cambridge, 1982), p. 129.
12. Quoted in Newby, *Plain Folk*, pp. 168, 169, 173.
13. Quoted in Montgomery, *Fall*, p. 239, and Stephen Meyer III, *The Five Dollar Day* (Albany, 1981), p. 85.
14. Quoted in James R. Green, *The World of the Worker* (New York, 1980), p. 18, and Meyer, *Five Dollar Day*, p. 89.
15. Quoted in Kessler-Harris, *Out to Work*, p. 146.
16. John R. Commons, *Labor and Administration* (New York, 1923), p. 365.
17. Quoted in Montgomery, *Fall*, p. 59.
18. Quoted in ibid., p. 90.
19. Quoted in Brody, *Workers*, p. 29.
20. Quoted in David Brody, *The Butcher Workman* (Cambridge, 1964), p. 39.
21. Quoted in Barrett, *Work and Community*, pp. 158–59, 165.
22. Quoted in Susan A. Glenn, *Daughters of the Shtetl* (Ithaca, 1990), p. 174.
23. Quoted in Irving Howe, *World of Our Fathers* (New York, 1976), p. 298.
24. Quoted in Brody, *Workers*, pp. 35–36.
25. Quoted in Hareven, *Family Time*, p. 189, and John Bodnar, *Workers' World* (Baltimore, 1982), p. 40.
26. Bodnar, *Workers' World*, p. 47.
27. Ibid., p. 105.
28. Quoted in Gary R. Mormino and George E. Pozzetta, *The Immigrant World of Ybor City* (Urbana, 1987), p. 144.
29. David M. Emmons, *The Butte Irish* (Urbana, 1989), p. 198.
30. Roy Rosenzweig, *Eight Hours for What We Will* (Cambridge, 1983), p. 61; observer quoted in Perry R. Duis, *The Saloon* (Urbana, 1983), p. 201.
31. Quoted in Ardis Cameron, *Radicals of the Worst Sort* (Urbana, 1993), p. 101.
32. Quoted in Rosenzweig, *Eight Hours*, p. 151.
33. Quoted in David Nasaw, *Going Out* (New York, 1993), p. 168.

3. IMMIGRANTS IN INDUSTRIAL AMERICA

1. Kate Holladay Claghorn, "The Assimilation of Races," in Mary Beard, ed., *Women's Work in Municipalities* (New York, 1915), p. 174, and Robert Hunter, *Poverty* (New York, 1904), pp. 262–63.

2. Quoted in Ewa Morawska, *For Bread with Butter* (New York, 1985), p. 72.

3. Quoted in Elizabeth Ewen, *Immigrant Women in the Land of Dollars* (New York, 1985), p. 56.

4. Quoted in Judith E. Smith, *Family Connections* (Albany, 1985), p. 95, and Hareven, *Family Time*, p. 86.

5. Quoted in Mark Wyman, *Round-Trip to America* (Ithaca, 1993), p. 6.

6. Quoted in ibid., p. 96.

7. Quoted in Jeffrey Gurock, "From Exception to Role Model," *American Jewish History* 76 (June 1987), p. 463.

8. Quoted in Daniel M. Bluestone, " 'The Pushcart Evil,' " *Journal of Urban History* 18 (November 1991), p. 73, and Smith, *Family Connections*, p. 40.

9. Quoted in Alixa Naff, *Becoming American* (Carbondale, 1985), pp. 169–70, 165.

10. Robert E. Park and Herbert A. Miller, *Old World Traits Transplanted* (New York, 1921), pp. 121–22.

11. Quoted in Ronald M. Takaki, *Strangers from a Different Shore* (New York, 1989), p. 240.

12. Quoted in Robert Anthony Orsi, *The Madonna of 115th Street* (New Haven, 1985), p. 57.

13. Quoted in Howe, *World*, p. 185, and Takaki, *Strangers*, p. 118.

14. Quoted in Park and Miller, *Old World Traits*, pp. 127–28, 131.

15. Quoted in Takaki, *Strangers*, p. 280, and Park and Miller, *Old World Traits*, p. 133.

16. Quoted in Ewen, *Immigrant Women*, p. 192.

17. Quoted in Morawska, *For Bread*, p. 132, and M. Mark Stolarik, "Immigration, Education, and the Social Mobility of Slovaks, 1870–1930," in Randall M. Miller and Thomas D. Marzik, eds., *Immigrants and Religion in Urban America* (Philadelphia, 1977), pp. 107–8.

18. Quoted in Stephan F. Brumberg, *Going to America: Going to School* (New York, 1986), pp. 68, 12, 8, 146, and Takaki, *Strangers*, p. 257.

19. Quoted in Victor R. Green, *American Immigrant Leaders, 1800–1910* (Baltimore, 1987), pp. 100, 113, 121, 119.
20. Quoted in Yuji Ichioka, *The Issei* (New York, 1988), pp. 200, 219, 221.

4. RURAL AMERICANS AND INDUSTRIAL CAPITALISM

1. Quoted in Deborah Fink, *Agrarian Women* (Chapel Hill, 1992), p. 143.
2. Quoted in William L. Bowers, *The Country Life Movement in America* (Port Washington, 1974), p. 117.
3. Quoted in Dona Brown, *Inventing New England* (Washington, 1995), p. 144.
4. Ned Cobb quoted in Theodore Rosengarten, *All God's Dangers* (New York, 1974), p. 108; white tenant quoted in Newby, *Plain Folk*, p. 43.
5. Quoted in Newby, *Plain Folk*, p. 51.
6. Quoted in Wayne Flint, *Poor but Proud: Alabama's Poor Whites* (Tuscaloosa, 1989), p. 83.
7. Quoted in Newby, *Plain Folk*, pp. 2, 1.
8. Quoted in Ronald D. Eller, *Miners, Millhands and Mountaineers* (Knoxville, 1982), p. 22.
9. Quoted in Brier, *Who Built America?*, Vol. 2, p. 104.
10. Quoted in Caroline Gilman and Mary Jane Schneider, *The Way to Independence* (St. Paul, 1987), pp. 183, 198.
11. Quoted in ibid., pp. 209–10, 222.
12. Quoted in ibid., p. 223.
13. Quoted in Melissa L. Meyer, *The White Earth Tragedy* (Lincoln, NE, 1994), p. 113.
14. Quoted in ibid., p. 77.
15. Bowers, *Country Life*, p. 103.
16. Quoted in David B. Tyack, *The One Best System* (Cambridge, 1974), p. 21.
17. Quoted in William Link, *Paradox of Southern Progressivism* (Chapel Hill, 1992), pp. 272, 310.
18. Quoted in David B. Danbom, *The Resisted Revolution* (Ames, 1979), p. 82.
19. Quoted in Newby, *Plain Folk*, p. 409.

20. Quoted in Roy V. Scott, *The Reluctant Farmer* (Urbana, 1970), p. 10, and Danbom, *Resisted Revolution*, pp. 39, 88.

21. Quoted in Theodore Mitchell and Robert Lowe, "To Sow Contentment," *Journal of Social History* 24 (Winter 1990), p. 326, and Grant Mc-Connell, *The Decline of Agrarian Democracy* (Berkeley, 1953), p. 42.

22. Quoted in Danbom, *Resisted Revolution*, p. 89.

23. Quoted in ibid.

5. AFRICAN-AMERICANS' QUEST FOR FREEDOM

1. Quoted in Neil R. McMillen, *Dark Journey* (Urbana, 1989), p. 41.

2. Quoted in ibid., p. 25.

3. Quoted in John Dittmer, *Black Georgia in the Progressive Era* (Urbana, 1977), p. 135.

4. Quoted in McMillen, *Dark Journey*, p. 121.

5. Quoted in Elizabeth Clark-Lewis, *Living In, Living Out* (Washington, 1994), p. 48.

6. Quoted in ibid., pp. 41–42.

7. Quoted in Ronald L. Lewis, *Black Coal Miners in America* (Lexington, KY, 1987), p. 125.

8. Quoted in Norman L. Crockett, *The Black Towns* (Lawrence, KS, 1979), p. 46.

9. Quoted in Clark-Lewis, *Living In, Living Out*, p. 66.

10. Quoted in Lester Lamon, *Black Tenneseeans* (Knoxville, 1977), p. 120.

11. Quoted in Lewis, *Black Coal Miners*, p. 55.

12. Ibid., p. 135.

13. Quoted in Clark-Lewis, *Living In, Living Out*, p. 111.

14. Quoted in Elizabeth Clark-Lewis, " 'This Work Had an End,' " in Carol Groneman and Mary Beth Norton, eds., *"To Toil the Livelong Day"* (Ithaca, 1987), pp. 206–7.

15. Quoted in McMillen, *Dark Journey*, pp. 90, 91.

16. Bodnar, *Workers' World*, p. 29.

17. Quoted in James D. Anderson, *The Education of Blacks in the South, 1860–1935* (Chapel Hill, 1988), p. 166.

18. J. J. Watson, "Churches and Religious Conditions," *Annals of the American Academy of Political and Social Science* (September 1913), p. 120.

19. William Wells Brown, *My Southern Home* (Upper Saddle River, NJ, 1968), p. 193.

20. Rev. W. H. Holloway, "A Black Belt County, Georgia," in W. E. B. Du Bois, ed., *The Negro Church* (Atlanta, 1903), p. 58.
21. Quoted in McMillan, *Dark Journey*, p. 183.
22. Quoted in Elsa Barley Brown, "Maggie Lena Walker and the Independent Order of Saint Luke," in Linda K. Kerber and Jane Sherron De Hart, eds., *Women's America*, 4th ed. (New York, 1995), p. 235.
23. Booker T. Washington, "The Atlanta Exposition Address," September 18, 1895, in Washington, *Up From Slavery: An Autobiography* (New York, 1900), pp. 218–25.
24. Quoted in Brier, *Who Built America?*, Vol. 2, p. 202.
25. Quoted in August Meier and Elliott Rudwick, *Along the Color Line* (Urbana, 1976), p. 270.
26. Quoted in Herbert Shapiro, *White Violence and Black Response* (Amherst, 1988), p. 63, and McMillen, *Dark Journey*, p. 226.
27. Quoted in James Grossman, *Land of Hope* (Chicago, 1989), p. 36, and Emmet J. Scott, "Additional Letters of Negro Migrants of 1916–1918," *Journal of Negro History* 4 (October 1919), pp. 437, 438, 451; Johnson quoted in Grossman, *Land of Hope*, p. 60.
28. Haynes quoted in Carole Marks, *Farewell—We're Good and Gone* (Bloomington, 1989), p. 2. *Dallas Express* article in Malaika Adero, ed., *Up South* (New York, 1993), p. xviii.
29. Quoted in Grossman, *Land of Hope*, p. 58.
30. Quoted in ibid., p. 119.

6. WHITE-COLLAR WORKERS
IN CORPORATE AMERICA

1. Quoted in Roslyn L. Feldberg, " 'Union Fever': Organizing among Clerical Workers, 1900–1930," *Radical America* 14 (1980), p. 58.
2. Quoted in Jurgen Kocka, *White Collar Workers in America, 1890–1940* (London, 1980), pp. 88–89.
3. Quoted in Cindy Sondik Aron, *Ladies and Gentlemen of the Civil Service* (New York, 1987), p. 34.
4. Quoted in Gary Cross and Peter Shergold, " 'We Think We Are of the Oppressed': Gender, White Collar Work, and Grievances of Late Nineteenth-Century Women," *Labor History* 28 (1987), p. 47.
5. Quoted in Sharon Hartman Strom, *Beyond the Typewriter* (Urbana, 1992), p. 176.

6. Quoted in Aron, *Ladies and Gentlemen*, pp. 125–26.
7. Quoted in Strom, *Beyond the Typewriter*, p. 320.
8. Quoted in Margery W. Davies, *Woman's Place Is at the Typewriter* (Philadelphia, 1982), p. 131.
9. Quoted in Aron, *Ladies and Gentlemen*, p. 38.
10. Quoted in Davies, *Woman's Place*, pp. 77–78.
11. Quoted in Kocka, *White Collar Workers*, p. 90.
12. Quoted in Alice Kessler-Harris, "Independence and Virtue in the Lives of Wage-Earning Women," in Judith Friedlander, ed., *Women in Culture and Politics* (Bloomington, 1986), p. 10.
13. Quoted in William R. Leach, "Transformations in a Culture of Consumption," *Journal of American History* 71 (1984), p. 332.
14. Quoted in Cross and Shergold, " 'We Think We Are of the Oppressed,' " p. 50.
15. Quoted in Stephen H. Norwood, *Labor's Flaming Youth* (Urbana, 1990), pp. 35–36, 38.
16. Ibid, pp. 1, 48–49.

7. THE COMPETITION FOR CONTROL OF THE PROFESSIONS

1. Quoted in Paul Starr, *The Social Transformation of American Medicine* (New York, 1982), p. 164; *AAUP Bulletin* 1 (December 1915), p. 26.
2. Quoted in Samuel Haber, *The Quest for Authority and Honor in the American Professions, 1750–1900* (Chicago, 1991), p. 251.
3. Quoted in George Rosen, *The Structure of American Medical Practice* (Philadelphia, 1983), p. 30.
4. Quoted in James G. Burrow, *Organized Medicine in the Progressive Era* (Baltimore, 1977), pp. 43, 45.
5. Quoted in Rosen, *Structure*, p. 34.
6. Quoted in ibid., p. 42.
7. Quoted in John S. Haller, Jr., *American Medicine in Transition* (Urbana, 1981), p. 250.
8. Quoted in Starr, *Transformation of American Medicine*, p. 165.
9. Quoted in Haber, *Quest for Authority*, p. 228.
10. Quoted in Jerold S. Auerbach, *Unequal Justice* (New York, 1976), p. 63.

11. Quoted in Wayne K. Hobson, *The American Legal Profession and the Organizational Society* (New York, 1986), p. 283.
12. Quoted in Auerbach, *Unequal Justice*, p. 66.
13. Quoted in ibid., p. 33.
14. Quoted in Edwin T. Layton, Jr., *The Revolt of the Engineers* (Cleveland, 1971), p. 37.
15. Quoted in ibid., p. 146.
16. *AAUP Bulletin* 1 (December 1915), p. 28.
17. Quoted in Margaret W. Rossiter, *Women Scientists in America* (Baltimore, 1982), p. 68.
18. A. F. Weber, "Labor Legislation, National and International," *Journal of the American Social Science Association* 45 (September 1907), p. 36.
19. Quoted in Dee Garrison, *Apostles of Culture* (New York, 1979), p. 214.

8. THE PROGRESSIVE DISCOURSE IN AMERICAN POLITICS

1. Wilson, *New Freedom*, p. 27.
2. Addams, *Twenty Years at Hull House*, p. 309; Samuel Jones, *The New Right* (New York, 1899), pp. 469, 477.
3. Walter Rauschenbusch, *Christianity and the Social Crisis* (New York, 1907), p. 209.
4. Rheta Childe Dorr, *What Eight Million Women Want* (Boston, 1910), p. 327.
5. Quoted in John Milton Cooper, *Pivotal Decades* (New York, 1990), p. 88.
6. Quoted in Sidney E. Zimbalist, *Historic Themes and Landmarks in Social Welfare Research* (New York, 1977), p. 124.
7. Quoted in Martin J. Schiesl, *The Politics of Efficiency* (Berkeley, 1977), p. 167.
8. De Witt, *Progressive Movement*, p. 244.
9. "National Unity Versus Class Cleavage," in William H. Harbaugh, ed., *The Writings of Theodore Roosevelt* (Indianapolis, 1967), p. 20.
10. Rauschenbusch, *Christianity and the Social Crisis*, p. 336; Herbert Croly, *The Promise of American Life* (New York, 1909), p. xiv; James Harvey Robinson, *The New History* (New York, 1912), p. 251.
11. Quoted in Cooper, *Pivotal Decades*, p. 173.

12. Otis Pease, ed., *The Progressive Years* (New York, 1962), p. 326.
13. Wilson, *New Freedom*, pp. 227, 284; quoted in Cooper, *Pivotal Decades*, pp. 180, 182.
14. Quoted in Ronald Steel, *Walter Lippmann and the American Century* (Boston, 1980), p. 42.
15. Walter Lippmann, *A Preface to Politics*, paperback edition (Ann Arbor, 1962), pp. 25–26, 237.
16. Walter Lippmann, *Drift and Mastery*, paperback edition (New York, 1961), p. 151.

9. THE GREAT WAR AND
THE COMPETITION FOR CONTROL

1. Quoted in Ronald Schaeffer, *America in the Great War* (New York, 1991), p. 58.
2. Quoted in ibid., p. 57.
3. Quoted in Nell Irvin Painter, *Standing at Armageddon* (New York, 1987), p. 329.
4. Quoted in Sanford Jacoby, *Employing Bureaucracy* (New York, 1985), p. 135.
5. Quoted in Stuart Brandes, *American Welfare Capitalism* (Chicago, 1970), p. 127.
6. Quoted in Neil A. Wynn, *Progressivism to Prosperity* (New York, 1986), p. 98.
7. Quoted in Montgomery, *Fall of the House of Labor*, pp. 384–85.
8. Quoted in David Brody, *Labor in Crisis* (Philadelphia, 1965), p. 81.
9. Quoted in Brandes, *Welfare Capitalism*, p. 134.
10. Quoted in Strom, *Beyond the Typewriter*, pp. 201, 202.
11. Quoted in Danbom, *Resisted Revolution*, p. 102.
12. Quoted in ibid., p. 106.
13. Quoted in David Kennedy, *Over Here* (Oxford, 1980), pp. 120–21, and Danbom, *Resisted Revolution*, p. 108.
14. Quoted in Marine W. Greenwald, *Women, Work and War* (Westport, 1980), pp. 24, 27.
15. Du Bois in *The Crisis*, 16 (1918), p. 111; Simmons quoted in Kenneth W. Goings and Gerald L. Smith, " 'Unhidden Transcripts,' " *Journal of Urban History* 21 (March 1995), p. 390.

16. Quoted in Schaffer, *America in the Great War*, p. 79.
17. *Tifton Gazette* quoted in Dittmer, *Black Georgia*, p. 190.
18. Quoted in Dittmer, *Black Georgia*, p. 198, and Lamon, *Black Tennesseans*, p. 235.
19. Quoted in Hunter, "Domination and Resistance," *Labor History* 34 (Spring–Summer 1993), p. 215.
20. Claude McKay, "If We Must Die," in Robert T. Kerlin, *The Voice of the Negro, 1919* (New York, 1968), p. 186, and Arthur E. Barbeau and Florette Henri, *The Unknown Soldiers* (Philadelphia, 1974), p. 182.
21. Quoted in John F. McClymer, *War and Welfare* (Westport, 1980), pp. 113–14.
22. Quoted in Frederick Luebke, *The Bonds of Loyalty* (De Kalb, 1974), pp. 142, 146.
23. Quoted in Auerbach, *Unequal Justice*, pp. 114–15.
24. Quoted in Garrison, *Apostles of Culture*, p. 220.
25. Quoted in Wynn, *Progressivism to Prosperity*, pp. 36–37.
26. Quoted in Carol Gruber, *Mars and Minerva* (Baton Rouge, 1975), pp. 108, 125.
27. Quoted in Stuart Rochester, *American Liberal Disillusionment* (University Park, 1977), p. 42; Kennedy, *Over Here*, p. 39; John A. Thompson, *Reformers and War* (Cambridge, 1987), pp. 212–13; and Stephen Vaughn, *Holding Fast the Inner Lines* (Chapel Hill, 1980), p. 56.
28. Quoted in Chambers, *Tyranny of Change*, p. 244.
29. Quoted in Wynn, *Progressivism to Prosperity*, pp. 118–19.
30. Quoted in Alan Dawley, *Struggles for Justice* (Cambridge, 1991), p. 207; Stephen Vaughn, *Holding Fast the Inner Line* (Chapel Hill, 1980), p. 20, and ibid., p. 60.
31. Quoted in Kennedy, *Over Here*, p. 246, and McClymer, *War and Welfare*, p. 172.
32. Quoted in Cooper, *Pivotal Decades*, p. 308.
33. Quoted in Kennedy, *Over Here*, p. 90, and Rochester, *Liberal Disillusionment*, p. 95.
34. Frederic C. Howe, *The Confessions of a Reformer* (New York, 1925), p. 328; Baker quoted in Rochester, *Liberal Disillusionment*, p. 95.

BIBLIOGRAPHICAL ESSAY

Two classic interpretations of the Progressive Era are Richard Hofstadter, *The Age of Reform: From Bryan to F.D.R.* (New York, 1955), which emphasized status anxieties as a cause of the Populist and progressive reform movements, and Robert H. Wiebe, *The Search for Order, 1877–1920* (New York, 1967), which viewed the years from 1877 to the end of World War I as an era of bureaucratic rationalization in which a nation of "island communities" became a modern society. Several recent chronological surveys have integrated social history into political narratives, including Nell Irvin Painter, *Standing at Armageddon: The United States, 1877–1919* (New York, 1987), Alan Dawley, *Struggles for Justice: Social Responsibility and the Liberal State* (Cambridge, MA, 1991), and John Whiteclay Chambers II, *The Tyranny of Change: America in the Progressive Era, 1890–1920*, 2nd ed. (New York, 1992).

PROLOGUE: CRISIS IN THE 1890S

Many of the sources on the 1890s are included in the topical chapter bibliographies below. On national politics in the 1890s, see Lewis L. Gould, *The Presidency of William McKinley* (Lawrence, KS, 1980), Morton Keller, *Affairs of State: Public Life in Late Nineteenth Century America* (Cambridge, MA, 1977), Richard E. Welch, Jr., *The Presidencies of Grover Cleveland* (Lawrence, KS, 1988), and H. W. Brands, *The Reckless Decade: America in the 1890s* (New York, 1995).

The farmer protests of the late nineteenth century have interested historians since John D. Hicks published *The Populist Revolt* (Minneapolis, 1931). I have relied most heavily upon Lawrence Goodwyn, *Democratic*

Promise: The Populist Moment in America (New York, 1976), and Robert
C. McMath, Jr., *American Populism: A Social History, 1877–1898* (New
York, 1993). Narratives of the 1896 election include Paul W. Glad, *Mc-
Kinley, Bryan and the People* (Philadelphia, 1964), and Stanley L. Jones,
The Presidential Election of 1896 (Madison, WI, 1964). On Coxey's
march, see Carlos A. Schwantes, *Coxey's Army: An American Odyssey*
(Lincoln, NE, 1985).

1. OWNERS, MANAGERS, AND CORPORATE CAPITALISM

Glenn Porter, *The Rise of Big Business, 1860–1920*, 2nd ed. (Wheeling, IL,
1992), provides a succinct and authoritative survey of the emergence of large
business combinations, but Thomas C. Cochran, *American Business in the
Twentieth Century* (Cambridge, MA, 1972), is also useful. On the spate of
corporate mergers at the turn of the century, see Naomi Lamoreaux, *The
Great Merger Movement in American Business, 1895–1904* (Cambridge, MA,
1985). The definitive work on the development of centralized corporate man-
agement, on which I have relied heavily, is Alfred D. Chandler, Jr., *The
Visible Hand: The Managerial Revolution in American Business* (Cambridge,
MA, 1977), which built upon case studies in his earlier book, *Strategy and
Structure: Chapters in the History of the Industrial Enterprise* (Cambridge,
MA, 1962).

On the changing roles and relationships among managers and foremen in
large corporations, I found most useful Daniel Nelson, *Managers and Workers: Origins of the New Factory System in the United States, 1880–1920*
(Madison, WI, 1975), Sanford M. Jacoby, *Employing Bureaucracy: Managers, Unions, and the Transformation of Work in American Industry, 1900–
1945* (New York, 1985), Dan Clawson, *Bureaucracy and the Labor Process:
The Transformation of U.S. Industry, 1860–1920* (New York, 1980), JoAnne
Yates, *Control Through Communication: The Rise of System in American
Management* (Baltimore, 1989), and James R. Beniger, *The Control Revolution: Technological and Economic Origins of the Information Society* (Cambridge, MA, 1986). Olivier Zunz, *Making America Corporate, 1870–1920*
(Chicago, 1990), examines the work lives of middle managers and salesmen
in several corporations.

Daniel Wren, *The Evolution of Management Thought*, 2nd ed. (New York,

1979), offers a useful survey of the idea of systematic management. Of the vast literature on Frederick W. Taylor and scientific management, the most valuable are Samuel Haber, *Efficiency and Uplift: Scientific Management in the Progressive Era, 1890–1920* (Chicago, 1964), David F. Noble, *America by Design: Science, Technology and the Rise of Corporate Capitalism* (New York, 1977), and Daniel Nelson, *Frederick W. Taylor and the Rise of Scientific Management* (Madison, WI, 1980). Stuart D. Brandes examines corporate welfare programs in *American Welfare Capitalism, 1880–1940* (Chicago, 1976).

Historians have devoted much less attention to small businesses in the era of corporate capitalism. A few of the essays in Stuart W. Bruchey, ed., *Small Business in American Life* (New York, 1980), cover this period. James H. Soltow, *Origins of Small Business: Metal Fabricators and Machinery Makers in New England, 1890–1957* (Philadelphia, 1965), and Philip Scranton, *Figured Tapestry: Production, Markets, and Power in Philadelphia Textiles, 1885–1941* (New York, 1989), present valuable case studies of small manufacturers.

There is a vast literature on the history of government regulation of business in this period. The most sophisticated analysis of federal antitrust policy is Martin J. Sklar, *The Corporate Reconstruction of American Capitalism, 1890–1916: The Market, the Law, and Politics* (New York, 1988), elaborated further in *The United States as a Developing Country: Studies in U.S. History in the Progressive Era and the 1920s* (New York, 1992). See also Morton Keller, *Regulating a New Economy: Public Policy and Economic Change in America, 1900–1933* (Cambridge, MA, 1990). Gabriel Kolko, *The Triumph of Conservatism: A Re-interpretation of American History, 1900–1916* (New York, 1963), argues that corporate leaders used government to eliminate unprofitable competition, and James Weinstein, *The Corporate Ideal in the Liberal State: 1900–1918* (Boston, 1968), explores the ideology of corporate liberalism.

The classic work on businessmen's involvement in reform is Robert H. Wiebe, *Businessmen and Reform: A Study of the Progressive Movement* (Cambridge, MA, 1962). State and local studies include Mansel G. Blackford, *The Politics of Business in California, 1890–1920* (Columbus, 1977), and Judith Sealander, *Grand Plans: Business Progressivism and Social Change in Ohio's Miami Valley, 1890–1929* (Lexington, KY, 1988).

2. INDUSTRIAL WORKERS' STRUGGLE
FOR CONTROL

The essays and articles of Herbert G. Gutman collected in *Work, Culture and Society in Industrializing America* (New York, 1977) and in Ira Berlin, ed., *Power and Culture: Essays on the American Working Class* (New York, 1987), have greatly influenced historians of the American working class. The most important examination of worker struggle for control in this period, on which I have drawn heavily, is David Montgomery, *The Fall of the House of Labor: The Workplace, the State and American Labor Activism, 1865–1925* (New York, 1987), supplemented by Montgomery's earlier volume, *Workers' Control in America: Studies in the History of Work, Technology, and Labor Struggles* (New York, 1979). Useful surveys of the period include David Brody, *Workers in Industrial America: Essays on the Twentieth Century Struggle*, 2nd ed. (New York, 1993), Melvyn Dubofsky, *Industrialism and the American Worker, 1865–1920*, 2nd ed. (Arlington Heights, IL, 1985), James R. Green, *The World of the Worker: Labor in Twentieth Century America* (New York, 1980), and Daniel Nelson, *Farm and Factory: Workers in the Midwest, 1880–1990* (Bloomington, 1995). Surveys of women workers include Alice Kessler-Harris, *Out to Work: A History of Wage-Earning Women in the United States* (New York, 1982), and Leslie Woodcock Tentler, *Wage Earning Women: Industrial Work and Family Life in the United States, 1900–1930* (New York, 1979).

Francis Couvares provides an excellent portrait of the decline of skilled iron and glass craftsmen in *The Remaking of Pittsburgh: Class and Culture in an Industrializing City, 1877–1919* (Albany, 1984). Important studies of coal miners include David A. Corbin, *Life, Work and Rebellion in the Fields: The Southern West Virginia Coal Miners, 1880–1922* (Urbana, 1981), John Bodnar, *Anthracite People: Families, Unions and Work, 1900–1940* (Harrisburg, 1983), and Perry Blatz, *Democratic Miners: Work and Labor Relations in the Anthracite Coal Industry, 1875–1925* (Albany, 1994). James Barrett provides an insightful analysis of meatpackers in *Work and Community in the Jungle: Chicago's Packinghouse Workers, 1894–1922* (Urbana, 1987). On autoworkers, I have relied substantially on Stephen Meyer III, *The Five Dollar Day: Labor Management and Social Control in the Ford Motor Company, 1908–1921* (Albany, 1981). On cigar makers, see Patricia A. Cooper, *Once a Cigar Maker: Men, Women, and Work Culture in American Cigar*

Factories, 1900–1919 (Urbana, 1987). Tamara K. Hareven, *Family Time and Industrial Time* (New York, 1982), offers a rich portrait of textile workers in the Amoskeag mills, on which I have drawn. I. A. Newby, *Plain Folk in the New South: Social Change and Cultural Persistence, 1880–1915* (Baton Rouge, 1989), Jacqueline Dowd Hall, et al., *Like a Family: The Making of a Southern Cotton Mill World* (Chapel Hill, 1987), and Douglas Flamming, *Creating the Modern South: Millhands and Managers in Dalton, Georgia, 1884–1984* (Chapel Hill, 1992), offer a vivid picture of the lives of Southern textile workers. On common laborers, see Montgomery, *Fall of the House of Labor*, and Jacqueline Jones, *The Dispossessed: America's Underclass from the Civil War to the Present* (New York, 1992).

The historical literature on the labor movement and organized worker protest is voluminous. Bruno Ramirez, *When Workers Fight: The Politics of Industrial Relations in the Progressive Era, 1898–1916* (Westport, CT, 1978), surveys worker-employer bargaining in this period. P. K. Edwards, *Strikes in the United States* (New York, 1981), provides a thorough survey of walkouts. On the conflict at Homestead, see Leon Wolff, *Lockout: The Story of the Homestead Strike of 1892* (New York, 1965). On the success of garment workers in the years after 1909, see Susan Glenn, *Daughters of the Shtetl: Life and Labor in the Immigrant Generation* (Ithaca, 1990), and Meredith Tax, *The Rising of the Women: Feminist Solidarity and Class Conflict, 1880–1917* (New York, 1980). The Women's Trade Union League is examined in Nancy Schrom Dye, *As Equals and as Sisters: Feminism, Unionism and the Women's Trade Union League of New York* (Columbia, MO, 1980), and Elizabeth Anne Payne, *Reform, Labor and Feminism: Margaret Dreier Robins and the Women's Trade Union League* (Urbana, 1988). Major studies of the Wobblies include Patrick Renshaw, *The Wobblies: The Story of Syndicalism in the United States* (Garden City, NY, 1967), Melvyn Dubofsky, *We Shall Be All: A History of the Industrial Workers of the World* (Chicago, 1969), and two books by Joseph R. Conlin, *Bread and Roses Too: Studies of the Wobblies* (Westport, CT, 1969) and *At the Point of Production: The Local History of the I.W.W.* (Westport, CT, 1981).

There is also a substantial literature on workers and politics. Marc Karson surveys the AFL's political activities in *American Labor Unions and Politics, 1900–1918* (Carbondale, 1958). Irwin Yellowitz, *Labor and the Progressive Movement in New York State, 1897–1916* (Ithaca, 1965), and Gary M. Fink,

Labor's Search for Political Order: The Political Behavior of the Missouri Labor Movement, 1890–1940 (Columbia, MO, 1973), look at state-level politics. Socialist politics in this period is explored by Howard Quint, *The Forging of American Socialism* (Columbia, SC, 1953), David Shannon, *The Socialist Party of America* (New York, 1955), John H. M. Laslett, *Labor and the Left: A Study of Socialist and Radical Influences in the American Labor Movement, 1881–1924* (New York, 1970), and James Weinstein, *The Decline of Socialism in America, 1912–1925* (New York, 1967).

John Bodnar, *The Transplanted: A History of Immigrants in Urban America* (Bloomington, 1985), provides an excellent description of the immigrant family economy. In *Workers' World: Kinship, Community, and Protest in an Industrial Society, 1900–1940* (Baltimore, 1982), Bodnar offers firsthand accounts of the family economy and worker enclaves in industrial Pennsylvania. Tamara K. Hareven and Randolph Langenbach, *Amoskeag: Life and Work in an American Factory City* (New York, 1978), provides similar accounts of Manchester, New Hampshire. On homework, see Eileen Boris, *Home to Work: Motherhood and the Politics of Industrial Homework in the United States* (New York, 1994).

John T. Cumbler, *Working-Class Community in America: Work, Leisure and Struggle in Two Industrial Cities, 1880–1930* (Westport, CT, 1979), compares worker communities in Lynn and Fall River, Massachusetts. Gary R. Mormino and George E. Pozzetta, *The Immigrant World of Ybor City: Italians and their Latin Neighbors in Tampa, 1885–1985* (Urbana, 1987), explains the development of a radical culture there, and David Emmons, *The Butte Irish: Class and Ethnicity in an American Mining Town, 1875–1925* (Urbana, 1989), shows why a conservative Irish worker community emerged in this Montana town.

The most important book on worker leisure in this period is Roy Rosenzweig's pioneering study *Eight Hours for What We Will: Workers and Leisure in an Industrial City, 1870–1920* (New York, 1983). Dominick Cavallo examines reformers of the playground movement in *Muscles and Morals: Organized Playgrounds and Urban Reform, 1880–1920* (Philadelphia, 1981). See also Couvares, *The Remaking of Pittsburgh*, and Ardis Cameron, *Radicals of the Worst Sort: Laboring Women in Lawrence, Massachusetts, 1960–1912* (Urbana, 1993). On the saloon, see Perry R. Duis, *The Saloon: Public Drinking in Chicago and Boston, 1880–1920* (Urbana, 1983).

3. IMMIGRANTS IN INDUSTRIAL AMERICA

A classic interpretation of the immigrant experience is Oscar Handlin, *The Uprooted: The Epic Story of the Great Migrations That Made the American People* (New York, 1951), which movingly describes the alienation of peasants forced to come to America. The most comprehensive alternative to Handlin's argument is Bodnar, *The Transplanted*. Among the many other general surveys of immigration to America, I have found Roger Daniels, *Coming to America: A History of Immigration and Ethnicity in American Life* (New York, 1990), useful for its treatment of specific immigrant groups. See also Maldwyn Allen Jones, *American Immigration*, 2nd ed. (Chicago, 1992), and Thomas Archdeacon, *Becoming American: An Ethnic History* (New York, 1983).

Among the hundreds of histories of specific immigrant groups, I have found the following most helpful: On Italians, Virginia Yans-McLaughlin, *Family and Community: Italian Immigrants in Buffalo, 1880–1930* (Ithaca, 1977), Donna Gabaccia, *From Sicily to Elizabeth Street: Housing and Social Change among Italian Immigrants, 1880–1930* (Albany, 1984), and Dino Cinel, *From Italy to San Francisco: The Immigrant Experience* (Stanford, 1982). On Jews, Irving Howe, *World of Our Fathers: The Journey of the East European Jews to America and the Life They Found and Made* (New York, 1976), and Gerald Sorin, *A Time for Building: The Third Migration, 1880–1920* (Baltimore, 1992). On Poles, Dominic Pacyga, *Polish Immigrants and Industrial Chicago: Workers on the South Side, 1880–1922* (Columbus, OH, 1991), and Joseph John Parot, *Polish Catholics in Chicago, 1850–1920* (De Kalb, IL, 1981). On Germans, Hartmut Keil and John B. Jentz, eds., *German Workers in Industrial Chicago, 1850–1910: A Comparative Perspective* (De Kalb, IL, 1983). On the Irish, Kerby Miller, *Emigrants and Exiles: Ireland and the Irish Exodus to North America* (New York, 1985), and Hasia R. Diner, *Erin's Daughters in America: Immigrant Women in the Nineteenth Century* (Baltimore, 1983). On Swedes, Philip J. Anderson and Dag Blanck, eds., *Swedish-American Life in Chicago: Cultural and Urban Aspects of an Immigrant People, 1850–1930* (Urbana, 1992). On the Chinese, Shih-shan Henry Tsai, *The Chinese Experience in America* (Bloomington, 1986), and Sucheng Chan, *This Bittersweet Soil: The Chinese in California Agriculture, 1869–1910* (Berkeley, 1986). On the Japanese, Yuji Ichioka, *The Issei: The World of the First Generation Japanese Immigrants, 1885–1924* (New York,

1988), Brian Masaru Hayashi, *"For the Sake of Our Japanese Brethren":
Assimilation, Nationalism, and Protestantism among the Japanese of Los An-
geles, 1895–1942* (Stanford, 1995), and Edna Bonacich and John Modell,
*The Economic Basis of Ethnic Solidarity: Small Business in the Japanese-
American Community* (Berkeley, 1980). On Greeks, Theodore Saloutos, *The
Greeks in the United States* (Cambridge, MA, 1964). On French Canadians,
Bruno Ramirez, *On the Move: French Canadian and Italian Migrants in the
North Atlantic Economy, 1860–1914* (Toronto, 1991). On Syrians, Alixa Naff,
Becoming American: The Early Arab Immigrant Experience (Carbondale,
1985). On Mexicans, Mario T. Garcia, *Desert Immigrants: The Mexicans of
El Paso, 1880–1920* (New Haven, 1981), and George J. Sanchez, *Becoming
Mexican American: Ethnicity, Culture and Identity in Chicano Los Angeles,
1900–1945* (New York, 1993). On Slovaks, June Granatir Alexander, *The
Immigrant Church and Community: Pittsburgh's Slovak Catholics and Lu-
therans, 1880–1915* (Pittsburgh, 1987). And on Cape Verdeans, Marilyn
Halter, *Between Race and Ethnicity: Cape Verdean American Immigrants,
1860–1965* (Urbana, 1993). Studies of two or more groups I have found most
useful include Ewa Morawska, *For Bread with Butter: The Life Worlds of
East Central Europeans in Johnstown, Pennsylvania, 1890–1940* (New York,
1985), Ronald Takaki, *Strangers from a Different Shore: A History of Asian
Americans* (New York, 1989), and Judith E. Smith, *Family Connections: A
History of Italian and Jewish Immigrant Lives in Providence, Rhode Island,
1900–1940* (Albany, 1985).

Mark Wyman, *Round-Trip to America: The Immigrants Return to Europe,
1880–1930* (Ithaca, 1993), discusses how home governments encouraged
repatriation. Robert Anthony Orsi, *The Madonna of 115th Street: Faith and
Community in Italian Harlem, 1880–1950* (New Haven, 1985), is a splendid
case study of Italian immigrant religion. There is no general history of either
immigrant peddling or small business, but Scott Cummings, ed., *Self-Help
in Urban America: Patterns of Minority Business Enterprise* (Port Washington,
NY, 1980), has useful essays on mutual aid societies. Robert E. Park, *The
Immigrant Press and Its Control* (New York, 1922), is still valuable.

On Catholic parochial education, see James W. Sanders, *The Education
of an Urban Minority: Catholics in Chicago, 1833–1965* (New York, 1977),
and M. Mark Stolarik's essay on Slovaks in Randall M. Miller and Thomas
S. Marzik, eds., *Immigrants and Religion in Urban America* (Philadelphia,

1977). Other than Stephan F. Brumberg, *Going to America, Going to School: The Jewish Immigrant Public School Encounter in Turn-of-the-Century New York City* (New York, 1986), and Leonard Covello, *The Social Background of the Italo-American School Child* (Leiden, 1967), relatively little has been written on how immigrant children experienced public schools. My discussion of immigrant leaders and Americanization draws heavily on Victor R. Greene, *American Immigrant Leaders, 1800–1910: Marginality and Identity* (Baltimore, 1987).

4. RURAL AMERICANS AND INDUSTRIAL CAPITALISM

Numerous social histories of American farmers in this period have been published in the last decade. David B. Danbom, *Born in the Country: A History of Rural America* (Baltimore, 1995), provides an excellent recent survey. On Southern agriculture, I have found Pete Daniel, *Breaking the Land: The Transformation of Cotton, Tobacco, and Rice Cultures Since 1880* (Urbana, 1985), extremely useful. See also Gilbert C. Fite, *Cotton Fields No More: Southern Agriculture, 1865–1980* (Lexington, KY, 1984).

On farmer protest and collective action, in addition to the sources on Populism listed above see Theodore Saloutos and John D. Hicks, *Agricultural Discontent in the Middle West, 1900–1939* (Madison, WI, 1951), and Theodore Saloutos, *Farmer Movements in the South, 1865–1933* (Berkeley, 1960).

Case studies of how farmers lived and adapted to change outside the South include Jane Marie Penderson, *Between Memory and Reality: Family and Community in Rural Wisconsin, 1870–1970* (Madison, WI, 1992), Hal S. Barron, *Those Who Stayed Behind: Rural Society in Nineteenth-Century New England* (New York, 1984), Kathleen Neils Conzen's essay on German farmers in St. Martin, Minnesota, in Steven Hahn and Jonathan Prude, eds., *The Countryside in the Age of Capitalist Transformation: Essays in the Social History of Rural America* (Chapel Hill, 1985), Carol K. Coburn, *Life at Four Corners: Religion, Gender, and Education in a German-Lutheran Community, 1868–1945* (Lawrence, KS, 1992), J. Sanford Rikoon, *Threshing in the Midwest, 1820–1940: A Study of Traditional Culture and Technological Change* (Bloomington, 1988), Jon Gjerde, *From Peasants to Farmers: The Migration from Balestrand, Norway, to the Upper Middle West* (New York, 1985), Jane Adams, *The Transformation of Rural Life: Southern Illinois, 1890–1990*

(Chapel Hill, 1994), and Marilyn P. Watkins, *Rural Democracy: Family Farmers and Politics in Western Washington, 1890–1925* (Ithaca, 1995). Eric E. Lampard, *The Rise of the Dairy Industry in Wisconsin: A Study in Agricultural Change, 1880–1920* (Madison, WI, 1963), remains valuable. Dona Brown, *Inventing New England: Regional Tourism in the Nineteenth Century* (Washington, DC, 1995), describes the efforts of New Hampshire and Vermont to attract farm vacationers. On women's roles in farming and in rural communities, I have made substantial use of Mary Neth, *Preserving the Family Farm: Women, Community, and the Foundations of Agribusiness in the Midwest, 1900–1940* (Baltimore, 1995), Deborah Fink, *Agrarian Women: Wives and Mothers in Rural Nebraska, 1880–1940* (Chapel Hill, 1992), Nancy Grey Osterud, *Bonds of Community: The Lives of Farm Women in Nineteenth-Century New York* (Ithaca, 1991), Joan M. Jensen, *Promise to the Land: Essays on Rural Women* (Albuquerque, 1991), and Glenda Riley, *The Female Frontier: A Comparative View of Women on the Prairie and the Plains* (Lawrence, KS, 1988).

From the rich literature on Southern tenant farmers and poor landowners, I have relied most heavily on Newby, *Plain Folk*, Pete Daniel, *Standing at the Crossroads: Southern Life Since 1900* (New York, 1986), Jack Temple Kirby, *The Countercultural South* (Athens, GA, 1995), Ted Ownby, *Subduing Satan: Religion, Recreation, and Manhood in the Rural South, 1865–1920* (Chapel Hill, 1990), and two books by Wayne Flynt, *Poor but Proud: Alabama's Poor Whites* (Tuscaloosa, 1989), and *Dixie's Forgotten People: The South's Poor Whites* (Bloomington, 1979). Peonage is examined in Pete Daniel, *The Shadow of Slavery: Peonage in the South, 1901–1969* (Urbana, 1972).

In the sources for Chapter 5, below, I discuss the extensive writings on the migration of African-Americans to the North. The migration of white Southerners has not been well documented, but a start has been made in Jack Temple Kirby, "The Southern Exodus, 1910–1960: A Primer for Historians," *Journal of Southern History* 49 (November 1983), pp. 585–600, Neil Fligstein, *Going North: Migration of Blacks and Whites from the South, 1900–1950* (New York, 1981), and Lorraine Garkovich, *Population and Community in Rural America* (New York, 1989).

My discussion of black subsistence farming in the South Carolina low country is based on John Scott Strickland's article in Hahn and Prude, eds.,

The Countryside in the Age of Capitalist Transformation. Subsistence farming and the displacement of Appalachian mountain folk is discussed by Ronald D. Eller, *Miners, Millhands, and Mountaineers: Industrialization of the Appalachian South, 1880–1930* (Knoxville, 1982). The effects of Southwestern prairie rice cultivation on Cajun farmers is discussed briefly in Glenn R. Conrad, ed., *The Cajuns: Essays on Their History and Culture*, 2nd ed. (Lafayette, LA, 1978). On Hispanic farmers displaced by Anglo settlement in the Southwest, see Sarah Deutsch, *No Separate Refuge: Culture, Class and Gender on an Anglo-Hispanic Frontier in the American Southwest, 1880–1940* (New York, 1987).

On the impact of the Dawes Act and the allotment policy for Native Americans, see Frederick E. Hoxie, *A Final Promise: The Campaign to Assimilate the Indians, 1880–1920* (Lincoln, NE, 1984). My discussion of the Hidatsa is based on Carolyn Gilman, *The Way to Independence: Memories of a Hidatsa Indian Family, 1840–1920* (St. Paul, 1987); my discussion of the Anishinaabe comes from Melissa L. Meyer, *The White Earth Tragedy: Ethnicity and Dispossession at a Minnesota Anishinaabe Reservation, 1889–1920* (Lincoln, NE, 1994).

The Country Life Movement and farmers' resistance to it are discussed in William L. Bowers, *The Country Life Movement in America, 1900–1920* (Port Washington, NY, 1974), and David Danbom, *The Resisted Revolution: Urban America and the Industrialization of Agriculture, 1900–1930* (Ames, 1979). On resistance to school centralization, see William A. Link, *A Hard Country and a Lonely Place: Schooling, Society, and Reform in Rural Virginia, 1870–1920* (Chapel Hill, 1986), and *The Paradox of Southern Progressivism, 1880–1930* (Chapel Hill, 1992), Wayne E. Fuller, *The Old Country School: The Story of Rural Education in the Middle West* (Chicago, 1982), and David B. Tyack, *The One Best System: A History of American Urban Education* (Cambridge, MA, 1974). On the agricultural extension movement, see Roy V. Scott, *The Reluctant Farmer: The Rise of Agricultural Extension to 1914* (Urbana, 1970).

5. AFRICAN-AMERICANS' QUEST FOR FREEDOM

August Meier, *Negro Thought in America, 1880–1915: Racial Ideologies in the Age of Booker T. Washington* (Ann Arbor, 1963), remains a useful survey of the African-American experience in the Progressive Era. Numerous books examine individual states and cities in this period. Neil R. McMillen, *Dark Journey: Black Mississippians in the Age of Jim Crow* (Urbana, 1989), is meticulously researched and well written. Also valuable are John Dittmer, *Black Georgia in the Progressive Era, 1900–1920* (Urbana, 1977), Lester Lamon, *Black Tennesseans, 1900–1930* (Knoxville, 1977), and Fon Louise Gordon, *Caste and Class: The Black Experience in Arkansas, 1880–1920* (Athens, 1995), Earl Lewis, *In Their Own Interests: Race, Class, and Power in Twentieth-Century Norfolk, Virginia* (Berkeley, 1991), and George C. Wright, *Life Behind a Veil: Blacks in Louisville, Kentucky, 1865–1930* (Baton Rouge, 1985). My account of the People's Grocery violence in Memphis comes from Kenneth W. Goings and Gerald L. Smith, " 'Unhidden' Transcripts: Memphis and African American Agency, 1862–1920," *Journal of Urban History* 21 (March 1995), pp. 372–94. Elizabeth Bethel, *Promiseland: A Century of Life in a Negro Community* (Philadelphia, 1981), uses oral history to document the experience of a rural community of black landowners.

On the development of all-black towns, see Norman Crockett, *The Black Towns* (Lawrence, KS, 1979), and Kenneth M. Hamilton, *Black Towns and Profit: Promotion and Development in the Trans-Appalachian West, 1877–1915* (Urbana, 1991). Edwin S. Redkey, *Black Exodus: Black Nationalist and Back-to-Africa Movements, 1890–1910* (New Haven, 1969), tells the story of those who sought to return to Africa. William Cohen, *At Freedom's Edge: Black Mobility and the Southern White Quest for Racial Control, 1861–1915* (Baton Rouge, 1991), carefully details the white South's efforts to control black movement before the Great Migration.

The development of Northern urban communities in these years has received a great deal of attention. Early studies of ghetto formation include Gilbert Osofsky, *Harlem: The Making of a Ghetto: Negro New York, 1890–1930* (New York, 1963), Allan Spear, *Black Chicago: The Making of a Negro Ghetto, 1890–1920* (Chicago, 1967), and Kenneth Kusmer, *A Ghetto Takes Shape: Black Cleveland, 1870–1930* (Urbana, 1976). More recent studies have focused on the lives of African-Americans as workers and city residents. See Joe W. Trotter, Jr., *Black Milwaukee: The Making of an Industrial Proletariat, 1915–1945* (Urbana, 1985), Peter Gottlieb, *Making Their Own Way: Southern Blacks' Migration to Pittsburgh, 1916–30* (Urbana, 1987), Roger Lane, *The Roots of Violence in Black Philadelphia, 1860–1900* (Cambridge,

MA, 1986), Douglas H. Daniels, *Pioneer Urbanites: A Social and Cultural History of Black San Francisco* (Philadelphia, 1979), Albert S. Broussard, *Black San Francisco: The Struggle for Racial Equality in the West, 1900–1954* (Lawrence, KS, 1993), Quintard Taylor, *The Forging of a Black Community: Seattle's Central District from 1870 Through the Civil Rights Era* (Seattle, 1994), and Richard W. Thomas, *Life for Us Is What We Make It: Building Black Community in Detroit, 1915–1945* (Bloomington, 1992). On African-American industrial and urban workers, see Ronald L. Lewis, *Black Coal Miners in America: Race, Class and Community Conflict, 1780–1980* (Lexington, KY, 1987), Joe William Trotter, Jr., *Coal, Class and Color: Blacks in Southern West Virginia, 1915–1932* (Urbana, 1990), Eric Arnesen, *Waterfront Workers in New Orleans: Race, Class and Politics, 1863–1923* (New York, 1991), Daniel Rosenberg, *New Orleans Dockworkers: Race, Labor and Unionism, 1892–1923* (Albany, 1988), and Dennis C. Dickerson, *Out of the Crucible: Black Steelworkers in Western Pennsylvania, 1875–1980* (Albany, 1986). William H. Harris, *The Harder We Run: Black Workers Since the Civil War* (New York, 1982), is an excellent survey. Elizabeth Clark-Lewis, *Living In, Living Out: African American Domestics in Washington, D.C., 1910–1940* (Washington, DC, 1994), is an extraordinarily rich history, based largely on interviews with women who migrated from the South to Washington. Tera W. Hunter, "Domination and Resistance: The Politics of Wage Household Labor in New South Atlanta," *Labor History* 34 (Spring–Summer 1993), pp. 205–20, shows how black washerwomen and other domestic workers maintained a degree of control over their work.

Violence against African-Americans in the South and their response to it are examined in W. Fitzhugh Brundage, *Lynching in the New South: Georgia and Virginia, 1880–1930* (Urbana, 1993), and Herbert Shapiro, *White Violence and Black Response: From Reconstruction to Montgomery* (Amherst, 1988). August Meier and Elliott Rudwick describe resistance to streetcar segregation in Southern cities in *Along the Color Line: Explorations in the Black Experience* (Urbana, 1976). Robin D. G. Kelley, *Race Rebels: Culture, Politics and the Black Working Class* (New York, 1994), examines the ways in which Southern African-Americans in this period resisted domination by whites.

My description of the efforts of African-American communities to build "Rosenwald schools" is based on James D. Anderson, *The Education of*

Blacks in the South, 1860–1935 (Chapel Hill, 1988). Histories of black religious life in this period include William E. Montgomery, *Under Their Own Vine and Fig Tree: The African-American Church in the South, 1865–1900* (Baton Rouge, 1993), C. Eric Lincoln and Lawrence H. Mamiya, *The Black Church in the African-American Experience* (Durham, 1990), Clarence Taylor, *The Black Churches of Brooklyn* (New York, 1994), Robert Gregg, *Sparks from the Anvil of Oppression: Philadelphia's African Methodists and Southern Migrants, 1890–1940* (Philadelphia, 1993), and James T. Campbell, *Songs of Zion: The African Methodist Episcopal Church in the United States and South Africa* (New York, 1995).

A vast historical literature documents the Great Migration and debates its causes. I have relied heavily on James Grossman, *Land of Hope: Chicago, Black Southerners, and the Great Migration* (Chicago, 1989), which argues that the migration represented a grass-roots effort at emancipation. See also Carole Marks, *Farewell—We're Good and Gone: The Great Black Migration* (Bloomington, 1989). Older historical studies include Fligstein, *Going North*, Florette Henri, *Black Migration: Movement North, 1900–1920: The Road from Myth to Man* (Garden City, NY, 1975), and Arna Bontemps and Jack Conroy, *They Seek a City* (Garden City, NY, 1945).

6. WHITE-COLLAR WORKERS IN CORPORATE AMERICA

No single work surveys white-collar work in the Progressive Era. Stuart Blumin, *The Emergence of the Middle Class: Social Experience in the American City, 1760–1900* (New York, 1989), examines the development of middle-class identity in the nineteenth century, but ends in 1900. Zunz, *Making America Corporate*, argues that white-collar employees created a corporate work culture. Jurgen Kocka, *White Collar Workers in America, 1890–1940: A Social-Political History in International Perspective* (London, 1980), compares salesclerks and clerical workers for manufacturing firms in the United States and Germany. Christopher P. Wilson, *White Collar Fictions: Class and Social Representation in American Literature, 1885–1925* (Athens, GA, 1992), looks at how American writers of the era portrayed white-collar workers.

Cindy Sondik Aron, *Ladies and Gentlemen of the Civil Service: Middle Class Workers in Victorian America* (New York, 1987), examines perceptively the men and women who staffed federal government agencies in the years between the Civil War and 1900. Margery W. Davies, *Woman's Place Is at the Typewriter: Office Work and Office Workers, 1870–1930* (Philadelphia, 1982), explores the feminization of office work, and Sharon H. Strom, *Beyond the Typewriter: Gender, Class and the Origins of Modern American Office Work, 1900–1930* (Urbana, 1992), provides rich detail on male and female clerical workers. See also Elyce J. Rotella, *From Home to Office: U.S. Women at Work, 1870–1930* (Ann Arbor, 1980), and Angel Kwolek-Folland, *Engendering Business: Men and Women in the Corporate Office, 1870–1930* (Baltimore, 1994). On high school education and clerical work, see Ileen A. DeVault, *Sons and Daughters of Labor: Class and Clerical Work in Turn-of-the-Century Pittsburgh* (Ithaca, 1990), John L. Rury, *Education and Women's Work: Female Schooling and the Division of Labor in Urban America, 1870–1930* (Albany, 1991), and Harvey Kantor, *Learning to Earn: School, Work and Vocational Reform in California, 1880–1930* (Madison, WI, 1988). On telephone operators, see Stephen H. Norwood, *Labor's Flaming Youth: Telephone Operators and Worker Militancy, 1878–1923* (Urbana, 1990). The best work on salesclerks is Susan Porter Benson, *Counter Cultures: Saleswomen, Managers and Customers in American Department Stores, 1890–1940* (Urbana, 1986).

7. THE COMPETITION FOR CONTROL OF THE PROFESSIONS

Burton Bledstein, *The Culture of Professionalism: The Middle Class and the Development of Higher Education in America* (New York, 1976), traces the development of a professional identity in this period. Samuel Haber, *The Quest for Authority and Honor in the American Professions, 1750–1900* (Chicago, 1991), reexamines the history of lawyers, the clergy, professors, engineers, and physicians.

Paul Starr, *The Social Transformation of American Medicine: The Rise of a Sovereign Profession and the Making of a Vast Industry* (New York, 1982), provides a superb analysis of the professionalization of medicine, upon which I have drawn heavily. Other important works include John S. Haller, Jr., *American Medicine in Transition, 1840–1910* (Urbana, 1981), George Rosen, *The Structure of American Medical Practice, 1875–1941* (Philadelphia, 1983), and James G. Burrow, *Organized Medicine in the Progressive Era: The*

Move Toward Monopoly (Baltimore, 1977). On black physicians, see Herbert M. Morais, *The History of the Negro in Medicine* (New York, 1967). The development of hospitals in this period is examined in Charles E. Rosenberg, *The Care of Strangers: The Rise of America's Hospital System* (New York, 1987), and David Rosner, *A Once Charitable Enterprise: Hospitals and Health Care in Brooklyn and New York, 1885–1915* (New York, 1982). Studies of women physicians include Regina M. Morantz-Sanchez, *Sympathy and Science: Women Physicians in American Medicine* (New York, 1985), and Mary Roth Walsh, *"Doctors Wanted: No Women Need Apply": Sexual Barriers in the Medical Profession, 1835–1975* (New Haven, 1977). See also Barbara Sicherman, *Alice Hamilton, A Life in Letters* (Cambridge, MA, 1984).

No one book surveys comprehensively the legal profession in these years. Lawrence M. Friedman, *A History of American Law* (New York, 1973), ends with a general sketch of the twentieth century. Jerold S. Auerbach, *Unequal Justice: Lawyers and Social Change in Modern America* (New York, 1976), examines bigotry in the legal elite and its service to the wealthy. Several of the articles in Gerard W. Gawalt, ed., *The New High Priests: Lawyers in Post-Civil War America* (Westport, CT, 1984), illuminate the dynamics of professionalization in this period. Wayne K. Hobson, *The American Legal Profession and the Organizational Society, 1890–1930* (New York, 1986), has a wealth of information. Robert Stevens, *Law School: Legal Education from the 1850s to the 1980s* (Chapel Hill, 1983), traces the rise of university law schools and their impact on the profession. On women attorneys, see Karen Berger Morello, *The Invisible Bar: The Woman Lawyer in America, 1638 to the Present* (New York, 1986). On African-American lawyers, see Kenneth S. Tollett, "Black Lawyers, Their Education and the Black Community," *Howard Law Journal*, 17 (1972), pp. 326–57.

The most useful study of the professionalization of engineering in this period is Edwin T. Layton, Jr., *The Revolt of the Engineers: Social Responsibility and the American Engineering Profession* (Cleveland, 1971), on which much of my account is based, but see also Monte A. Calvert, *The Mechanical Engineer in America, 1830–1910* (Baltimore, 1967). Kenneth E. Trombley, *The Life and Times of a Happy Liberal: A Biography of Morris Llewellyn Cooke* (New York, 1954), is admiring and uncritical.

Laurence R. Veysey, *The Emergence of the American University* (Chicago, 1965), explores the rise of the modern university. The professionalization of the social sciences is examined in Dorothy Ross, *The Origins of American Social Science* (Cambridge, MA, 1991), Mary O. Furner, *Advocacy and Objectivity: A Crisis in the Professionalization of American Social Science, 1865–1905* (Lexington, KY, 1975), and Thomas L. Haskell, *The Emergence of Professional Social Science: The American Social Science Association and the Nineteenth-Century Crisis of Authority* (Urbana, 1977). On professors' lack of job security, see Walter Metzger, *Academic Freedom in the Age of the University* (New York, 1955). Jessie Bernard, *Academic Women* (University Park, PA, 1964) is an important early study of women professors, but see also Margaret W. Rossiter, *Women Scientists in America: Struggles and Strategies to 1940* (Baltimore, 1982). Robert Clarke, *Ellen Swallow: The Woman Who Founded Ecology* (Chicago, 1973), discusses the emergence of home economics.

The role of university professors in La Follette's administration is described in Charles McCarthy, *The Wisconsin Idea* (New York, 1912), and Russel B. Nye, *Midwestern Progressive Politics: A Historical Study of Its Origins and Development, 1870–1958* (East Lansing, 1951), and in several La Follette biographies (see below). Steven J. Diner, *A City and Its Universities: Public Policy in Chicago, 1892–1919* (Chapel Hill, 1980), examines professors' involvement in reform and public policy in Progressive Era Chicago. Barry D. Karl traces Merriam's career in *Charles E. Merriam and the Study of Politics* (Chicago, 1974). The activities of professors in the American Association for Labor Legislation are analyzed in Theda Skocpol, *Protecting Soldiers and Mothers: The Political Origins of Social Policy in the United States* (Cambridge, MA, 1992). JoAnne Brown, *The Definition of a Profession: The Authority of Metaphor in the History of Intelligence Testing, 1890–1930* (Princeton, 1992), describes the applications of measurement psychology.

The only systematic discussion of the professionalization of the clergy in this period is in Haber, *The Quest for Authority and Honor*, which ends in 1900. Brief discussions of professional status and training of clergy can be found in denominational histories, histories of theological seminaries, and studies of the social gospel movement. On women in the Protestant ministry, see Cynthia Grant Tucker, *Prophetic Sisterhood: Liberal Women Ministers of the Frontier, 1880–1930* (Boston, 1990).

Although a full history of teachers in this period remains to be written, Donald Warren, ed., *American Teachers: Histories of a Profession at Work*

(New York, 1989), provides a start. Teacher unionization in this period is well documented in Marjorie Murphy, *Blackboard Unions: The AFT and the NEA, 1900–1980* (Ithaca, 1990). On Richman, see Selma Cantor Berrol, *Julia Richman: A Notable Woman* (Philadelphia, 1993). On Young, see Joan K. Smith, *Ella Flagg Young: Portrait of a Leader* (Ames, 1979). On women college students in this period, see Lynn D. Gordon, *Gender and Higher Education in the Progressive Era* (New Haven, 1990).

My discussion of librarians draws heavily on Dee Garrison, *Apostles of Culture: The Public Librarian and American Society, 1876–1920* (New York, 1979). On the history of nursing in this period, see Susan Reverby, *Ordered to Care: The Dilemma of American Nursing, 1850–1945* (New York, 1987), and Darlene Clark Hine, *Black Women in White: Racial Conflict and Co-operation in the Nursing Profession, 1890–1950* (Bloomington, 1989). Barbara Melosh, *"The Physician's Hand": Work Culture and Conflict in American Nursing* (Philadelphia, 1982), although concerned with the years after 1920, provides a valuable perspective on this period. The standard work on the professionalization of social work is Roy Lubove, *The Professional Altruist: The Emergence of Social Work as a Career, 1880–1930* (Cambridge, MA, 1965). See also Clarke A. Chambers, "Women in the Creation of Social Work," *Social Service Review* 60 (March 1986), pp. 1–33.

8. THE PROGRESSIVE DISCOURSE IN AMERICAN POLITICS

The most thorough and balanced assessment of progressive reform is Arthur Link and Richard L. McCormick, *Progressivism* (Arlington Heights, IL, 1983). Many historians have attempted to illuminate the transformation of ideas that underlay progressive reform. Eric Goldman, *Rendezvous with Destiny* (New York, 1953), celebrated the writers and intellectuals engaged in dissolving the conservative thought of the late nineteenth century. More recent examinations of progressive ideas include David W. Noble's *The Progressive Mind, 1890–1917*, rev. ed. (Minneapolis, 1981), David B. Danbom, *"The World of Hope": Progressives and the Struggle for an Ethical Public Life* (Philadelphia, 1987), and Robert M. Crunden, *Ministers of Reform: The Progressives' Achievement in American Civilization, 1889–1920* (New York, 1982).

Of numerous books on women and public life during the Progressive Era, see especially Sheila M. Rothman, *Women's Proper Place: A History of Changing Ideals and Practices, 1870 to the Present* (New York, 1978), Nancy F. Cott, *The Grounding of Modern Feminism* (New Haven, 1987), Anne Firor Scott, *Natural Allies: Women's Associations in American History* (Urbana, 1991), Karen J. Blair, *The Clubwoman as Feminist: True Womanhood Redefined, 1868–1914* (New York, 1980), and *The Torchbearers: Women and Their Amateur Arts Associations in America, 1890–1930* (Bloomington, 1994). Mary Beard, *Woman's Work in Municipalities* (New York, 1915), documents in extraordinary detail the work of women's organizations in cities. The fullest scholarly treatment of the National Congress of Mothers/PTA is in Molly Ladd-Taylor, *Mother-Work: Women, Child Welfare and the State, 1890–1930* (Urbana, 1994). On women's philanthropy in the Progressive Era, see Kathleen McCarthy, *Noblesse Oblige: Charity and Cultural Philanthropy in Chicago, 1849–1929* (Chicago, 1982). Cynthia Neverdon-Morton, *Afro-American Women of the South and the Advancement of the Race, 1895–1925* (Knoxville, 1989), and Dorothy Salem, *To Better Our World: Black Women in Organized Reform, 1890–1920* (Brooklyn, 1990), survey voluntary associations and clubs among African-American women.

On women's religious activities, see especially Patricia R. Hill, *The World Their Household: The American Woman's Foreign Mission Movement and Cultural Transformation* (Ann Arbor, 1985), Regina G. Kunzel, *Fallen Women, Problem Girls: Unmarried Mothers and the Professionalization of Social Work, 1890–1945* (New Haven, 1993), Ruth Bordin, *Women and Temperance: The Quest for Power and Liberty, 1873–1900* (Philadelphia, 1981), and *Frances Willard: A Biography* (Chapel Hill, 1986), Ian Tyrrell, *Woman's World/Woman's Empire: The Women's Christian Temperance Union in International Perspective, 1880–1930* (Chapel Hill, 1991), and Evelyn Brooks Higgenbotham's thoughtful study, *Righteous Discontent: The Women's Movement in the Black Baptist Church, 1880–1920* (Cambridge, MA, 1993).

On changes in city government in this period, see Jon C. Teaford, *The Unheralded Triumph: City Government in America, 1870–1900* (Baltimore, 1983), Kenneth Fox, *Better City Government: Innovation in American Urban Politics, 1850–1937* (Philadelphia, 1977), Martin J. Schiesl, *The Politics of Efficiency: Municipal Administration and Reform in America, 1880–1920* (Berkeley, 1977), Bradley R. Rice, *Progressive Cities: The Commission Government Movement in America, 1901–1920* (Austin, 1977), Paul S. Boyer,

Urban Masses and Moral Order in America, 1820–1920 (Cambridge, MA, 1978), and Ernest S. Griffith, *A History of American City Government: The Progressive Years and Their Aftermath, 1900–1920* (New York, 1974). On big-city machines' relationship with reform, see John D. Buenker, *Urban Liberalism and Progressive Reform* (New York, 1973), and Kenneth Finegold, *Experts and Politicians: Reform Challenges to Machine Politics in New York, Cleveland, and Chicago* (Princeton, 1995).

Allen F. Davis, *Spearheads for Reform: The Social Settlements and the Progressive Era, 1890–1914* (New York, 1967), remains the best source on settlements' role in reform. More recent studies include Judith Trolander, *Professionalism and Social Change: From the Settlement House Movement to Neighborhood Centers, 1886 to the Present* (New York, 1987), Rivka Shpak Lissak, *Pluralism and Progressives: Hull House and the New Immigrants, 1890–1919* (Chicago, 1989), Elisabeth Lasch-Quinn, *Black Neighbors: Race and the Limits of Reform in the American Settlement House Movement, 1890–1945* (Chapel Hill, 1993), Mina Carson, *Settlement Folk: Social Thought and the American Settlement Movement, 1885–1930* (Chicago, 1990), and Ruth Hutchinson Crocker, *Social Work and Social Order: The Settlement Movement in Two Industrial Cities, 1889–1930* (Urbana, 1992). My discussion of Florence Kelley relies heavily on the first volume of Kathryn Kish Sklar's thorough and insightful biography, *Florence Kelley and the Nation's Work: The Rise of Women's Political Culture, 1830–1900* (New Haven, 1995).

On the history of child saving and the juvenile court, see Anthony Platt, *The Child Savers: The Invention of Delinquency* (Chicago, 1969), and Steven Schlossman, *Love and the American Delinquent: The Theory and Practice of "Progressive" Juvenile Justice, 1825–1920* (Chicago, 1977). The housing reform movement is examined in Roy Lubove, *The Progressives and the Slums: Tenement House Reform in New York City, 1890–1917* (Pittsburgh, 1962), and somewhat polemically in Thomas L. Philpott, *The Slum and the Ghetto: Neighborhood Deterioration and Middle-Class Reform, Chicago, 1880–1920* (New York, 1978).

Numerous books have examined progressive politics in individual states. On La Follette's Wisconsin, see David P. Thelen, *The New Citizenship: Origins of Progressivism in Wisconsin, 1885–1900* (Columbia, MO, 1972) and *Robert M. La Follette and the Insurgent Spirit* (Boston, 1976), and Carl R.

Burgchardt, *Robert M. La Follette, Sr.: The Voice of Conscience* (New York, 1992). Nye, *Midwestern Progressive Politics*, examines progressivism in several Midwestern states. Of numerous other state studies, see especially Thomas R. Pegram, *Partisans and Progressives: Private Interest and Public Policy in Illinois, 1870–1922* (Urbana, 1992), Robert W. Cherny, *Populism, Progressivism and the Transformation of Nebraska Politics, 1885–1915* (Lincoln, NE, 1981), David Thelen, *Paths of Resistance: Tradition and Dignity in Industrializing Missouri* (New York, 1986), George E. Mowry, *The California Progressives* (Berkeley, 1951), and Richard L. McCormick, *From Realignment to Reform: Political Change in New York State, 1893–1910* (Ithaca, 1981). On Progressivism in Southern states, see William A. Link, *The Paradox of Southern Progressivism, 1880–1930* (Chapel Hill, 1992), Dewey W. Grantham, Jr., *Hoke Smith and the Politics of the New South* (Baton Rouge, 1958), and William F. Holmes, *The White Chief: James Kimble Vardaman* (Baton Rouge, 1970).

Skocpol, *Protecting Soldiers and Mothers*, provides a splendid analysis of maternalist social policy, on which I have relied heavily. Linda Gordon, *Pitied but Not Entitled: Single Mothers and the History of Welfare, 1890–1935* (New York, 1994), places contemporary debates about "welfare" in historical perspective. Samuel P. Hays examines the conservation movement in *Conservation and the Gospel of Efficiency: The Progressive Conservation Movement, 1890–1920* (Cambridge, MA, 1959).

The literature on national politics in these years is vast. Major works on Theodore Roosevelt include William H. Harbaugh, *The Life and Times of Theodore Roosevelt*, rev. ed. (New York, 1963), Edmund Morris, *The Rise of Theodore Roosevelt* (New York, 1979), and David McCullough, *Mornings on Horseback* (New York, 1981). On Wilson, see Arthur S. Link's monumental *Wilson*, 5 vols. (Princeton, 1947–65), and Kendrick Clements, *Woodrow Wilson, World Statesman* (Boston, 1987). John Milton Cooper, Jr., *The Warrior and the Priest: Woodrow Wilson and Theodore Roosevelt* (Cambridge, MA, 1983), compares these two dominant political figures. Biographies of Taft include Henry F. Pringle, *The Life and Times of William Howard Taft*, 2 vols. (New York, 1939), and Donald R. Anderson, *William Howard Taft: A Conservative's Conception of the Presidency* (Ithaca, 1973). On Bryan, see Paolo E. Coletta, *William Jennings Bryan*, 3 vols. (Lincoln, NE, 1964–69), and LeRoy Ashby, *William Jennings Bryan: Champion of Democracy* (Boston, 1987). Debs's career is examined in Nick Salvatore, *Eugene V. Debs: Citizen and Socialist* (Urbana, 1982).

The most comprehensive study of the muckraking journalists is Louis Filler, *The Muckrakers: Crusaders for American Liberalism* (Chicago, 1950). On the survey research movement, see Clarke A. Chambers, *Paul U. Kellogg and the Survey: Voices for Social Welfare and Social Justice* (Minneapolis, 1971). The U.S. Children's Bureau is considered at length by Skocpol, *Protecting Soldiers and Mothers*, Ladd-Taylor, *Mother-Work*, and Robyn Muncy, *Creating a Female Dominion in American Reform, 1890–1935* (New York, 1991). On woman suffrage, see Anne F. Scott and Andrew M. Scott, *One Half the People: The Fight for Woman Suffrage* (Philadelphia, 1975), Eleanor Flexner, *Century of Struggle: The Woman's Rights Movement in the United States*, rev. ed. (Cambridge, MA, 1975), and Aileen Kraditor, *The Ideas of the Woman Suffrage Movement, 1890–1920* (New York, 1965).

My account of Walter Lippmann's early life and his career in the Progressive Era draws upon Ronald Steel's splendid biography, *Walter Lippmann and the American Century* (Boston, 1980). Also valuable is Charles Forcey's *Crossroads of Liberalism: Croly, Weyl, Lippmann and the Progressive Era, 1900–1925* (New York, 1961). On the decline of party politics as a result of the changes begun in the Progressive Era, see Richard L. McCormick, *The Party Period and Public Policy: American Politics from the Age of Jackson to the Progressive Era* (New York, 1986), Walter Dean Burnham, *Critical Elections and the Mainspring of American Politics* (New York, 1970), Michael E. McGerr, *The Decline of Popular Politics: The American North, 1865–1928* (New York, 1986), and Paul Kleppner, *Who Voted? The Dynamics of Electoral Turnout, 1870–1980* (New York, 1982) and *Continuity and Change in American Electoral Politics, 1893–1928* (New York, 1987).

9. THE GREAT WAR AND THE COMPETITION FOR CONTROL

My discussion of World War I and its immediate aftermath draws substantially on several excellent histories of the domestic side of the war: David M. Kennedy, *Over Here: The First World War and American Society* (New York, 1980), Neil A. Wynn, *From Progressivism to Prosperity: World War I and American Society* (New York, 1986), Ronald Schaffer, *America in the Great War: The Rise of the War Welfare State* (New York, 1991), Burl Noggle,

Into the Twenties: The United States from Armistice to Normalcy (Urbana, 1974), and Robert H. Ferrell, *Woodrow Wilson and World War I, 1917–1921* (New York, 1985).

Many war agencies have received book-length treatment: William J. Breen, *Uncle Sam at Home: Civilian Mobilization, Wartime Federalism and the Council of National Defense, 1917–1919* (Westport, CT, 1984), Robert D. Cuff, *The War Industries Board: Business-Government Relations During World War I* (Baltimore, 1973), Valerie Jean Conner, *The National War Labor Board: Stability, Social Justice, and the Voluntary State in World War I* (Chapel Hill, 1983), John Whiteclay Chambers II, *To Raise an Army: The Draft Comes to Modern America* (New York, 1987), and Nancy K. Bristow, *Making Men Moral: Social Engineering During the Great War* (New York, 1996), on the Commission on Training Camp Activities. Stephen Vaughn, *Holding Fast the Inner Lines: Democracy, Nationalism and the Committee on Public Information* (Chapel Hill, 1980), is supplemented by an older study, James R. Mock and Cedric Larson, *Words That Won the War: The Story of the Committee on Public Information, 1917–1919* (Princeton, 1939).

Two valuable studies of reformers and the war are John A. Thompson, *Reformers and War: American Progressive Publicists and the First World War* (Cambridge, MA, 1987), and Stuart I. Rochester, *American Liberal Disillusionment in the Wake of World War I* (University Park, PA, 1977). Carol S. Gruber, *Mars and Minerva: World War I and the Uses of the Higher Learning in America* (Baton Rouge, 1975), and George T. Blakey, *Historians on the Homefront: American Propagandists for the Great War* (Lexington, KY, 1970), examine professors and universities. John F. McClymer, *War and Welfare: Social Engineering in America, 1890–1925* (Westport, CT, 1980), considers the role of social welfare experts in the war mobilization, particularly in Americanization activities. On psychologists and mental testing, see Daniel J. Kelves, "Testing the Army's Intelligence: Psychologists and the Military in World War I," *Journal of American History* 55 (December 1968), pp. 565–81.

Richard Polenberg, *Fighting Faiths: The Abrams Case, the Supreme Court, and Free Speech* (New York, 1987), Paul L. Murphy, *World War I and the Origins of Civil Liberties in the United States* (New York, 1979), and Harry N. Scheiber, *The Wilson Administration and Civil Liberties, 1917–1921* (Ithaca, 1960), examine the repression of wartime civil liberties, and Robert K.

Murray, *Red Scare: A Study in National Hysteria, 1919–1920* (Minneapolis, 1955), analyzes the antiradical campaign immediately afterward.

Many of the books cited above on industrial and white-collar workers, immigrants, African-Americans, and farmers discuss the World War I period. In addition, on workers, see Maurine Weiner Greenwald, *Women, War and Work: The Impact of World War I on Women Workers in the United States* (Westport, CT, 1980), and David Brody, *Labor in Crisis: The Steel Strike of 1919* (Philadelphia, 1965). On African-Americans, see Arthur Barbeau and Florette Henri, *The Unknown Soldiers: Black American Troops in World War I* (Philadelphia, 1974), Arthur I. Waskow, *From Race Riot to Sit-In, 1919 and the 1960s: A Study in the Connections Between Conflict and Violence* (Garden City, NY, 1966), and William M. Tuttle, Jr., *Race Riot: Chicago in the Red Summer of 1919* (New York, 1970). On immigrants, see Frederick C. Luebke, *Bonds of Loyalty: German-Americans and World War I* (De Kalb, IL, 1974), and Joseph P. O'Grady, ed., *The Immigrants' Influence on Wilson's Peace Policies* (Lexington, KY, 1967).

INDEX

Baker, Josephine, 181–82
Baker, Newton D., 260
Baker, Ray Stannard, 36, 204,
264
Balfour Declaration, 256
Baltimore Bar Association, 186
banking and currency reform, 223,
224
Baptists, 121
Barnes, Odessa Minnie, 129
Baruch, Bernard M., 235
Bashara, Salem, 83
Beaufort-Savannah steamship line,
148
Becker, Carl, 262
Bell Telephone System, 171, 173
Belmont, August, 25
Bemis, Edward, 191
Berger, Victor, 68, 236
Bergeron, Antonia, 80–81
Bethlehem Steel Company, 35, 38
Birmingham Trades Council, 135
Birth of a Nation, The (film), 147
blue-collar workers, see workers
boarders, 70, 130
Bohemians, 93
Bond, Willard F., 138, 139
Bookkeepers and Accountants
Union, 162
Boston Common, 228
Bourne, Randolph, 260
Bowen, Louise deKoven, 23
boycotts, 148, 171, 210
Brandeis, Louis, 36, 65, 185, 210,
221, 225–26
Breckinridge, Sophonisba P., 195

Brewer, David, 184
Brewster, Mary, 22
Brophy, John, 50–51
Brotherhood of Timber Workers,
136
Brown, William Wells, 142
Bryan, William Jennings, 26–28,
215, 216
Buffalo Bird Woman, 118
Bunyan, John, 204

Cahan, Abraham, 93, 99
Cajuns, 114
California, University of, 101
California Alien Land Act (1913),
86
Call, 229, 262
Call, Homer, 62
Canadians, 72, 77, 80–81, 87–89,
96
Candler, Asa, 42
capitalism, corporate, 4, 6–8, 12–
15, 30, 234; African-Americans
and, 130; farmers and, 102, 103,
122, 124; impact on managers
of, 40; office workers and, 156;
progressive discourse and, 200;
small entrepreneurs and, 45;
social consequences of, 21; see
also corporations; welfare
capitalism
Carnegie, Andrew, 32, 53
Carnegie Foundation for the
Advancement of Teaching, 180
Carnegie Steel, 19, 32, 52–53

Catholics, 5, 8, 71, 81, 86–89, 95–
    97, 99, 177, 191
Cato, Will, 128
Catt, Carrie Chapman, 228
Cattell, James McKeen, 258
cattle ranchers, 114–15
Census Bureau, U.S., 155, 157–59,
    242
chain stores, 42, 44, 45, 82
Charities and Commons, 205
charity organization movement, 193–
    95, 257
Charles, Robert, 149
Chattanooga Medical College, 181
Cherokee Indians, 119
Cheyenne Indians, 119
Chicago, University of, 69, 190–93,
    195, 197
Chicago Commons, 194, 195
Chicago Defender, 153
Chicago Normal School, 197
Chicago School of Civics and
    Philanthropy, 195
Chicago Teachers Union, 197
child labor, 11, 21, 23, 46, 55, 69,
    210, 212, 215, 216, 220, 225,
    260
children, 8; African-American, 139,
    141, 151; farm, 104–7, 109–10,
    112; health care for, 181–82;
    immigrant, 83, 94–98; libraries
    for, 198; recreation of, 74, 203
Children's Bureau, U.S., 217, 227,
    263
Chinese, 85, 92–94, 97, 256
Choctaw Indians, 119

Christianity and the Social Crisis
    (Rauschenbusch), 218
churches, *see* religious institutions
cigar makers, 52, 71
city governments: machine-
    dominated, *see* machine politics,
    urban; reform of, 205–9
Civic Federation of Chicago, 20
civil rights, battle for, 145–50, 248
Civil War, 17, 24
Claghorn, Kate Holladay, 76
Clark-Lewis, Elizabeth, 129
Clarkson, Grosvenor B., 262
Clayton Antitrust Act (1914), 48, 224
clergymen, 177–78; African-
    American, 142–43
clerical workers, 156–65
Cleveland, Grover, 20, 25, 26, 222
Cloak Operators Union, 65
clubwomen, 21, 23, 27, 29, 202,
    206, 210, 212, 227, 249
coal mines, *see* miners
Cobb, Ned, 109
Coca-Cola, 42
Coffin, Howard E., 235
Cohen, Rose, 92
College Settlement, 22
Colored Farmers' National
    Alliance, 18, 133–34
Colored Joint Stock Company, 134
Colored Knights of Pythias, 143
Colored State Poultry Association,
    134
Columbia University, 190, 195,
    218, 258
Comer, Braxton Bragg, 136

institutions of, 86–90; restriction of, 256, 257; self-employment of, 82–86; settlement houses for, 21–23, 194; as unskilled laborers, 60; working-class culture of, 69–74; during World War I, 236, 253–56

Immigration Commission, U.S., 59, 69, 80, 141

Indian Affairs, Bureau of, 117

Indians, see Native Americans

Industrial Commission, U.S., 45, 92

industrialism, 12, 13, 14; African-Americans and, 125; agriculture and, 102; consumer goods and, 168; immigration and, 78; professional specialization and, 177; social change and, 5; in South, 112; see also corporations

industrial operatives, 54–59, 61–62

Industrial Workers of the World (IWW), 66–67, 136, 236

insurance companies, 164, 167

intellectuals, 200, 219–20, 228–30; African-American, 143; immigrant, 93, 101; during World War I, 259–64

Interior, U.S. Department of, 253

International Association of Machinists (IAM), 54, 240

International Harvester, 4, 39, 58, 165–66

International Ladies' Garment Workers' Union (ILGWU), 64–66

International Molders' and Foundry Workers' Union, 240

Interstate Commerce Commission (ICC), 16, 36, 215, 216, 263

investigative journalism, 203–5

Irish, 71–72, 77, 81, 169; businesses of, 83, 84; and Catholic Church, 87, 88, 95; in labor movement, 169, 174; as teachers, 196; during World War I, 256

ironworkers, 51, 53

Italians, 8, 60, 69, 77, 79–81; businesses of, 83; and Catholic Church, 87, 89; education of, 94–95; in labor movement, 11–12, 63, 66, 71; mutual aid societies of, 91; newspapers for, 93

Japanese, 77, 85–86, 93, 96, 100–1, 256

Jefferson, Thomas, 223

Jewish Daily Forward, 66, 93, 99

Jewish Theological Seminary, 178

Jews, 5, 79, 93, 94, 173, 228, 256; businesses of, 79, 82–85; education of, 96–98; in labor movement, 11–12, 63, 65, 66, 71; mutual benefit societies of, 91; in professions, 185, 191, 196; synagogues of, 87, 89–90; theological institutions of, 77–78

Johns Hopkins University, 180, 190

Johnson, Hiram, 212, 260

Johnson, James Weldon, 147, 151

Johnson, Tom, 207–8

Jones, Samuel, 24, 28, 201, 207
Joseph, Jacob, 90
journalism, investigative, 203–5
*Journal of the American Medical
    Association*, 176, 183
Jungle, The (Sinclair), 215
Justice Department, U.S., 214, 217,
    236, 253
juvenile court, 23

Kagan, Israel Meir Ha-Kohen, 82
Kanipe, Rosa, 109–10
Kelley, Florence, 22–23, 28, 210,
    217
Kellogg, Paul, 205, 257
Kellor, Frances, 220, 253
Kiolbassa, Peter, 99
Kirby, Jack, 113
Knights of Labor, 18–19, 61
Knights of Pythias, 166
Koreans, 93
Kosciuszko, Thaddeus, 99
Kruszka, Michael, 100

Labor, U.S. Department of, 48, 238,
    261
labor movement, *see* unions
Lacey, Virginia, 137
La Follette, Robert M., 192, 211,
    216, 218, 224, 225
laissez-faire ideology, 14, 16, 191,
    200, 203, 222
land grant universities, 121, 123,
    190

Lathrop, Julia, 195, 227, 260
lawyers, 9, 11, 176, 177, 183–88,
    256–58
Lazarus, Emma, 76
Lease, Mary, 14, 16, 28
legal profession, *see* lawyers
Leiserson's Shirtwaist Company, 64
leisure-time activities, working-
    class, 10–11, 73–75
Lemlich, Clara, 64–65
librarians, 9, 178, 195, 197–98,
    257
Lindsay, Ben, 262
Lindsay, Samuel McCune, 195
Lippmann, Walter, 219, 228–30,
    259–60
Lithuanians, 88
London, Meyer, 58
Low, Seth, 207
Lunn, George, 229
Lutherans, 87, 95, 96, 254, 255
lynching, 127–29, 148, 149, 248–
    50, 254

McClure, S. S., 204
McCormick Harvesting, 42, 166
machine politics, urban, 12, 208;
    African-American, 145; exposés
    of, 204
machinists, 53–54
Mack, Julian, 260
McKay, Claude, 251–52
McKinley, William, 27, 28, 185,
    212, 213, 222
McKinley Steel Company, 236

Worman, H. A., 58
Wrigley Chewing Gum Company,
   42, 43

Yale University, 190, 258
Yerkes, Robert, 259
Young, Ella Flagg, 197

Young Men's Christian Association
   (YMCA), 129, 144, 261
Young Women's Christian
   Association (YWCA), 144
Yu, Alice, 97

Zionists, 97